# REASON and RHETORIC:
the intellectual foundations
of 20th-century liberal
educational policy

WALTER FEINBERG
The University of Illinois

# REASON and RHETORIC

the intellectual
foundations of
20th century
liberal educational
policy

JOHN WILEY & SONS, INC.
New York • London • Sydney • Toronto

*To Eleanor*

Copyright © 1975, by John Wiley & Sons, Inc.

All rights reserved. Published simultaneously in Canada.

No part of this book may be reproduced by any means, nor transmitted, nor translated into a machine language without the written permission of the publisher.

**Library of Congress Cataloging in Publication Data:**

Feinberg, Walter, 1937-
    Reason and Rhetoric.
    Includes bibliographical references.

    1. Education—Philosophy—History.  I. Title.
LA21.F44          370.1         74-16009
ISBN 0-471-25697-8

Printed in the United States of America

10 9 8 7 6 5 4 3 2 1

# PREFACE

The confusion of the times often seems to find an outlet in debates about public schooling and when I began this study the winds were powerful, sweeping the schools in opposite currents. The influence of the Conant volumes were still being felt with the concurrent attempt to centralize facilities and to identify talent with, so it seemed, a minimum emphasis on racial or class background. But it was a time too when the voice of dissent was being sounded and, as it was at Ocean-Hill Brownsville, translated into institutional form. Suddenly, and with little warning, the nature of the conflict shifted as the old alignments broke down. Integration, first proposed in the name of equality, was challenged as inequitable and other liberal reforms were addressed as illiberal.

At that time I still sensed that the need was to explain the new dissent to the liberal, to show him that the conflict was not a difference of ends, but of means only. This study was conceived as a liberal project, addressed to a liberal audience whose basic goals were to go unchallenged. But the course of events has changed that. The book is an examination and critique of the liberal assumptions that have underwritten the process of schooling in the United States. It is an examination of the ideas of some liberal educational theorists about progress, technology, freedom and equality and it is an attempt to show how their ideas about progress and technology influenced and limited their notions of freedom and equality.

Schooling in America is a liberal institution conceived by liberal theorists and carried out by liberal practitioners and therefore any intelligent change in the education of the American people must be predicted on an understanding of the liberal thought and structure which dominates the institution of schooling.[1]

---

[1] In defense of the liberal position, some argue that despite the liberal rhetoric of the educational establishment, the schools remain rigid, conservative institutions. This position overlooks the fact that many major aspects of liberal reform are taken for granted by educators. For example, the professionalization and certification of teachers arose very much out of liberal progressive concerns as did the accreditation of universities. Moreover, most of the textbooks from Curti to Commager have a liberal orientation, and John Dewey remains the one philosopher with whom virtually every American teacher has some familiarity. At the university level, liberal ideas have dominated teacher education, political science, psychology, and economic departments.

The phrase "the education of the American people" is an indication of another shift in focus—I was originally concerned with the schooling of the American child. The university and other institutions which educate were outside of the study presumably disassociated with the greater educational problems of the times. Subsequent events have made this stance inadequate. American schooling from Kindergarten through graduate school operates to reinforce certain basic aspects of the American political, economic and moral structure. They can be isolated only for functional reasons, and these are no longer functional essays.

The events which altered the focus of this book are not subtle and I can claim no special powers of observation in perceiving them. They are, beginning with Vietnam, the most powerful events of recent times. Vietnam was the beginning, but My Lai, Cambodia, and then Jackson and Kent State—and more recently Watergate[2]—all contributed to a deeper questioning of liberal thought and behavior.

These events—except for Vietnam, the liberal's war—are not sufficient to indict liberal theory and practice alone. The guns fired at Jackson and Kent State were not held by liberal hands. But the hands belonged to people who were supervised by liberal politicians, educated by liberal institutions, and judged by a liberal society. The fact that the

[2] The view of Watergate as a vindication of American *political* institutions is correct, but only partially so. What is equally as significant as Nixon's resignation is his landslide election and the number of liberals who supported him. Given the tone of his entire political career, together with the fact that the outline of Watergate was already known, it is not unreasonable to conclude that many people not committed to his conservative ideology voted for him because of the same qualities which later brought his administration under investigation. The difference was that whereas his cunningness could be overlooked as necessary for the *illusion* of peace with honor in Vietnam, it could not be excused once it became a publicly shared rather than a privately shared fact. It is one thing for each of us to know individually that a man is shady, but it is another for each of us to know that the other person knows it, and to know too that he knows that we know it. The conservative who suggests that Congress' earlier reluctance to investigate closely the Bobby Baker scandal indicates an anti-Nixon bias in the Watergate case may have a very important insight. His only problem is that he uses it as an excuse to vindicate Nixon rather than to examine the influences of the economic and political power structure on American cultural life. Indeed there may be no more significant sign of the problems with our educational institutions than the ease with which the centers of power can manipulate emotions to their own end.

vi

war that precipitated these events was a liberal war does not absolve others from personal responsibility. The problem with the liberal theory arises from its inability to see events as signs of serious structural problems, and therefore it tends to treat them as administrative rather than moral concerns. Thus we find liberal theorists discouraging an analysis of the basic political and moral structure of American society and the extent to which it has generated the unfortunate events of recent times.

Although the public schools provide a receptive audience for liberal thought, they are not its primary forum. The university serves this function and unless checked by his faculty the university administrator's voice is taken as the voice of the forum. To the events of Cambodia, of Jackson and Kent State, the official voice was conspicuous not only in its initial silence, but also in its firmness in interpreting the protest that followed as the threat to the idea of academic freedom and university autonomy. One of the more prominent administrators, having gained his own ribbons in a series of student strikes, could discuss the shootings by the national guard at Kent as the act of men who were distraught by the abusive language that students had hurled at them, thus leaving the impression that it was excusable to confront four letter words with a round of bullets.[3]

The schools have become an instrument of national continuity—a means by which one generation makes itself known to the next. The procedures, skills, routine and information which are allowed into the schoolroom as knowledge is an indication of how the older generation wishes to be known and a reasonable guide to what the next generation will be expected to accept in an unquestioning way. The philosophy that has articulated the modern form of intelligence is the focus of this book.

In writing this book I had the good fortune to have access to the work in progress of a number of graduate students and colleagues at the University of Illinois and elsewhere. I have profited by James Anderson's research on black education and by discussions with Ronald Goodenow concerning his research on the progressive response to black education. Russ Marks' work on the testing movement and Morris Sammons' research on distributive justice were also very helpful in preparing this book. I am also grateful to David Tyack for his initial en-

---

[3] See Hayakawa's review of Michener's book, *Kent State: What Happened and Why. Boston Herald,* Sunday, August 15, 1971.

couragement in this project and to Noam Chomsky, Johan Galtung, Maxine Greene and Beth Singer for their comments on various sections of the manuscript. My research on Dewey was aided by the assistance of my colleague Joe Burnett of the University of Illinois, who made available his extensive file on Dewey's writings. Joanne Boynston of the Dewey project at Southern Illinois University was also helpful in this regard. Kenneth Benne allowed me access to his files on the Bureau of Intercultural Education and he, along with Marx Wartofsky, were instrumental in the development of my interest in Dewey and the liberal tradition generally. B. Othanel Smith and Brand Blanshard patiently answered my questions about aspects of the progressive movement and Professor Blanshard generously provided me with a copy of his report on the churches in the Polish community.

A number of colleagues both at Illinois and elsewhere read sections of this manuscript and tried to convince me to change the errors of my ways. For these attempts I am indebted to Laszlo Hetenyi, Phillip Hugley, Clarence Karier, Foster McMurray, David Nyberg, Alan Peshkin, Hugh Petrie, Elisabeth Shapiro, Michael Shapiro, Mobin Shorish, Donald Tunnell and Paul Violas. William O. Stanley retired from the University of Illinois before the earlier drafts were completed, but I profited much from his passionate defense of liberal educational and political theory.

I am especially indebted to Paul Nash for his comments on an earlier draft of the entire manuscript. Richard Hult and Mickey Becker were helpful in researching different aspects of the book. A number of graduate students in the College of Education at the University of Illinois participated in a seminar where an earlier draft of this book was discussed. These sessions were very helpful to me.

During the course of writing this book my point of view changed more than once and I was forced to return to earlier chapters in order to revise them. Without the persistent advice of Ronald Szoke, who as my research assistant, served to remind me of what I had not yet considered, and of Henry Rosemont, who did not allow his friendship to interfere with his sharp and perceptive criticisms, this book would have been completed significantly earlier.

The early phases of this study were supported by the University of Illinois Research Board and the Department of History and Philosophy of Education. The manuscript was patiently typed by Cindy Goken. Part of Chapter One originally appeared in a slightly altered form as an article in *Educational Theory* and Sections of Chapter Three were originally published as part of an article which appeared in the *T. C. Record*. Sections were first presented in draft form as papers at the State University of New York at Buffalo, the Inter University Center Course on Peace and Conflict Resolution, Dubrovnik, Yugoslavia, The Cambridge (England) Philosophy of Education Society, and the Universities of Oslo and Trompso in Norway. I am grateful to the students and staff of these institutions for their comments and criticisms.

My wife Eleanor's research on Frank Parsons provided insight into some related aspects of twentieth century educational reform. This and many other things I appreciate.

# CONTENTS

Page

INTRODUCTION: THE IDEOLOGY OF LIBERALISM    1

    I. Political Philosophy and Political Practice    1
    II. Liberal Ideology    4
    III. Facts and Images    8
    IV. Moral Dilemmas    12
    V. Liberal and Progressive Educational Theory:
        The Problem of Freedom    13
    VI. Technology and Freedom    19
    VII. The Organization of the Book    21

CHAPTER ONE   FROM A PHILOSOPHY OF MAN TO A
SCIENCE OF MANAGEMENT    25

    I. Introduction    25
    II. The Beginnings of "A Science of Education"    26
    III. The Science of Education at the Turn of the Century    28
    IV. The Idea of Educational Science in the
        Twentieth Century    40
    V. A Case of Shifting Priorities: The Influence
        of Darwin    42
    VI. William Graham Sumner's Scientific Prohibitions    43
    VII. Science and Reform    47
    VIII. Conclusion    54

CHAPTER TWO   OBJECTIVITY AND IDEOLOGY    57

    I. Introduction    57
    II. The Testing Movement    58
    III. The Efficiency Movement    62
    IV. Some Problems with the "Scientific" Justifications
        of the Testing Movement    64

V.  Some Ideological Aspects of the Testing and
    Efficiency Movements                                    67
VI.  The Liberal Progressive Response to the Testing
     and Efficiency Movements                              75
VII.  The Limits of the Challenge                          79
VIII.  Dewey on Work and Education                         80
IX.  Dewey's views in a Concrete Setting                   84
X.  Summary                                                91


CHAPTER THREE   THE DEMOCRATIC IDEAL
AND LIBERAL EDUCATIONAL POLICY                             93

I.  Introduction                                           93
II.  The Social Context of Progressive Reform              94
III.  The Conflict Between Technological and Communal
      Values in Progressive Thought                        97
IV.  The Democratic Ideal and Educational Reform          100
V.  The Liberal Ideal and its Functional Limits           102
VI.  Dewey and the Polish Community                        103
VII.  Dewey and P.S. 26                                    108
VIII.  Liberals and Progressives on Negro Education        111
IX.  The Bureau of Intercultural Education:
     The Response of Later Progressives to the
     Problems of Minority Groups                           121
X.  Summary                                                132


CHAPTER FOUR   THE UNDERLYING CONSISTENCY OF
TWENTIETH-CENTURY EDUCATIONAL REFORM                      135

I.  Introduction                                          135
II.  Liberal Policy and the Distribution of Knowledge     137
III.  Rites of Passage and Educational Reform             139
IV.  Social Tension and the Rhythm of
     Educational Reform                                   141

Page

V. The Life-Adjustment Movement and its Critics    143

VI. Later Educational Reforms    153

VII. Summary    166

CHAPTER FIVE    **THE IMAGE OF PROGRESS:
HISTORY IN THE SERVICE OF REFORM**    167

I. Introduction    167

II. The Inspirational Side of Liberal Theory    168

III. History in the Service of Nation and School    169

IV. History as an Instrument of Reform    172

V. Progressive History: Charles Beard    177

VI. Beard and the Idea of Progress in the
School Textbooks    182

VII. James Harvey Robinson and the Progressive
Evolution of the Human Mind    185

VIII. History in the Service of the Common Man    188

IX. The Idea of Progress Evaluated    191

X. Progress in Later School Texts    194

XI. The Idea of Progress and Educational Histories    196

XII. Summary    199

CHAPTER SIX    **THE LIBERAL'S IMAGE OF SOCIETY:
INTELLIGENCE AT THE SERVICE OF POWER**    201

I. Introduction    201

II. Marxism in Retreat    203

III. The Progressive Ideal of Management    207

IV. Conflicting Classes or Pressuring Groups    210

V. Legitimizing Power    215

VI. Serving Power    223

VII. The Critic from Within    227

VIII. Summary Comments    233

xiii

CHAPTER SEVEN   **EDUCATION IN A JUST SOCIETY:
THE LIMITS OF LIBERAL EDUCATIONAL REFORM**   235

    I.   Introduction   235

    II.   The Issue of Manipulation   236

    III.   Manipulation and Its Evaluation   240

    IV.   Manipulation and Progressive Education   243

    V.   The Progressives' Point of View   250

    VI.   Beyond Revisionists Critiques   255

    VII.   Against Equality of Educational Opportunity   262

    VIII.   A Concluding Evaluation of Twentieth-Century
Educational Reform   283

Index   285

# REASON and RHETORIC:
the intellectual foundations
of 20th-century liberal
educational policy

*Even if the words remain the same they mean something very different when they are uttered by a minority struggling against repressive measures and when expressed by a group that, having attained power, then uses ideas that were once weapons of emancipation as instruments for keeping the power and wealth it has obtained. Ideas that at one time are means of producing social change assume another guise when they are used as a means of preventing further social change.*

John Dewey

# INTRODUCTION:
# The Ideology of Liberalism

## I. POLITICAL PHILOSOPHY
## AND POLITICAL PRACTICE

Because this is partly a study of liberal and progressive educational philosophy, I will begin by discussing the method of examination. Philosophers have sometimes claimed that their discipline is the study of pure thought. By this they mean that they are concerned not with the motives that spirit an argument, nor with the consequences to which thinking in a particular way may lead, but with the structure of thinking, with the logic of the arguments, and the consistency and rigor with which a string of propositions are held together. My general inclination is to be skeptical about this claim and to suggest that, at least when it comes to political philosophy, an area under which educational thought naturally falls, motives and consequences are difficult to separate from the structure of thought itself. Among the largest decisions a political philosopher makes is the argument that he chooses to accept as a legitimate object of criticism and what he chooses to accept as unalterable aspects of human and institutional relationships. What is offered as pure thought invariably lends support to one institutional position and weakens another.[1] Liberal thought in America arose, for example, as a reaction to the Social Darwinism that preceded it, but what is most significant for today's problems is not that aspect of Social Darwinism that was challenged but the aspects that went unchallenged by contemporary liberal thinkers. (See Chapter One.)

It is a mistake to completely abstract a political or an educational philosophy from the historical context out of which it arose and to treat it as pure thought. For when such philosophy is abstracted from the concrete historical situation, the resolution of many of its initial concerns and subsequent tensions are lost. For example, there is a tension between two fundamental liberal commitments. First there is a commitment to the values of democracy and community and second there is a commitment to the use of scientific intelligence in social affairs.[2] Precisely how this tension was worked out in liberal thought will be decided less by the various philosophical attempts to smooth it over and more by the recommendations about specific social issues. Thus historical

---

[1] This point has been made often enough by liberal theorists constituting, for example, a large part of Gunnar Myrdal's critique of William Graham Summer. The analysis has less frequently been applied to liberal theory itself. Nevertheless, a liberal endeavor such as Daniel Bell's *End of Ideology* should serve to illustrate that liberals have no special immunity. Bell begins by heralding the passage of ideological thinking and ends by applauding the goal of a technological society run from the top with the help and advice of the "dispassionate" expert.

However, while a political philosophy does lend support to one institutional position or another, a distinction needs to be made between long-range and short-range support. Certainly once a political philosophy is articulated it gains a certain independence from its initial author and may, in time, be used to argue for institutional arrangements which were not entailed in the original intent. Karl Marx was perhaps the first to recognize this aspect of political thought, and liberals such as Dewey were in general agreement. It should not be thought that the process stopped with the formation of liberal political theory. Regarding the present work, for example, the author admits to sharing a number of assumptions with modern-day liberals. We would both agree, for example, that men ought to be free and that it is bad when they are not. However, I believe that the liberal created a rather special view of freedom, one that was designed to meet the contingencies of the first half of the twentieth century.

[2] For further views on the nature of this tension see my article, "The Conflict Between Intelligence and Community in the Social Philosophy of John Dewey," *Educational Theory,* Vol. 19, Summer 1969, No. 3, pp. 236-249.

data are used in this study in order to understand how such tensions were resolved and to reveal aspects of the liberal past that persist as significant trends in the present. Therefore this study differs in approach from both those that treat liberal thought only as a philosophical system and those that look only at its historical impact on educational institutions. Here an examination of the thought and activity of liberal educators on concrete issues is used to show how various tensions in their philosophical system were resolved.

John Dewey, who is mentioned frequently in this book, once wrote a book, *German Philosophy and Politics,* where, in a revised edition written just prior to World War II, he argued that most of German cultural and philosophical thought quite naturally reached its fruition in the figure of Hitler, a position that itself supports the view that philosophy is more than pure thought (although, more than likely, Dewey's concern was simply to support the cause of the allies). The question of political causation is, however, more complicated than Dewey's book would have us believe, and it would be unfortunate if this work, critical as it is of the liberal progressive tradition in education, were to simplify things in this way and to assume, for example, that the liberal legacy reached its natural and inevitable fruition in the more unfortunate events of recent times. The problem here is to reveal intellectual influences that helped to form our view of the world, and to appraise their adequacy as guides for the future.

Discussions of a political and educational nature most naturally center on issues of intentions and consequences, and philosophers debate whether or not intentions are causes. Academic philosophers will no doubt continue to ponder this issue, but there is another way to look at intentions and consequences. Sometimes we say that a man acted with the very best of intentions but that the consequences of his act were not what he wished. At other times we say that a man acted out of a selfish intent, and yet the consequences served others. A frequent interpretation of the liberal educator is that his intentions were well designed, but that for reasons beyond his control schooling did not often work out the way that he wished. The question of how a person's intentions are to be judged, however, depends partly on the evaluation of the principles that are believed to be guiding his actions. As the evaluation of these principles are placed in a different light, then so too are the actions that are performed in their name. The point of this study is to go beyond both the questions of intentions and of consequences and to reveal and examine some of the very fundamental assumptions that were made by liberal educators about schooling and society and about the place of children and citizens in both of these. Such assumptions when used to guide action in the real world are said to constitute the liberal ideology.

## II. LIBERAL IDEOLOGY

The people who come under scrutiny in these pages would probably resent the suggestion that they were governed by ideological considerations since many viewed themselves as combatting the ignorance that they thought accompanied ideological thinking. They believed themselves to be scientific in their outlook. They saw themselves to be problem solvers who took issues as they came, keeping in mind only the requirements of scientific intelligence. I hope to show that they were more than problem solvers; they were committed to an ideology as well.

The meaning of the term "ideology" is difficult to pin down, and I am not using it in its most common meaning. For many people "ideology" suggests a set of articulated propositions about life, propositions that guide action in a programmatic, nonpragmatic fashion. The ideologue is thought of as the doctrinaire Marxist who awaits and perpetuates the coming revolution with little regard for the events that actually surround him or for the feelings or desires of others. Or, the word conjures up images of religious zealots waiting for the world to end as the sun is rising over the hill to usher in another day. These images seem to me to be simpleminded and patronizing as if only other people were afflicted with the "disease" while those of us who are clearheaded and sensitive to the day's events go along making the world run better.

I am using the term ideology with as little disapproval as possible. The point is not that some men are ideologues and others are not but that all men are ideologues insofar as we all function within a set of ideas that remain unexamined and unquestioned. I do not say that the liberal educator was an uncritical man. This is not the point. The point is simply that liberal educators held some significant ideas in uncritical ways, and that, insofar as those ideas still guide our debates and influence our actions and judgments, it is important to understand what they are.[3] Ironically, John Dewey himself noted that we do not doubt everything at once: we doubt some things while accepting others as fixed. The problem now under consideration is to uncover some of those things that Dewey and the liberal circle in general accepted as fixed.

"Ideology" as it is used here is much closer in meaning to the way that Karl Mannheim used the term in his volume, *Ideology and Utopia*, than it is to its ordinary usage. Mannheim emphasized the fact that people hold varying images about what their society is like, and that such images determine to a large extent how they react to different events. Mannheim's treatise analyzed what happens with regard to these images when a society begins to break down, and much of what he had to say is pertinent today because the liberal's view of the world has undergone serious challenge and is in the process of decay. Mannheim used both the words "ideology" and "utopia" to represent organizing principles that evolve out of man's attempt to understand his social world. The events of the present are significant as signs that point to a more complicated network of relationships, and the ideas we have of the past and the future serve to order these events, stamping them with different qualities and significances. An event is imagined to be part of a temporal sequence where what is important is not the event itself but what is believed will follow it. As Mannheim explains it "Events which at first glance present themselves as mere chronological accumulations . . . take on the character of destiny."[4]

In practical experience we cannot doubt everything at once (Dewey

---

[3] There is another aspect to this issue and that is the question as to whether any objective criteria exists by which a truth claim may be assessed. My immediate concern is not to address this issue but to highlight what I believe to be the ideological elements in liberal educational thought. I intend to do this first by identifying some ambiguities that are present in liberal political and educational philosophy and second by demonstrating that liberal educational activity often lent support to one social form rather than another while liberal rhetoric obscured the moral ambiguity involved. Thus more central to this study than the method by which a truth claim is assessed is the implications that are entailed for the treatment of people and cultures by those who do believe, rightly or wrongly, that they have a more adequate grasp of reality.

[4] Karl Mannheim, *Ideology and Utopia* (New York: Harvest Books), 1936, p. 209.

was correct about this), and, even more important, what we do eventually question is guided by the issues that loom largest for us—and these issues are partly a function of the times in which we live. But it is not intelligent any longer for people of one age to live by the accepted "truths" of another. Therefore, "ideology" is always in the process of being discovered, and its discovery is always painful because it involves ideas that still persist and have been granted quasi-sacred status.

Most of the world is beyond the sight and sound of people, and much of the world is invisible and silent. People function only slightly with their senses. Their guide is the image they have of their world, an image built up in mysterious ways—but on which the senses serve as pointers on a map. Man's image of his social world indicates to him the limits and the consequences of particular human acts. It is a mental grid of the possible and the desirable. Actions that fall within this grid will not violate his sensibilities.

But this image is not always as explicit as it can be. Without a thorough analysis rhetoric hides as much as it reveals, and our actions alter our rhetoric. Ideas, as Dewey said, have consequences, but it sometimes requires living through some of those consequences to find out what the ideas really are and to understand the rhetoric on a deeper level.

To uncover an ideology is to reveal what people have accepted as possible and thereby to reveal the limits that they have placed on their own actions. The process of revealing a contemporary and influential ideology is not the same as the process of revealing an object that lies hidden under a rug, for example. If an ideology is a powerful one, it has stamped the consciousness of those who attempt to examine it, and its revelation involves not only the question of what is out there but also how we see and understand what is out there. To a certain extent the question of reality (what is out there) must be put aside and in its place the question of value must be raised. Different times generate different concerns, and what one generation accepts as irrevocably part of the nature of things subsequent generations must see as issues of human choice and value. This is a fundamental requirement of responsibility. Therefore, much of this book attempts to uncover the images of history, society, and equality that were held by liberal educators.

The concept of an image can be used as a way to uncover and

analyze different ideological stances, and, as an *instrument of analysis,* it belongs primarily to the person who is examining a belief system— not to the person who holds it. As an instrument of analysis, its function is to highlight *as a belief* a fundamental concept that has previously been granted the status of reality. The Newtonian view of space, as an example, was not spoken of as an image of space by those who believed it was true.[5] To those people, the idea that space might be other than a container in which things were held was unthinkable. Reality was quite as Newton has proposed; he was not *imagining* space, he was *describing* it. But as soon as people recognize serious problems that this view cannot explain, it becomes reasonable to speak of it as an image of space.

Because the concept of the image belongs to the person who is examining beliefs about reality, it does not require the *immediate* assumption that there is a reality against which these beliefs are to be measured. It does, however, require a commitment to certain values that themselves may be only partially revealed. To reveal an image is not necessary to argue explicitly for a better image or to replace one theory of reality with another, nor does the revelation of an image necessarily disclose the point of view from which the image is to be evaluated. This requires a more explicit evaluation (Chapter Seven). The purpose is, instead, to reveal particular ways in which the human drive for explanation and closure have been met without itself yet attempting to explain or to close.

The revelation of an image is the condition for responsibility in that it takes a particular commitment to reality and elevates it to an object of human value and choice. But as judged by dominant standards, it is also irresponsible, for it underplays the historical circumstances that gave rise to the image that is being revealed. It does this, however, in order to highlight the very basis of moral judgment and to avoid looking at human action as simply part of the nature of things. Therefore, it is consciously irresponsible in this regard. History is important in understanding a decision, indeed it can even be used to *properly* justify a decision that under ideal circumstances may be questionable. But when decisions that may have once been justifiable as resulting from peculiar historical and social forces become the firm basis of moral judgments, it is important to begin by removing them from their context in order to

[5] I am indebted to Henry Rosemont, Jr., for this example.

highlight the principles they hide and eventually judge their moral worth. For example, many liberal decisions about schooling arose as an attempt to deal with industrial and technological developments of the times, but they also expressed a view of man and of freedom, articulated in liberal writings, that can be challenged. So in this study the emphasis is placed on the principles and images that arose out of concrete historical situations. We are concerned with the social images that different people held and that served thereby as their justification for educational practice.

## III. FACTS AND IMAGES

Louis Wirth, in his preface to Karl Mannheim's *Ideology and Utopia,* wrote:

A society is possible in the last analysis because the individuals in it carry around in their head some sort of picture of that society. Our society, however, in this period of minute division of labour, of extreme heterogeneity and profound conflict of interest, has come to a pass where these pictures are blurred and incongruous.[6]

The statement expressed a commonly accepted observation: the stability of society depends in large measure on each individual having a general awareness of how his function contributes to the society at large and how the society at large enables him to continue in his function. In most cases stability also depends on an acceptance of this relationship as both just and fair. *Ideology and Utopia* was written by Mannheim to describe the factors involved when this picture begins to break down, when the fundamental view held by one large segment of society is not held by others. Both the ideological mode that looks to the past and the utopian one that looks to the future have some representative validity. Advocates of both are able to bring facts to bear in support of their respective positions. But their primary function is to organize the facts of experience, and because each orders these differently and partially, their representative value is incomplete. In this sense, Mannheim is writing about some of the structural elements involved in the images that people have of their social world.

[6] Karl Mannheim, *Ideology and Utopia* (New York: Harvest Books), 1936, Preface by Louis Wirth, p. xxiii.

The image not only creates expectations about what will happen, it also provides a *way* of finding out and judging what will happen. Because of this, it has a significant bearing on what is accepted as evidence (and this eventually has a bearing on what does happen). Michael Polanyi cited as an example of a similar point the rejection of many scientists and doctors of the legitimacy of early findings in hypnosis. Because the explanation of the experimenter about the ability of certain metals to control mental operations were at variance with what was known about those metals, the *fact* of hypnosis was also dismissed. In political and educational theory one of the basic images involves the relation between man (or the child) and the institutions that contain him (such as the school), and goodness or badness has been varyingly assigned to either man or his institutions. Man is sometimes seen as naturally good and his institutions corrupting, or he is viewed as savagelike, and the institution is taken to be a civilizing factor. The significance of these images is not in their conformity or lack of conformity to fact, for there is sufficient evidence to warrant either point of view. Indeed, the image does not really concern a factual judgment but is more like a working principle. If it is believed that the child is naturally good, yet bad children are observed, the image directs one to look beyond the behavior of the child to the structure and process of the institutions that surround him. For example, A. S. Neill, in *Summerhill*, argued that the child develops best in an environment in which restrictions have been minimized pointing to his experience at Summerhill for support of this generalization. However, on those occasions when he finds a child for whom Summerhill does not work, he supposes that the oppressiveness of society has been overbearing, thus rendering any remediation ineffective. Neill's basic assumption about childhood is not a factual statement subject to any significant verification. It is more like a pointer that tells us where to look for the solution to a difficulty that we wish to resolve. It tells us to look towards the restrictiveness of society for the difficulties that may be found in the child. Of course, no less an image is entailed in the view that claims that the basic problems of children arise from a breakdown in the authority of institutions and the subsequent ungirding of the child's "true" nature. It should not be thought, however, that we can do without such images and simply evaluate the facts as they come. We only can choose among a finite number of images, and our choice helps determine how the facts do come.[7]

Liberal educators may have differed about many things, but they also shared a wide area in common, an area that was reinforced by certain images about the relation between education and technology. It was this area of agreement that determined the boundaries that were placed on educational inquiry and that strongly influenced judgments and evaluations about schools (see especially Chapter Three and Four).

There is, furthermore, a question as to the limits that are placed on *our* understanding of an image that differs from our own. One of the functions of an ideology is to influence the meaning and use of a language. "In every concept, in every concrete meaning, there is contained a crystallization of the experiences of a group. When someone says 'kingdom' he is using the term in the sense in which it has meaning for a certain group."[8] The meaning is drastically different for a person who was brought up revering the glory and grandeur of the kingdom than it is for one who has learned about it as simply another form of administrative structure.[9] There is an area of meaning that cannot be shared completely. It might be possible for an outsider to observe and record all of the verbal associations that are made by a native when the term "kingdom" is uttered; it is not likely that he will conjure up the same emotions or that he will, under certain conditions (e.g., when the kingdom is threatened), act in the same way. (Part of the reason for the likelihood of an unshared area of meaning is to be found in the

---

[7] Of course, people can often give good reasons for the images they hold citing evidence to support them and arguing to explain examples that seem to counter their basic beliefs. But no single image has a monopoly on all good evidence and arguments. Indeed, what one person may hold as evidence in support of one image, another may see as merely an exception to a general principle and, therefore, explainable on other grounds. Witness, for example, the way in which the admitted fact of bad men has been explained by those who believe man to be basically good and the way in which the fact of good men can be explained by one who believes that man is essentially self-serving. However, the fact that communication does not always break down (if it did, perhaps we would not even understand what a breakdown means) is an indication that certain images are shared. Even people who have drastically different views of human nature may agree about whether a person is acting badly at a particular time although they may still disagree about the essential cause.

[8] Manheim, *op. cit.*, p. 22.

[9] Ibid., p. 22.

educational modes of society. It is one thing for a young child to listen
to the folktales, legends, and stories of his society for the first time, and
then again, but it is quite another thing for an adult, having heard
different stories from a different culture, to listen to them. While the
outsider can tell us what goes on "in a native's head" when he hears a
certain word, it is less likely that he can make it happen "in his
own head" when he hears that same word.)

Thus there is a natural tendency to intellectualize the images of
others. Only if we had experienced all of the conditions that gave rise
to the image could we do otherwise, but if this were the case, the image
would be ours—we would own it, and we would not be examining it.
When a group of people possess a common set of images about the social
and political world, and react to the same symbols in a similar and
reinforcing way, we say that they share an ideology. However, they do
not say this. There is, for example, a tendency among recent revisionist
scholars of education to criticize the liberal educators of the past for their
attempts to use the schools as instruments of social control and
engineering. Yet those who argued that the schools should be used in
this way were often reacting to a set of events that they believed could
be handled in no other way, and thus "social engineering" had a
different evaluative force. Nevertheless, the events of recent times and
the reaction of the general public to them—the willingness to accept
Vietnam for so long without question, the inability to see the larger
significance of Watergate—places the idea of social engineering in a
different light.

It is easy, on recognizing the images of another group as an
ideology, to dismiss it as falling short of the absolute truth. This
response overlooks the fact that by developing a common set of reactions
an ideology serves a functional purpose. Within a group that adheres to
a common viewpoint, arguments and disputations may still occur, but
when they do they presuppose a common frame of reference and a
mutually acceptable set of credentials. The arguments reinforce what is
common and strengthen the relationship. When a common ideology
breaks down arguments still may occur, but then no one really believes
that words alone will convince a serious opponent.

Ideologies have their roots in the invisible, soundless world, but
they relate to real things that can be seen. Different ideologies force us,
however, to see them differently. The legal structure, for example,
consists largely of statements about how we are expected to see property

relations and what we are, therefore, to respect as ownership. But ownership can be seen in many ways, some of them exclusive of others. Does occupancy or possession define ownership, or is it defined by a title handed down from one generation to the next or by the fact that we have "mixed our labor" with an object and made something useful out of it? Or is it determined by some prior idea of a just distribution? Presumably the law will tell us, but what if it is the law along with the ideology that embodies it that is being challenged? This particular ideological issue is of crucial importance to education, for the way it is answered will strongly influence the distribution of educational resources. (See Chapter Seven.)

In the last analysis however, the revelation of an image is only the first step in altering the total ideological structure. Unless one wishes to remain satisfied with the view that his ideology is his and mine is mine— a view that sounds reasonable but that can lead to insufferable conflicts— the examination of an ideology must eventually lead to an evaluation of issues on moral grounds. (See Chapter Seven.)

## IV.  MORAL  DILEMMAS

The treatment of the image presented here still presupposes that the drive for consistency is the precondition of moral and intellectual inquiry. Yet having a drive does not guarantee its fulfillment. The twentieth century has been a century of violence, killing, and destruction on a scale never before seen. During the 1940s in Europe alone 44 million people died in the name of one moral system or another and this number may not match that of Asia. Therefore, it is appropriate that we try to understand the ways in which theories about the world can influence our moral judgments sometimes to the point of overlooking the destruction that might be carried out even in the name of the theory. As we start this inquiry, it is clearly the case that our own moral posture and the peculiar problems of our times are both consciously and unconsciously guiding the inquiry. Yet it may be possible to uncover some glimpse of the areas in which that posture may possibly break down and, hence, where our most cherished norms need themselves to be reevaluated. Schooling may seem an odd subject to focus on for this study, but debates about the school reflect profoundly larger debates about the appropriate direction of society, and what we are willing to do to our children is a strong indication of what we are willing to do to each other. The movement known as progressive education comprises a significant focus of this study not because it was more prone than others to be on the fringe of its own moral view. Indeed, it is my opinion that it was less likely to do that. It has been chosen mainly because its theories comprise some of the most sophisticated attempts to think about education and because its practices were of some significance in the development of twentieth-century American schooling and educational policy. It has been chosen, too, for a personal reason. We live at a time when idealism breaks down quickly. In the early part of the 1960s some young people asked themselves what they were willing to die for and they answered in a militant but also in a nonviolent manner. Some joined the Peace Corps, others organized voter registration in Mississippi, others marched at Selma, and some died as a result of their commitment. Assassinations and war have intervened since that time, and for some the idealism that ushered in the 1960s has turned to hopelessness, accommodation, and, for a very few, senseless violence, which only mirrors but does not correct the structural violence of the larger society. There is a parallel in progressive thought. The idealism of progressive education, now somewhat jaded, survived two world wars and a depression, but in the process the idealism itself faded. Progressive education had its heroes, yet as the social context of the times have changed so too must these men and their works be reassessed. Although there is always a certain difficulty that accompanies the decline of an idea, there is also an opportunity to show how a changing context can affect profoundly the meaning of events and can lead to reassessment of fundamental principles.

## V. LIBERAL AND PROGRESSIVE EDUCATIONAL THEORY: THE PROBLEM OF FREEDOM

This study concentrates on people who I believe were central in the development of educational reform theory. Many of them were in the progressive education movement, but some were peripheral to it, and a few were opposed to it. But the question as to who was central and who was not is a subjective one, and no clear-cut criterion is available. For the moment, however, it will suffice to say that I believe that people such as John Dewey, George Herbert Mead, Edward L. Thorndike, Charles Beard, Arthur Bently, George Counts, Harold Rugg, and William Head Kilpatrick provided much of the theory behind progressive reform. Obviously these men did not agree on all things, and some are only peripherally related to schooling. Yet I believe that through them and others a family of ideas developed that became associated with liberal educational reform, and that these ideas had a powerful impact on the schools at many different levels and in many different ways.

Unlike other treatments of educational reform, however, the one offered here does not focus on the specific pedagogical practices or recommendations. These are not left out of consideration, but when they are examined, they are analyzed in order to reveal other things. The more central consideration is the relationship between schooling and society, a relationship that is not absent from traditional treatments of progressive thought, but one that is explored here in a new light.

Progressive education is best understood as a branch of American liberal thought that began to develop at the beginning of the twentieth century in reaction to what was seen as unfortunate social effects of classical liberal philosophy. Liberal thinkers and reformers addressed the injustices and hardships that they believed resulted from an ethics built on the demands of private industry and capitalism. Countering what they often called economic anarchy, they developed a philosophy that demanded an expanded role for public and governmental institutions. What liberals did for institutions in general, educational liberals did for the school: they provided the justification for expanding its influence on the lives of children.

While liberal educational reformers addressed the larger issues of educational policy, progressive educators are best known for their innovative proposals regarding teaching. The progressive teacher's concern was "the whole child" as the cliche went, but the idea of the whole child was indeed much more than a simple cliche. The idea that the school was to address the moral, social, emotional, and intellectual aspects of childhood arose as a reaction to the perceived breakdown in community believed to be associated with the developing industrial society. Thus the school was to pick up where it was thought the family, the church, and the community had been forced to leave off. This view of schooling entailed a new role for the teacher who was to be the orchestrator of an environment where intellectual, emotional, and spiritual growth would develop naturally, as many believed had been the case in preindustrial America.

Progressive education can therefore be seen as a sub-branch of liberal educational reform in general. Whereas liberal reform was interested in the larger policy questions that would extend the general influence of schooling, progressive educators were concerned to develop specific classroom techniques that would ease the process of growing up in industrial America.

A central justification of modern-day reform liberalism was based on a philosophical analysis of the concept of freedom and of the applicability of this concept in terms of the real conditions of the modern world. Contemporary liberals objected to the laissez-faire view of freedom on the grounds that it granted most men only the right to be free but not the means to achieve freedom. There is little need to reiterate the familiar history of this era in order to understand the power of the contemporary liberal's critique (man had the right to eat but only if he had the money to buy his food). The contemporary liberal believed that his proposals offered the means to make abstract freedom concrete. His job was to complete what the classical liberal had begun.

Although I have much sympathy with the contemporary liberal's critique of laissez-faire society, I believe that his view of freedom was misleading—that it did not propose to develop a society whereby men could achieve what they willed but, instead, one whereby the majority of men would will what they could achieve. A brief analysis of the concept of freedom will be helpful in establishing a framework for the elaboration of this point in the chapters that follow.

Almost all analyses of freedom contain the same factors—the differences arising from the way in which these factors are put together. One of these is an internal factor that I call the human will. This will embraces, among other things, man's needs, wants, and desires. It is indicative of man's purposeful striving and suggests acts that are performed to satisfy some deprivation. The second factor in the concept of freedom is indicated by something that begins as external to man's will, which I call his environment. Freedom consists of the appropriation (or the possibility of appropriation) of one of these to the other. Man finds his satisfaction in his environment, and it is the interaction of his will with the external world that provides the index of his freedoms. However, the nature of the environment should not be taken narrowly.

For some the essential environment is to be found in the accumulation of physical objects which can satisfy man's material needs. For others it consists of something else, a set of unchangeable laws, a spiritual substance or an institutional arrangement.

The will and the something external to it constitute the two major ingredients of freedom. But it is the relationship between these two that constitute varying views of freedom. In common language, we say: "He is free to choose what he wants," but this has two different meanings. First, it means that there are no external constraints that hinder his choice—that no one is twisting his arms or holding a gun at his head. However, it can mean that the object of his desire is available to him—that he has only to exercise his will in order to obtain it. These two meanings are not precisely the same. To say that there are no external constraints does not mean that there are no restraints whatsoever. For example, "He is free to become a nuclear physicist" might sometimes more accurately be rendered "He is free to try to become a nuclear physicist" where the statement suggests disparagingly that there are no external barriers present to him alone—("what does it matter if he is black, or Jewish he is free.") but that internal barriers may well be present ("only his own intellectual limits stand in the way"). This was the view of freedom held by the classical liberal.

Another meaning of the statement, "He is free to do as he wishes," indicates that there are no barriers whatsoever. "You are now free to walk out the door," or, more precisely, "If you wish to walk out the door, then nothing will stop you." In this case, freedom consists of a correspondence between what is desired and what, in fact, can be achieved. Regarding this view of freedom, the two essential ingredients can be related in rather dramatically different ways, each revealing a different view of freedom. On the one hand, there is the will that desires something, and, on the other hand, there is the something that is desired. Freedom is the appropriation of one of these factors to the other, but we do not yet know which factor is to be appropriated to the other.

Suppose, for example, that we take the will to be the independent variable. Then freedom consists in molding that which is external to the dictates of the will. To illustrate further, assume that the *nature* of man dictates that he seeks pleasure and, furthermore, that objects $A$, $B$, and $C$ will bring him pleasure, but that objects $X$, $Y$, and $Z$ will only produce sorrow and pain; a man is then free when he is so able to manipulate his world as to achieve *A, B,* or *C* and to avoid *X, Y,* and *Z*. Or to make the matter more concrete, a man who has a burning desire to read a book by D. H. Lawrence exercises his freedom when, in fact, he is able to find a copy of his works and read it.[10]

Freedom as a correspondence between the will and the object of its desire contains another possibility. Suppose that the environment, or an important aspect of it, (and not the will), is taken as the independent variable. In this case, the correspondence must be achieved by making an adjustment in the will. The history of philosophy is replete with views that have proposed just such an adjustment. The stoics' demand that man overcome his passion and achieve freedom by embracing the universal and necessary principle of reason, Spinoza's association of freedom with the intellectual love of God, Hegel's appeal that men attach themselves to the historically necessary movement of the nation and state, and Marx's claim that freedom is found only when the dialectical process of history is understood and followed are all examples of views that associate freedom with the appropriate adjustment of the will. It should be mentioned that in few, if any, of these views is man ever completely passive with regards to the total environment. Once he has attached his will to the major external force, then he is quite capable of projecting other goals and manipulating parts of the environment to satisfy them. Critics of both Hegel and Marx especially have tended to miss this point. Man does not cease to desire once he has embraced the institution of the state or the laws of history, but what he now in fact desires can be achieved with the aid of the very forces that he has embraced. The chapters that follow explore the kinds of adjustments that liberal and progressive educators saw as desirable.

The classical liberal had assumed that freedom consisted of the absence of external man-made constraints—that a man could be free even if he did not actually achieve the object of his desires. He was free if his failure could be attributed to some personal inadequacy: a lack of energy, skill, intelligence, or luck. It was to the contemporary liberal's credit that he pointed out that the classical liberal had accepted only

---

[10] It would be quite futile for those who hold this view of freedom actually to maintain that freedom is achieved only when a desire for a very specific object such as *Lady Chatterley's Lover* is achieved. Instead, as with someone like Bentham, the point is that there are some simple psychological states that can, in fact, be satisfied by a variety of objects. This is why, for example, "pleasure" and "pain" are so much more convenient than Lady Chatterley.

legal constraints as real and assumed that if legal strictures were removed, all failure could be attributed to some internal lack. It was also to the new liberal's credit that he was able to demonstrate that a large network of extra-legal, oppressive institutions had grown up supported philosophically by the *laissez-faire* view of freedom.

Yet precisely because the contemporary liberal began his critique with an examination of the classical view of freedom, his own ideas on this subject have been generally misunderstood. It has been thought that because contemporary liberalism initiated its critique by highlighting the roadblocks that grew out of classical liberalism, that the new liberalism was about removing these roadblocks. In other words, it is thought that the new liberal was determined to help man alter his environment to suit his will, but this is only part of the story.[11]

Without doing a disservice to the reforms initiated by the contemporary liberal, I believe it would be more accurate to say that he removed some barriers and supported others. Yet his philosophy was so constructed as to convince himself and others that the latter were not barriers at all but were inevitable aspects of an external environment to which the will had to adjust itself in order for man to be free. The schools were a major instrument in making this adjustment.

It is tempting to undertake a discussion of when a barrier is real and when it is not, but this is a temptation I choose to avoid. What is

---

[11] Such an interpretation is found, for example, in Richard J. Bernstein's work on Dewey: "Freedom is based on the possibility of human choice, but it involves more than this possibility. Freedom requires the effective power to *act* in accordance with choice" [Richard J. Bernstein, *John Dewey* (New York: Washington Square Press), 1967, p. 140].

But in an indirect way Bernstein recognizes the other side of this issue:

Classical liberalism fails to realize the powerful influence that all social institutions can exert on shaping the quality and type of human individuality that is expressed. Dewey firmly believed that if complexes of social, economic, and political institutions were not deliberately controlled, they will result in the increase of human alienation and dehumanization (ibid., p. 139).

Yet if institutions do have such a large impact upon individuality, and if elements of the human will are included in the notion of individuality (as indeed they would be in Dewey's thought), then as institutions are controlled so, too, is the human will. Thus, perhaps part of the first quote from Bernstein could be rephrased: " 'Freedom requires the effective power to *act* in accord with choice' as choice has been deliberately determined by conscious institutional control."

significant for this study is that the acceptance of certain conditions as fixed can reinforce those conditions, and it was around such acceptance that the liberal concept of man and society was developed. An example will be useful to illustrate this point. Suppose that it is believed that schools exist to service an existing elite and to render the masses obedient to that elite. This belief may be true or it may be false, but the belief itself tells us little about how such a situation is to be evaluated. If it is also believed however, that every social group of a similar size is and *must* be governed by an elite that sets policy, leads the masses, and governs with the major intent of keeping itself in power then one kind of evaluation is called for. In this situation all government is, by necessity, a conspiracy against the masses, but because this is to be viewed as an unalterable aspect of human society the description of the "conspiracy" does not suggest a negative evaluation. Suppose now, however, that someone else describes the same society in the very same way, only now it is assumed that events had once been different and could be different again. In this instance the description demands an evaluation, and, more than likely, it will be a negative one.[12]


## VI. TECHNOLOGY AND FREEDOM

One of the fixed conditions that the liberal accepted was the continued growth of technology as the factor around which all other major aspects of man's social and intellectual activity was to be adjusted—including his will. By regarding the growth of technology in this way, he contributed to the development of the technological, expert society that we are experiencing now. As a consequence of this view, the liberal's recommendations for schooling were designed to adjust the student's will to the perceived inevitability of expanding technology.

But even further, if Dewey believed that "if complexes of social, economic, and political institutions are not deliberately controlled, they will result in an increase of human alienation and dehumanization," perhaps we now have reason to believe that as deliberate control has often intensified, human alienation and dehumanization has not abated.

[12] In social theory these two views are represented by Pareto and C. W. Mills, respectively.

Technology, of course, meant more than the use of simple tools to create commodities and satisfy human wants. It also indicated a high level of interdependence among various productive and social functions such that any given product was the result of many men interacting with each other and with the machine. Moreover such interaction had to be consciously planned and designed with the goals of production and efficiency in mind. The well-being of the worker also may be a consideration, but it is defined in terms that are consistent with the production goals. In this process, individuality was not denied, but it was more often seen as an aspect of consumption instead of a part of production itself. Indeed, one of the reasons that schooling was so attractive to progressives was that they recognized that the production process had lost its educative and humanizing significance, and they believed that the schools could serve as a substitute.

Technology suggested more than simply the way in which man and machine were related to each other. It also had implications for the way in which men were to think about themselves and others in the context of this interdependence between men and machines. Here the school played a major role in giving the child an understanding of his place in the large scheme of things. The recognition that the meaning of technology entails not only machines and their organization, but also the way in which men must come to think about these things, is shared by people of many different persuasions, such as a liberal like Karl Mannheim and an opponent of technological society, such as Jacques Ellul. Both would agree, for example, that technological society conditions people to view their world in pieces, with but a vague sense of how their own function fits into the larger complexity. That Ellul would judge this in a generally negative way and Mannheim would not is largely because they differ over whether the growth of technology is inevitable and natural to man.

Ellul[13] perceives liberal thought as an attempt to accommodate man's will to the expanding technology, arguing that such attempts contribute to the total envelopment of man by an artificial and external force. The liberal response to this kind of criticism has been that the critic made an untenable separation between what is natural and what

---

[13] Jacques Ellul, *The Technological Society* (New York: Vintage Books), 1964. See especially Chapter V.

is artificial, between what is technical and what is human. In other words, it is claimed that technology is not necessarily a barrier to man's will but is something that he can and should incorporate into his structure of thinking and desiring as an instrument in achieving his freedom.

These are difficult arguments to address because of the problems involved in deciding what is artificial and what is not. If Ellul is correct, then technology itself poses the greatest threat to man's freedom. If he is wrong, then perhaps it does offer man the promise of a new age of human development and freedom. I must admit that my own view is ambivalent. It would be absurd not to recognize the promises that could be realized to some extent by technology. Health, food growth, and population control are the most imperative and noteworthy examples. Of course, the scorecard is obscure and difficult to read as we can see by observing the "advances" that have been made in the instruments of war. But the scorecard alone will never tell us what we want to know. Are our problems of technology to be solved by more or less technology? My hope is to examine the thought and activity of people who believed that technology was not an essential threat to man and, therefore, not a barrier to his freedom. My intent is also to examine the images that sustained this view and to evaluate the principle that justified it.

## VII. THE ORGANIZATION
## OF THE BOOK

The organization of this book reflects my belief that technology has been the dominant influence in the development of twentieth-century educational reform. The first chapter shows the accommodations that were made by both conservative and progressive educators around 1900 to certain industrial and national trends, and it examines the way in which important developments in scientific thought influenced liberal ideas about social and educational change. Chapter Two looks at some of the ideological limitations that were in fact placed on "science" and "objectivity" and the impact that this had on schools. Chapter Three examines the liberal ideal of equality of opportunity and shows some conflicts that arose in progressive thought since this ideal was expected to serve both justice and technology at the same time.

Chapter Four looks at progressive education as an aspect of liberal educational reform and shows how both those who advocated a child-centered pedagogy and those who opposed it were serving similar ends. Chapters Five and Six highlight two key images that guided and sustained liberal, progressive thought. Chapter Five looks at the liberal image of history and Chapter Six at the image of society. The last chapter approaches the problem of evaluation and explores some of the different points from which a judgment of liberal, progressive educational policy can be made. It offers an alternative point of view.

One final word is in order here to distinguish this work from other recent critiques of educational reform.

Not so long ago, when Americans still looked upon their country as the cradle of liberty, scholars, sympathetic to the progressive education movement, felt compelled to defend it against charges from the right by denying that it was intent on coddling the young and thereby corrupting society. Although the rhetoric was sometimes sharp, with the lines of battle clearly drawn, there was a large area of agreement about the inherent rightfulness of American institutions and the promise of her future course of development, and there was agreement, too, about the important role of the school in keeping her direction sound. Granted, there were different visions of the future and of how to reach it, nevertheless, the past was clearly defined and defended by liberals and conservatives alike. This area of agreement was important for it assured that educational and social problems would be analyzed by examining people and policies rather than by a searching examination of the structural complex of which schools are a part.

For many years the progressive reformer and his scholarly defender enjoyed the advantage of never having their ideas fully tested. They could, therefore, point with pride to the programs that were successful, could cite the educational and psychological literature to support their arguments, and could explain away the failures by commenting on the inadequate funds available or by denying that a particular program was truly representative of the progressive ideal.

The 1960s proved to be as much an embarrassment as a boom to educational reform and to the large remnant of progressive-minded educators who successfully bid for the funds that suddenly had become available. After the questionable records of progressive like programs such as Upward Bound, and Head Start, it has again become fashionable to suggest that differences in school performance are the result of genetic variations in intelligence among the different races. Moreover, the most frequently cited research on schools now suggest that they have little to do with achievement or mobility.[14]

In light of these new developments, it is not surprising to find educational reform under attack from the left as well as the right. Ivan Illich argues that schools are and, of necessity must be an essential part of the present oppressive political structure. Others, such as Colin Greer, agree that the schools have served tö cover up the oppressive features of society but believe that they could do otherwise serving perhaps as a force for radical change.

Regardless of the differences among the new critics of educational reform, there is agreement that the rhetoric of the reformer has been used to mask the reality of the public schools. Greer's criticism of Cremin, perhaps the most prominent defender of progressive education, is that he takes the rhetoric of the reformer at face value and therefore overlooks what was really happening in schools. While on one level this criticism is correct and serves to point out the failure of liberal scholars to check the progress of schools against their own standards, on another level it is misguided and counter productive to a radical critique. For if it is accepted that the refomer's rhetoric and stated intentions were one thing, but the reality of the school was something else, and if we judge the failure of education to lie in the gap between rhetoric and reality then we have allowed the liberal ideal to remain supreme and free of criticism. But if it is the ideal itself that is lacking, and if the reality has in some ways been true to it, then such a criticism will miss the target by a large degree. I believe that the latter is the case.

[14] For an elaboration of these points, see H. Gintus and S. Bowles, "The Contradictions of Liberal Educational Reform" in *Work, Technology and Education: Dissenting Essays in The History and Philosophy of Education*. W. Feinberg and H. Rosemont, Jr., eds. (Chicago: The University of Illinois Press). 1975.

# CHAPTER ONE

# From a Philosophy of Man to a Science of Management

## I. INTRODUCTION

Although it has been customary to classify an educational theory according to whether or not it reflects a child-centered or a subject-matter point of view, this scheme is misleading because it obscures the most significant aspects of twentieth century educational theory. The length to which scientific and technological considerations have guided educational theory and rhetoric cuts across both child-centered and subject-matter theories. It is this consideration that divides educators who might be thought of as nineteenth-century prototypes from their twentieth century counterparts.

This chapter examines the influence of scientific models on twentieth-century educational theory by comparing the educational theories of representative child-centered and subject-centered educators of the nineteenth century with developments that stamped the character of twentieth-century theory.

## II. THE BEGINNINGS OF
## "A SCIENCE OF EDUCATION"

Progressive education, with its emphasis on a child-centered approach can be perceived on a number of different levels, and its appeal can be explained by its common-sense approach to problems of schools. Joseph Mayer Rice, for example, wrote a series of muckraking articles in 1892 that attracted a good deal of attention. Rice's work is a good starting point not only because it marked a period of heightened concern about schools[1] but because Rice's writings reveal much that is attractive about progressive, child-centered ideas.

Rice's survey of the public schools took him to a number of cities including New York, Chicago, St. Paul, Boston, and Philadelphia. He found most of the teaching in these cities to be mechanical, abstract, and artificial.

For example in describing a reading lesson in Chicago he wrote:

When some time had been spent in thus maneuvering the jaws, the teacher remarked: "Your tongues are not loose." Fifty pupils now put out their tongues and wagged them in all directions. What an idea these pupils must have received of the purpose of a school when from the start they were taught systematically how to make grimaces and wag their tongues! . . .
    In another classroom the pupils threw their glances around in a horrible manner while reading; they stared frightfully. I mentioned this to the principal who informed me in reply that this room was noted for the manner in which pupils used their eyes and that it was, in consequence, generally known as "the eye-room."[2]

In New York, Rice found similar mechanical and dehumanizing educational techniques. In the following he describes the practice of one school whose principal had consistently been rated excellent by the New York superintendent.

In order to reach the desired end, the school had been converted into the most dehumanizing institution that I have ever laid eyes upon, each child being treated as if he possessed a memory and the faculty of speech, but no individuality, no sensibility, no soul. . . .
    The spirit of the school is, "do what you like with the child,

---

[1] Lawrence Cremin stresses the influence of Rice on the public in his *The Transformation of the Schools* (New York: Vintage Books), 1961, pp. 6-7.
    [2] John M. Rice "The Public Schools of Chicago and St. Paul," *The Forum,* Vol. 15 (April 1893), pp. 206 and 208.

immobilize him, automize him, dehumanize him, but save, save the minutes." Everything is prohibited that is of no measurable advantage to the child, such as movement of the head or limb, when there is no logical reason why it should be moved at that time. I asked the principal whether the children were not allowed to move their heads. She answered, "why should they look behind when the teacher is in front of them: '" words too logical to be refuted.[3]

By bringing such educational practices to the public attention, Rice offered a powerful and persuasive case for educational reform. It is not surprising that in his first article he expressed what was soon to become the rallying cry of progressive reform: "I never forget . . . that the school exists for the benefit of the child and not for the benefit of boards of education, superintendents, and teachers".[4]

However, there was a deeper level to the issue of whether or not existing schools were fit places for children, and this had to do with the adequacy of the existing educational theory to meet the emerging needs of an industrial society.

Rice, like many others, perceived that American society was reaching the point of social and technological interdependence whereby schooling would become a much more essential part of American culture. He believed that it was no longer excusable to rely simply on the fortunate presence of a good teacher or a wise administrator to advance the kind of education now needed, and that to meet the demands of the new age, education must become scientific. He felt that it must be taken out of the hands of the ward bosses and given over to a group of scientifically trained professionals who would set standards according to statistically determined norms and evaluate instructions according to proven instruments.

Even though many of Rice's proposals may seem modest from contemporary standards, nevertheless they met with significant resistance from professional educators. At the thirty-sixth annual convention of the National Education Association (1897), for example, Rice lead a round-table discussion on the methods of teaching spelling. Even though his statistics showed that no evident difference existed after eight years in

---

[3] John M. Rice, "The Public School System of New York City", *The Forum,* Vol. 14 (January 1892), p. 617.

[4] John M. Rice, "Our Public School System: Evils in Baltimore", *The Forum,* Vol. 14 (October 1892), p. 146.

the ability to spell of students who spent 15 minutes a day studying as opposed to those who spent 30, Rice was sternly reprimanded for thinking that important educational questions could be answered by statistical data.[5] He was informed that spelling was taught not for its own sake but for its disciplinary value in training the faculties of the mind.[6]

While there would be doubtful mileage in trying to defend Rice's critics on this particular point, nevertheless the response indicates some awareness, albeit uninformed, of the limits of scientific understanding, and it is the loss of this awareness that significantly characterizes later educational reform theory. One need not agree with any of the substantial proposals of the earlier educators in order to appreciate this essential difference between representative nineteenth-century thinkers and their twentieth-century counterparts. Therefore in order to understand the essential characteristics of twentieth-century educational theory, one begins by looking at it against the background of nineteenth-century theory.

## III. THE IDEA OF A
## SCIENCE OF EDUCATION AT
## THE TURN OF THE CENTURY

On the surface, Rice's appeal to a science of education was not new. As early as 1825 James G. Carter ("father of the normal school") declared that a science of education was self-evident.[7] For the most part, however, nineteenth-century works that were offered as treatises on the science of education resembled elaborate synthetic works on ethics. This is not surprising since it was thought that science was strictly a means and the major problem for education was to discover the end. Rice, however, was proposing that educational theory should focus on means and techniques. This proposal marks him as a representative of twentieth-century educational reform.

From the time that James G. Carter affirmed his faith in the existence of an educational science to the time that the superintendents

---

[5] John M. Rice, *Scientific Management in Education* (New York: Hinds, Noble and Eldridge), 1912, pp. 17-18.

[6] James Robarts, "The Rise of Educational Science in America," Unpublished Ph.D. thesis, University of Illinois, 1963, p. 57.

[7] Robarts, p. 14.

criticized Rice for not understanding the true purpose of spelling, a good many educators had become firmly convinced that there indeed did exist something that could properly be called a science of education. Yet while its existence was certain, its attributes were less so, and the ways of its intervention in the world of teachers and students remained a mystery. Nevertheless there were many attempts to explicate its nature and to reveal its methods, and it is against the background of these attempts, as they were carried out in the nineteenth century, that we can better understand the distinctive elements of twentieth-century educational rhetoric and reform.

Nineteenth-century treatises on the science of education were basically treatises on ethics mixed with some theology and a generous portion of common-sense principles about classroom management and child psychology. Educators who are commonly thought of as child-centered or progressive, shared this treatment of science with their conservative counterparts. The differences between them resulted not from the way they perceived educational science in general but from the way in which they characterized its content. Thus different views on the nature of childhood often gave rise to different views of pedagogy. However, the arguments were carried on within a similar intellectual framework, where different parties made similar appeals to justify conflicting claims. This framework was significantly different than the Darwinian mold in which later educational theory was cast.

Most of the educators of this period did not perceive of the science of education as involving a procedure for systematically controlled observation and experimentation, nor did they see any need to study animals in order to understand human beings. Indeed as we will see, some were quite concerned to mark off an area of knowledge where such procedures were not allowed to apply. Instead, the "scientific" studies of this period involved the selection and interpretation of ideas about such things as the nature of childhood, the structure of knowledge, and the purposes of education as these had been articulated by philosophers throughout the ages. Once this information was collected the role of educational science was to deduce rules of practice from it.

In order to see how very close different sides of the educational establishment were on the issues of the science of education, we need but to look briefly at two representative figures. William Torrey Harris (1835-1909), the foremost Hegelian philosopher in the United States, and a practicing school administrator who served as the U. S. Commissioner of Education from 1889 to 1906, is an important representative of conservative educational thought at the turn of the nineteenth century. Francis W. Parker (1837-1902), whom Dewey once referred to as the father of progressive education, served as superintendent of schools in Quincy, Massachusetts, and as head of the Cook County Normal School, each of which became a showcase of progressive practice. We will see that what distinguishes Harris as a conservative from Parker as a progressive were the different views each held about the method of pedagogy and the organization of the classroom. We will see too that certain aspects of their political rhetoric appear to distinguish their points of view but that, in fact, this distinction is of little real significance. The important point for understanding the changes in education that were soon to come is found in the fact that Harris and Parker were in general agreement that a science of education must rest firmly upon a nonscientific examination of the nature of education itself, (or as Harris would put it, upon the conditions that must be assumed present in order for a being to be educatable).

Harris and Parker both wrote at a time when the Darwinian influence was gaining prominence in scholarly circles, and although Harris, more than Parker, consciously feared this influence the styles of *both* men were inimical to it. Harris expressed concern lest a science of education follow the Darwinian model and begin thereby to focus only on the common element between man and beast. He warned that there is a right and wrong kind of educational science. The wrong kind looks only at what is, describes it and draws its implications from it. The right kind looks at what is only in the light of a systematic examination of what ought to be and thus focuses on the distinctive elements of man rather than upon the common ones.

Thus Harris believed that the science of education rested upon and was limited by the study of ethics and philosophy. Only after something was known about the nature of man as an educatable being could a claim be made about what a science of education should investigate. This point is rather crucial and therefore requires an illustration. If one believes, contrary to Harris, that human education is exactly the same kind of phenomena as animal learning (only perhaps more complex), then it is quite reasonable to restrict the activity of the teacher to behaviors that might just as well characterize the animal trainer, such as introducing the proper reinforcements at the proper moment. If, however, one believes that there is something quite distinctive about human education, something that is not at all analogous to animal learning, then, while reinforcement might not be ruled out as a necessary part of teaching, it would never sufficiently characterize the educational process. In this respect, Harris' fear of the Darwinian influence of education was not without foundation.

Although Harris' arguments are largely of historical interest, they illustrate the reasons why he believed that limits could properly be placed on educational science. He argued that an understanding of the nature of education presupposed an understanding of the type of being that could be educated. He pointed out that two factors were crucial. First, it must be a being whose development is not totally dependent on external forces, and second, it must be a being that is capable of recognizing itself as a member of a species.

Harris' concept of education rested on his view of the self since selfhood was a necessary (although not a sufficient) condition for a being to be educatable. Harris thought individuality was the essential characteristic of selfhood involving the power of a being to modify an external world according to its own inclinations, that is, to make a difference. It is this aspect of selfhood, that tied together both men and animals, and it was as pure will—as animals—that children entered the world. But, he argued, a self that is educatable must have more than the capacity to make a difference in the world. It must also have the capacity *to see* itself making a difference. Thus it must be able to distinguish itself from its world; it must be able to understand the persistence of itself and its object through time, and it must have the capacity to consciously perceive the fact of its own activity. Ultimately, the educatable being must also be able to grasp the principles that unite him as a member of a common species to others and then to nature as a whole. Harris believed that these conditions were reflected in the various human faculties from bare recollection and memory to language and abstract thinking.[8]

The limits that Harris placed on educational science were grounded in his beliefs about the nature of the self although, as we will see, his position is not without certain political concerns. Harris believed that personhood, the eventual object of an educatable self, is developed only in the context of a political society where, as he put it, an individual

---

[8] W. T. Harris, "Educational Psychology: Outline of a System", *Journal of Speculative Philosophy*, Vol. 14 (April 1880), pp. 230-235.

contributes "himself to the services of others" and "gains for himself the service of all mankind."[9] However, such mutual service did not occur in a simple face to face personal way, but rather through the mediation of institutions where resources were developed and stored, and where people were trained and mutually supported. The educated man was the one who recognized and identified with these institutional relationships and who knowingly directed his energy towards maintaining and strengthening them.

Harris' belief that personhood was the result of the interaction of men in institutions set the tone for his recommendations about schooling. In preparing the child for his life as a member of the species, Harris proposed that the schools must prepare him for a "life in institutions,"[10] and a large part of that task involved imposing on the child behavior rendered necessary in order to secure concert of action, such forms as regularity, punctuality, silence and industry. "These are the four cardinal duties of the public school pupil."[11] Then in contrast to Rice, Harris noted that "we call these duties mechanical duties, but they underlie all higher ethics."[12]

Certainly there are significant deficiencies in Harris' treatment of early education, and it is questionable just how much they follow from his ideas about selfhood and educatability as opposed to a certain obvious desire for political stability. Nevertheless the structure of Harris' argument serves as a reminder that particular events are to be evaluated and judged to be educationally worthwhile only in a contextual framework. To illustrate this point, suppose that the educational scientist, taking up Harris' call for the development of regularity, and punctuality, proposed a set of techniques that assured us that in 99 percent of the cases children would acquire these attitudes quickly and efficiently. Using Harris' argument, one would have to withhold judgment about the *educational* value of such techniques until one were able to judge the insights that these children were likely to obtain, first as a result of possessing these "virtues," and second, as a result of participating in the total educational program of a school. The cardinal virtues were only the beginning. All subsequent education was to be con-

[9] W. T. Harris, "Compulsory Education in Relation to Crime and Social Morals," Washington: privately printed, 1885, p. 6.

[10] Ibid., p. 7.

[11] Ibid., p. 8.

[12] Ibid., p. 8.

cerned with the distinctive aspect of man and thus the subjects included in the curriculum were to be chosen for the insights they provide about the relationship of members of the human species to each other and to their environment.

It would be a mistake to overemphasize the educative source of Harris' proposals about schools, for certainly, as we shall see, there were other concerns operating. Nevertheless, in the light of recent attempts to use the schools as the training arm of industry, to deny to many children because of IQ scores or for some other equally distorted reason, access to human insight and culture, there is some merit in remembering that education does have something to do with the issue of what knowledge is of most worth, and that the way in which one answers this question should have a bearing on what is accepted as a legitimate educational science.

Whereas Harris viewed the child as a little beast who was yet to be molded into a person by education, Parker saw him as a divine being who must be free to develop from his own impulses and instincts. Parker saw the child as a natural scholar seeking knowledge simply by virtue of his being in the world and possessed of the grace and harmony, which all art strived to imitate.[13] The child was an inherently moral being, "a perfect unity of thought and action" who needed only to be provided the conditions whereby his attruism could be expressed. Given his romantic view of childhood, Parker believed that the school should not be a place that imposed an institutional form on the child but, instead, a community that allowed him to express his natural impulses in rich and varied ways.

The major differences between Harris and Parker resulted from the fact that the former rested his arguments largely on the institutional requirements laid down by society, and the latter rested his on what he thought were the immediate needs of the child. This crucial difference in belief also lead to an important difference in emphasis. Harris was concerned with providing a rational for the teaching of certain *essential* subjects whereas Parker's concern was largely with the *way* such subjects should be taught. For example, Parker argued that reading, mathematics, and science should be taught as natural extensions of the child's already existing inclination to know his world and to communicate his knowl-

[13] Francis W. Parker, *Talks on Pedagogics: Theory of Concentration,* (N.Y. and Chicago: E. L. Kellog and Co.), 1894, pp. 20-21.

edge. Harris, however, believed that such subjects *must* be taught because they were the conditions for worthwhile *future* activity and even more important, because they were the conditions for wothwhile activity in an urban, industrial age. "Mathematics and science," he wrote, "are necessary to the labourer in this age of machinery. The more knowledge the school has given him, the higher his rank as directive Power!"[14] This difference remains as one of the most important characteristics distinguishing the child centered educator from his subject centered counterpart. Yet, as we shall see, its significance depends ultimately on the larger social structure in which it is found.[15]

While Parker's pedagogical proposals were in sharp contrast to those of Harris, his views on educational science were not. He did not believe, as Rice did, that the goal of educational science was to establish a set of *statistical* norms, nor did he believe that educational practice could be measured by how well it approximated such norms. Instead, he wrote that the study of education involved the discovery of laws that govern behavior towards a certain end, and he believed such laws to be immutable and divine. Because he believed that such laws emanated from a god that permeated all things, he also believed that no amount of statistical evidence could contradict them. Thus educational science, in the strict sense, also played a subsidiary role in Parker's view. Once such laws were known, then the science of education could draw implications for the activities of teaching and learning.

However noble Parker's sentiments may have been, they were hardly "scientific" in any contemporary sense of that term. Nevertheless, when we examine the political and economic concerns expressed by both Parker and Harris we can see each giving recognition to forces which would soon render their views on educational science quaint and obsolete. For each, in his own way and with his own emphasis, saw that the school was becoming essential to the industrial life of the nation.

These concerns are more apparent in the thought of Harris whose philosophical arguments were bolstered by a vision that saw the school as the last stronghold against the forces of darkness and evil. In an appeal that was to become more common among later educators, he asked: "Why educate the children of the common labourers?" And he

[14] W. T. Harris, "Educational Needs of Urban Civilization", *Education,* Vol. 5 (May 1885) p. 447.
[15] See Chapter Four.

answered: "For your own well-being and the well-being of your children, the children of all must be educated. If you wish property safe from confiscation by a majority composed of communists, you must see to it that the people are educated so that each sees the sacredness of property, and its service to the world in making available to each the industry of the entire population of the earth."[16]

Although Harris alluded to the mutual dependence of all peoples, there was no doubt in his mind that the United States must establish and maintain its industrial leadership, nor was there any doubt of the essential role that the school needed to play in this project. "Either educate your people in the common school," warned Harris, "or your labour will not compete with other nations whose people are educated up to the capacity of inventing and directing machinery. If you cannot compete with other peoples in the matter of the use of machinery, you must recede from the front ranks of nations in every respect."[17] If there was any tension between Harris' belief in the mutual interdependence of people and institutions on the one hand and his call for American industrial superiority on the other, he did not seem to recognize it. The institutions that merited respect were purely Western and largely American ones. It is not exaggerating to say that Harris believed that it was the duty of America to carry the mantle of white civilization to the "subcultures" of the world and that is was their *good fortune* to be conquered by such an advanced society.

The white man proves his civilization to be superior to other civilizations just by this very influence which he exercises over the people that have lower forms of civilizations, forms that do not permit them to conquer nature and to make the elements into ministers of human power.[18]

Given Harris' belief that civilizations were to be judged by their ability to conquer nature, he was, of course, quite justified in concluding that the only way to judge the merits of one civilization over another was by "the influence" that it exercised. And given this standard of might all

[16] W. T. Harris "Why Educate The Children of The Common Laborer?," Harvard University, Weidner Library Collection.

[17] Harris, "Educational Needs . . ." p. 447.

[18] Harris, "An Educational Policy for Our New Possessions," *Educational Review* (reprint), 1889, p. 115.

strictly ethical norms become quite irrelevant, as not surprisingly do Harris' view of educational science.

In the forefront of Harris' ideas were the requirements that he projected on to the developing urban industrial society. These were then used to map what he thought to be an appropriate education system. His major goal was to find a way in which America could adjust to the emerging technology without a political revolution and without a drastic alteration in the distribution of wealth. Marx had already served notice on the defenders of capitalism that within its own technology were the seeds of its destruction, and Harris believed that the school was the instrument to assure that such seeds never blossomed. Yet such assurance required sound management more than it required sound ethics.

That the requirements of the developing urban industrial society governed much of Harris' writings about education is quite clear. That these were also important considerations in Parkers' writings is less obvious, but no less true. The reason for the obscurity in Parker's writing is that his political rhetoric, much like his educational, had a more radical tone than Harris. Thus while Harris was quite content to maintain the class structure as it was, Parker argued that the common school was an essential instrument for reducing "the isolation between classes," and indeed there are times when his rhetoric seems to echo the ideas of Karl Marx rather than W. T. Harris, but this is only an echo. In a somewhat typical expression of his social theory, for example, he noted that the history of man is the history of ideas developed for the benefit of all, being taken over by and for the benefit of the few.

The great founders and reformers of religion have, almost without exception, discovered divine truths, have brought into the world some great good for humanity. . . . But in the history of every great movement for good there comes the time when, seeing its influence, the dominant few grasp it and use it as a means of control.[19]

This passage is somewhat peculiar for it appears to have little bearing upon Parker's perception of political reality, or upon his practical educational activity. For example, in 1894 Parker read a *paper* before the National Education Association convention.[20] The *paper* was a

---

[19] Parker, *Talks on Pedagogics,* p. 402.
[20] Parker, "The Report of the Committee of Ten . . . Its Use for the Improvement of Teachers Now at Work in the Schools," *NEA Journal of Addresses and Proceedings,* Vol. 33, (1894).

commentary on the report of the Committee of Ten, which was a high level committee headed by Charles W. Eliot, then president of Harvard, appointed to assess the needs of American education and to make recommendations for improving it. Parker's response was friendly to the report, restricting itself to suggestions about how its findings be disseminated most effectively and is interspersed with his usual appeal for democracy, hence:

Three-fourth of the pupils in large cities leave school before beginning their fifth year; . . . The mass of children do not leave school on account of poverty, they leave because the street, the shop, and the manufactory are more attractive than the school. If children loved school work, most parents would work their fingers to the bone to keep them there. One hundred educators have firmly declared that there are no preferred classes, no rich and poor, not one education for college and another for business.[21]

And then, quoting Eliot in the report:

The secondary schools of the United States, taken as a whole, do not exist for the purpose of preparing boys and girls for colleges. Only an insignificant percentage of the graduates of these schools go to college or scientific schools. Their main function is to prepare for the duties of life that small portion of all the children in the country—a proportion small in number, but very important to the welfare of the nation—who show themselves able to profit by an education prolonged to the eighteenth year, and whose parents are able to support them while they remain so long in school.[22]

It is significant that Parker saw no contradiction between his interpretation of Eliot's statement that "there are no preferred classes, no rich and no poor, etc." and Eliot's own words," who show themselves able to profit by an education prolonged to the eighteenth year, and whose parents are able to support them while they remain so long in school." Nor did he see any great tension between his own child-centered approach to schooling and the justification by the committee of its recommendations on the basis of the welfare of the nation. Parker seemed quite willing to accept the economic division of labour and the social division of status as an expression of some fixed, unchangeable quality. He did not think it unduly elitist to request that the secondary schools

---

[21] Ibid., p. 449.
[22] Ibid., p. 449.

serve only those children whose parents could support a prolonged education. It may have been that the economic conditions of the times could permit no more, but Parker did not choose to accept the statement as conditioned by the times. If the isolation of the classes were to be broken down, it was not to be at the expense of the wealthy.

There is little reason to believe that Parker was very much aware of the plight of the urban masses or had much sympathy for them or much understanding of the turmoil that was developing around the labor scene. Parker's own work was supported partly by aid from Fields and Pullman. There is also evidence to suggest that Parker was more than simply an unwilling accomplice to the leadership of the large corporate concerns. His general reactions to the social events of his times reveals a point of view that is not obvious in, but not inconsistent with, his educational writings. Parker objected vigorously to labor unions, to collective bargaining for teachers, and to the labor strikes that occured in Chicago during the 1880s and 1890s. Indeed he would often take the students of the Cook County Normal School on excursions to the Pullman community outside of Chicago, pointing to it as an example of a model community. One such excursion was even planned during the summer of 1894 as the workers were striking against low wages and high rents.[23] The Haymarket strike in 1886 was an occasion for him to argue for more support for education before society fell into utter chaos, and he supported the court's conviction of the leaders of the strike as well as the death penalty on the grounds that "the advice to commit violence makes the adviser guilty of whatever bloodshed results."[24] He advocated universal education for all races while at the same time supporting the idea of segregated schools for the black and the yellow races until they had accommodated themselves to American custom and law.[25]

Given these considerations, it is significant that Parker used the phrase, "reduction of isolation" between classes when describing the mandate of the school. For surely he was not calling for the abolition of the class structure, or for an ethical justification of the large social and economic differences that existed. He was, instead, calling on more

---

[23] Jack K. Cambell, *Colonel Francis W. Parker, The Children's Crusader* (New York: Teachers College Press, Columbia University), 1967, p. 164.
[24] Ibid., p. 167.
[25] Ibid., p. 169.

understanding on the part of one group for the condition of the other, of the poor for the rich and perhaps, too, of the rich for the poor.

Having accepted the underlying goals of the emerging technological society, Harris and Parker had accepted, too, the very forces that were to quickly undermine their vision of the educational science. The issues that were to dominate schooling in the coming century were to be perceived not primarily as ethical but as managerial, and the science of education was no longer to be subordinate to debates about the nature of the child, man and education.

Industrialization meant that traditional modes of socialization—the family, the community, and the church—were to be subordinate to the school. Many of the patterns to which children were traditionally socialized were becoming less functional for more people. For example, as the careers of Harris and Parker were ending, apprenticeship training was becoming a relic of a bygone age, and it was becoming more and more difficult to "keep them down on the farm" after they had seen New York, Chicago, or Philadelphia. To some, schooling provided avenues of mobility that industrialization might have otherwise blocked, but to others, perhaps the majority, school provided a justification for accepting without anger a consistent pattern of status and wealth. Nevertheless, the school came to be perceived as a major avenue through which people could gain a share of the nation's wealth, and, as such, it became a battleground for conflicting interests. Later in the century, issues such as equality of educational opportunity, educational quotas, compensatory programs, talent identification, and national assessment were as much economic issues relating to access to the nation's resources as they were educational ones. Industrialization had brought schooling into the forefront of economic conflict, but sometimes the school, as the focus of hostility, masked the fact that the conflict was indeed economic. Economic issues were not alone in generating the conflicts that were to occur over the schools. There were other, related ones. Schools were often expected to shift the attitudes and loyalties of a large number of children, and it was sometimes difficult to convince parents that institutions other than the family and those chosen by it had an equal right in this endeavor. As the twentieth century progressed, educational scholars began to consciously concern themselves with the techniques of political socialization more than with the values to which children should be socialized.

Several educational questions of the twentieth century involved some deep and puzzling social and philosophical concerns (but many alternatives were being excluded just by virtue of industrialization and the way it was perceived). Educators chose to swim with the tide not against it. They felt that what was needed was not philosophy but courses in conflict resolution and behavior modification. Speculative discussions about the nature of childhood and man, unless they focused upon the manipulative character of each, were somewhat irrelevant in a society that required its schools to develop the attitudes and to satisfy the manpower needs that were thought to be required by its growing industrial machinery.

Certainly a science of education was needed, but it was not to be one that debated the merits of goals that reality, as accepted, had rendered irrelevant. If economic and political battles were to be fought on the concrete playgrounds of the school, then the educator had to know something about the techniques by which such conflicts could be resolved. And, if the schools were to service the industrial needs of the nation, then the educator had to know what those needs were and whether the schools were meeting them. Clearly, "education science" as perceived by Parker and Harris was less than "visionary" in this regard whereas science according to Rice was consonant with the coming age. As the nation entered the twentieth century, a transition had occured. Educational science was no longer to be subordinate to a philosophy of man, but was now to be merged with a science of management.

## IV. THE IDEA OF EDUCATIONAL
## SCIENCE IN THE TWENTIETH CENTURY

The major difference between the nineteenth- and twentieth-century educational theory is the extent that the requirements of science and technology found a place in the theory. In the nineteenth century, observations about the role of the school in a technological society were awkwardly grafted on to scholarly deliberations about the nature of man and education. In the twentieth-century educational theory, including the deliberations about the nature of man and education, was consciously designed to meet the shifting social and technological requirements. The fact that most nineteenth-century works on the science of education resembled elaborate treatises on ethics arguing for this or that as the fixed end of education meant that values, however they were defined, were viewed as stable entities. Thus the major problem was to determine what these values were and then to elaborate the implications that they held for classroom procedure. The uncomfortable way in which observations about the new industrial age were grafted on to the more elaborately argued ethical theory resulted from the fact that technology required the breakdown of many traditionally held values.

Many twentieth century educational theorists believed that the schools could be a major force in guiding social change, but they also recognized that if such change was to be consistant with developing technology, some previously accepted valves would have to be challenged. They believed that while the direction of technological change could not be predicted with certainty, its process could be speeded up and its consequences controlled by developing a flexible value structure, which recognized technological growth as the ultimate reality, and could be changed when necessity demanded. In order to do this, it was recognized that a new principle of justification was required —one that subordinated ethical issues to the directives of science and technology. Because the school was perceived as the major instrument for developing a new mode of thought, the principle had to be capable of justifying the assumption by the school of many of the functions traditionally assigned to other institutions such as the family or the church. Thus, science was to become the new ethic with conflicting factions appealing to scientific objectivity rather than to some set standard of moral value.

The social scientists and policy makers who laboured in the field of education in this century were born under the star of Darwin, and just as Harris had feared, this influence was to have a profound impact upon the direction of educational theory. Darwinian science as interpreted turned the explicit relationship between science and ethics on its head, subjecting all ethical systems to the final tests of "survival" and "scientific objectivity." Essays on educational science were to eventually turn from treatises on ethics to pages of charts, graphs and statistics, and Darwin's thought was to have precisely the impact on educational theory that Harris had warned against. A biological model of man was substituted for an ethical one which claimed his species uniqueness. Yet ironically, the Darwinian influence provided the link that had been missing from Harris' analysis of technological America by replacing a philosophy of man with a philosophy of management.

## V. A CASE OF SHIFTING PRIORITIES: THE INFLUENCE OF DARWIN

The significance of Darwin's *Origin of the Species* for social theory (1859) was to be found in the message that man, as a species, could no longer claim to be discontinuous with the rest of organic nature. Although the theological impact of this message has been well-publicized (the biblical version of the creation was to be seen as a myth meriting the same attention as any other myth), the ethical significance is not as well-known.

To a strict Darwinist, man could no longer accurately perceive himself as an advance over other species except by some rather mundane standards. To believe himself to be different in kind from others was to accept the idea of species uniqueness, and it was to assume a standard beyond nature by which species were graded from the least to the more perfect. However, *The Origin of the Species* provided no such standard, nor did it give any reason to believe that one existed.

To assert that man could no longer perceive himself as a species apart meant that he was subject to all the laws of other species, the major ones being the law of survival and of extinction. The human species had survived the struggle for existence not because it had the protection of a divine group of angels, but because it had been able to adapt to its changing environment.

With the angels thrown out, man's ethical systems were on tenuous ground. Neither he nor his values could claim uniqueness. Specific values had been challenged numerous times in the course of human history, and they either withstood the challenge or were replaced by other values. The implications of the new biology was more sweeping than any previous challenge. It was not simply a challenge to one set of values by another but to all values and to the assumptions upon which they rested. No matter what particular ethical system might have been in vogue in the past, it assumed an order by which events could be ranked from the more to the less perfect. The challenge was to the notion of a ranked order, not to any specific system of ranking. The threat was not to a single system of values, but to values in general and to the belief that behavior was to be judged by how closely it conformed to a specific set.

If variations in species were, as Darwin had said, generated randomly, and if the human species was simply another product of selection, then the variations that occurred among members of the human species must also be generated randomly. With uniqueness denied, the variations among individual members must be judged, as with those of other species, only by their contribution to the survival of the genotype. Any higher appeal was unwarranted because all such appeals were merely random generations to be judged by the contribution to the survival of the species. In education, the Darwinian revolution was to reverse the priorities that had been set in the nineteenth century. Ethical systems were to be seen as weapons in an evolutionary struggle, and were to be judged by scientific norms.

## VI. WILLIAM GRAHAM SUMNER'S SCIENTIFIC PROHIBITIONS

Most theoretical debates in the earlier parts of the twentieth century took place within the shadow of Darwin, with educators, whether reformers or not, feeling obliged to pay homage to the new biology. The most prominent philosophers and social scientists writing about schooling wrote in the shadow of Darwin. Some American writers, attracted as much by the thought of Spencer on social evolution as by the writings of Darwin on biology, expressed their affinity with evolutionary ideas in a conservative tone. But the conservative tone was different from that of the eighteenth century. William Graham Sumner (1840-1910), a Yale sociologist and a man who had forsaken the ministry for a role in social science, illustrated in his elaboration of Darwin and Spencer's views the way evolutionary theory was used by some American theorists to support conservative ideals. Sumner, like W. T. Harris, is a transitional figure in American social thought, and his ideas are a mirror image of W. T. Harris. Whereas Harris was to applaud the development of American technology, Sumner was sceptical about its fruits, but whereas Harris believed that science must remain subordinate to an ethical system, Sumner argued that values are ultimately to be judged by scientific standards.

Sumner took the laws of evolution to be as fixed and as absolute as the laws of physical bodies. The struggle for existence and the process of natural selection were seen as the mainstays of social stability. Men struggle with each other and with their life conditions to meet the ever-pressing demands of survival. Sumner perceived the struggle as neither planned nor rational. It arose out of the physical needs of the organism and was directed towards satisfying those needs. In the course of the struggle, some men came to understand that they could meet the demands of the environment only by subordinating their antagonisms towards one another and entering into a cooperative relationship. Thus societies were built not out of love but out of expedience; they were held together not by man's social nature but by the power of some to maintain order and by the conviction of most that order must be maintained. Antagonisms remain, but they were confined and limited.

Sumner believed that the limits were regulated by the folkways and the *mores* of the society, or the norms by virtue of which judgments about good and bad, right and wrong, beautiful and ugly were made. Such norms were not thought to be reflections of a God-given value system, but merely statements of social customs and traditions mirroring for the members of the society modes of behavior that had proved successful in meeting life conditions. Different societies met these conditions in different ways, each developing its own peculiar *mores*. Thus, Sumner believed that there was no basis other than survival on which to make judgments about the relative merits of one set of *mores* as apposed to another. The *mores* defined the limits of right and wrong for a particular society and were capable of making anything right.[26] The test of any set of *mores* was found in the fact that the society which expresses it has survived.

Man did not lose his competitive nature by the fact that he entered society. The *mores* placed limits on the expression of competition, they did not abolish it. Society benefited not by teaching men to be cooperative, but as an indirect result of the natural competitiveness that existed among them. Under competition people who achieved a position of status, authority, and power were those whose ideas and skills, exercised in their own self-interest, also served the interests of the largest number of people. Therefore Sumner perceived the division of people along class lines to be not only necessary but natural, and the competition among people for membership in the various classes was the only guarantee that the most useful skills would have the most far-reaching effects.

Sumner's belief in the laws of evolution, along with his implicit view that such laws not only described behavior but governed it, led him

[26] See William Graham Sumner, *Folkways* (New York: Dover), 1959, Chapter 1, Section 31, and Chapter 15.

to view social class distinctions as irrevocable aspects of social life. He believed that membership in any given class generally conformed to the value of an individual's contribution to society, and while there might be temporary mismatches between social class membership and the social worth of an individual, man's natural propensity for competition assured that such mismatches were eventually corrected. He perceived men to be born unequal; their variations in mental power, health, practical sense, and sheer luck were the ultimate determinants of their position on the social ladder. In every society the distribution of these qualities was approximately the same and thus, in every society the percentage of people falling into the various classes was also the same. After the relatively small class of men who provide the innovative thrust of a society came the very large mass of men who were instinctively conservative and who served as the bearers of the folkways and *mores*. The masses were the "core of the society."[27] Below them were a number of smaller classes, the illiterate, the proletariat, the defective, dependent, and delinquent, the members of which contributed virtually nothing to society.[28] These distinctions were rooted in the biological nature of man, and in the match between a man's particular nature and the needs of his particular society. Because the range of talent in a society was fixed, any attempt to level the classes was doomed to create chaos and to fail.

Sumner believed that there were definite limits to educational reform. To use the schools to identify talented children from lower class origins was an efficient way of running a society and provided some justification for universal education on the very lowest levels. To use them to obliterate the distinctions between the classes or to create harmony among naturally disharmonious elements was fruitless and ultimately dangerous. The net effect would be simply to spread limited resources among those who did not want an education and who could not benefit from it. Although society needed some people who were critical of the folkways and *mores* in order to judge whether or not they were continuing to meet the demands of life conditions, education was

---

[27] Ibid., p. 45.

[28] This statement has to be slightly qualified with regards to the illiterate and the proletariat to whom Sumner concedes some slight contributions. Yet the members of all of these classes, in his view, seek much more from society than they are able to contribute to it.

seen as conservative in its general thrust. The primary need was for the young to learn the folkways and the *mores* so that they could avoid the errors of the past while understanding the ways of the present. For most children schools should concentrate on ritualistic training into the *mores* and on the development of skills needed to function in society.[29] The major error of the school was to focus its energies on the abstractions to be found in books, abstractions which were irrelevant to the work that most youngsters would eventually undertake.

While Sumner's nostalgia for *laissez-faire* society placed him clearly in the nineteenth century as did the fact that he deemphasized the role of formal political institutions in consciously shaping behavior towards some future goal, his appeal to Darwin and to evolutionary theory placed him in the twentieth as well. The fact that a number of the most significant social theorists who expressed concern about education felt obliged not only to accept evolutionary theory, but to argue against the use that conservatives like Sumner made of it, is an indication of the significance of this line of thought.

Most twentieth-century educators were more hopeful about the developing technology than Sumner and had grander ideas about the role of the school in social reform. Yet their commitment to science and technology meant that Darwinian theory had to be given a new twist if it was to be used to justify educational reform. To the reform-minded educator, intent on developing a sense of national purpose in a group of new and disparate people, Sumner's version of evolution was clearly inadequate, and the implications he drew were merely an expression of that inadequacy. Confronted with a shift in population from the farm to the city, and with the influx of immigrants from new areas, confronted too with a change in the nature and climate of work, the reformer believed that the schools had to take on a larger and more direct role in the education of all children. He argued that the heavy air of the factories and the loneliness of the city resulted in the breakdown of concern and in a loss of community; that they created personal disorder and social disorganization. The family and the community could not main-

---

[29] The consistency with which Sumner held this view is questionable—see, for example, *Folkways* p. 632-633, where he emphasized the development of the critical faculty. The tension is another expression of the problem of adherence to a traditional culture where life conditions are reasonably stable on one hand, and the clear observation that technology was swiftly altering life conditions on the other.

tain primary responsibility for the education of the child because the structure of the family had changed and the community had broken down. Thus, he looked to the school as the instrument for achieving his vision of American society.

To accept Sumner's view of the minimum role of the school would have been to accept a situation which the reformer believed no longer existed, a situation where the major tasks of teaching such as the socializing of the child and the training of specific skills could be taught by the family and the community. The reformer argued that functions previously performed by other groups had to now be taken over by the school. The strength of his argument depended in part upon the accuracy of the descriptions of city and country life, but it depended too on his implicit acceptance of much of what Sumner had said about the relation between evolutionary theory and values. For to argue against Sumner's view of schooling on the grounds that it was dysfunctional for a given situation was to affirm the belief that particular values were to be judged as instruments of survival in a given social context and were to be discharged when that end could no longer be effectively served by them.

Nevertheless if schools were to be consciously used as major instruments of reform, Sumner's determinism had to be modified. Conscious human purpose had to replace the folkways and *mores* as guides to social change. Yet such purpose could be not simply the product of a free floating human will, but rather it had to be consistent with the requirements of industrial development that was taken to be the fixed direction of American society. Thus while Sumner's determinism had to be broken in some respects, it had to be maintained in others.

## VII. SCIENCE AND REFORM

Although the intent behind Sumner's sociology was to caution against deliberate and conscious social reform, his appeal to Darwin (as well as his elaboration of Spencer) expressed what was to become an important aspect of reform theory. Like Sumner, subsequent scholars turned their attention away from issues of man's destiny and to the question of his malleability.

Sumner's bias against reform was expressed in his rigid, mechanistic interpretation of Darwinian biology, and in his belief that changes in man's consciousness depended on changes in the natural physical environment. Because reformers believed that technology demanded sweeping alterations in man's consciousness, this particular aspect of his theory was unacceptable to them.

Like Sumner, the reformers of the twentieth century accepted the principles of evolution; unlike Sumner they emphasized the inevitability and the blessing of an industrial age, and they accepted the necessity of an elaborate social organization to keep it functioning. Many believed that the effects of large scale industry were inconsistent with those of the *laissez-faire* society that Sumner advocated, and they argued that the balance between production and consumption was too fragile, the discrepancy between effort and opportunity too large to be left to chance. Even though planning and cooperation were not primary categories of Darwinian theory, the reform theorist set about to make them such. Just as Sumner and Spencer had made the values of *laissez-faire* capitalism consistent with evolution, the reformer did the same with those of corporate industrial society. But if his reforms were to be adequately justified, two additional steps had to be completed in the formation of his theory. First the rigid mechanistic interpretation of Darwin had to be altered to allow for the possibility of conscious, deliberate, and beneficial reform and second, it had to be shown that the requirements of the new age were consistent not only with evolutionary theory, but with ethical principles as well.

Even before the publication of Sumner's *Folkways,* Charles Peirce (1839-1914) in an essay directed against Herbert Spencer[30] had set the logical stage for an interpretation of evolutionary theory that was to lend support to reform practice. He attacked the idea that the laws of evolution were to be understood as absolute governors of behavior; he argued that they too must be seen as the result of an evolutionary development, themselves subject to amendment. The laws of evolution must be viewed as creations of man, creations limited only by the present level of evolutionary progress. The implication was clear: man had now reached the stage where evolution had become a conscious phenomena to direct and to be directed by the purposes of men. Peirce's message was carried into the twentieth century by scholars like George Herbert Mead.

[30] See Charles S. Peirce, "The Architecture of Theory," *The Monist,* Vol. I, 1890-1891, pp. 161-176.

Mead (1863-1931) saw evolution as the natural process of social institutions, and he believed that man had reached the stage where he could direct social evolution according to his own purposes. Scientific intelligence was the latest link in the evolutionary chain and by reflecting upon the evolutionary process in nature man could understand how to advance himself and his institutions. "Society gets ahead not by fastening its vision upon a clearly outlined distant goal, but by bringing about the immediate adjustment of itself to its surroundings, which the immediate problem demands."[31]

If values and institutions were to be ultimately judged on a functional basis—by whether or not they aided the required adjustment—as Mead suggested, it had to be shown also that evolutionary processes were consistent with ethical norms, and that these norms were not to be equated simply with the existing folkways and *mores*. This link in the Social Darwinist argument was provided by Dewey. In an article published some years prior to Sumner's *Folkways* in the 1898 edition of the *Monist*, Dewey proposed that there is no contradiction between evolutionary theory and ethics, and that the essential precepts of the latter, such as cooperation and sympathy were outgrowths of the former. His argument centered on the observation that all of the relevant categories of evolution, such as struggle, survival, and adaptation when analyzed carefully were also appropriate categories for ethics. He concluded by affirming the need to rationally direct and form institutions to the changing character of the environment.

Dewey began his article by placing the ethical activities of man in the natural world and viewing them as instruments in the struggle for survival. The struggle was not, however, as Sumner would have it, one between man and man and between man and his "natural environment," as a whole. Instead, it involved man's attempt to overcome and to mold the ungirded effects of nature. In the process, man did not set himself over and against nature but he used one part of nature to bend another part to his will and desires. Human intelligence did not violate the natural order in establishing its will; it did not subdue nature; it intervened, but it did so as a part of nature that is conscious of its own process. Dewey argued that intelligence functioned to relate a narrow

[31] G. H. Mead, "Scientific Method and Moral Sciences", in *Mead-Selected Writings*. A. J. Reck, ed. (Indianapolis, The Library of Liberal Arts), 1964, pp. 265-266.

part of the environment to a wider context and to establish thereby a congruity between the two. Ethical man struggled with his environment, but only with a part of that environment; he used the remainder as an instrument in the struggle. Thus there was no absolute distinction between man's "ethical" behavior and his "natural" behavior; man must accept and use certain elements in the natural world (including his own intelligence) in order to behave ethically.

Ethical behavior was consistent with evolutionary activity because in the long run the survival of the fittest meant the survival of the ethically best. The success of ethical man's attempts to overcome the disparities of one part of his natural environment depended on his ability to incorporate other parts of that environment. And since part of such an environment included institutions and other men, the success of his struggle with nature depended upon man's ability to cooperate with other men. As Dewey puts it:

The conditions with respect to which the term "fit" must *now* be used include the existing social structure with all the habits, demands, and ideals which are found in it. . . . We have reason to conclude that the "fittest with respect to the whole of conditions" is the best; that, indeed, the only standard we have of the best is the discovery of that which maintains these conditions in their integrity. The unfit is practically the antisocial.[32]

Dewey illustrated his point by arguing that a society that cares for its old, its sick, and its feeble develops in this process habits of foresight that aid in its struggle for existence and contribute to the development of skills of warfare. "In a word, such conduct would pay in the struggle for existence as well as be morally commendable."[33]

Because Dewey's argument elaborated the canons by which many liberals were to judge social and individual actions it requires a closer examination, but first it will be useful to see its implications for schools and other social institutions. To illustrate these implications, it will be helpful to return to Sumner as a contrast to Dewey's ideas.

Behind Sumner's Social Darwinism was the view of a static natural environment. His model was one of primitive man struggling with life conditions and with other men for survival. Because the environment was taken as close and as visible, its effects could be understood by all.

---

[32] Dewey, "Evolution and Ethics", *The Monist,* April 1898, Vol. VIII, No. 3, p. 326.
[33] Ibid., p. 327.

Thus Sumner demphasized the function of what he called *enacted* institutions in shaping human attitudes and behavior. The environment and the institutions that grew out of it were the primary instrument for developing attitudes, but when institutions were deliberately created to shape attitudes beyond the requirements of the environment, Sumner believed that people would generally resist. Thus both successful reform and lasting revolutionary change were seen to be unlikely by Sumner, and enacted institutions were to have but a minor role in changing attitudes and in altering behavior. For Dewey, the model of the environment was somewhat different. It included all of those things that affected man and about which he was (or ought to be) concerned. His argument for the consistency between ethics and evolution was ultimately an argument for the flexibility of values in a situation where the environment is widening and changing. Institutions took on the role of channeling the natural inclinations of man (which are generally fixed) in ways that were consistent with the changing environment. "With man it is the intelligent and controlled foresight, the necessity of maintaining the institutions which have come down to us, while we make over these institutions so that they serve under changing conditions."[34]

Dewey believed that enacted institutions must take on a much more significant role in developing attitudes than Sumner would have them do. The environment was perceived to be not only the simple, primitive, and natural surroundings of man, but it included everything that had an effect on man—people as well as things. The present environment is in a process of expansion and change, and the role of the school and other institutions was not merely to reinforce the present values of society but to project and transmit the attitudes that would be needed in the future. Thus the school's role is to shape, transmit, and direct these attitudes. Education is the social instrument of natural selection. "Through . . . education certain forms of action are constantly stimulated and encouraged, while other forms are constantly objected to, repressed, and punished. What difference in principle exists between this . . . and what is ordinarily called natural selection."[35]

Dewey's argument bears closer examination for the light it throws on the character of educational theory. His insistence that ethical behavior pays off in the struggle for existence may or may not be true if it

[34] Ibid., p. 335.
[35] Ibid., p. 337.

is intended as a statement of fact. It is doubtful however whether Dewey is making merely a factual claim. The correlation between ethical acts and evolutionary processes was more than a mere accident. The struggle for existence, said Dewey,

. . . is found in the ethical process as it is in the cosmic, and it operates in the same way. So far as conditions have changed, so far as the environment is indefinitely more complex, wider and more variable, so far of necessity and as a biological and cosmic matter, not merely an ethical one, the functions selected differ.[36]

Human evolution differed from animal evolution only by the fact that it has entered the stage of "conscious deliberation and experimentation."[37]

Dewey's argument sounds like a series of factual propositions, but it is not. Instead of making strictly factual observations, Dewey was proposing a criterion by which ethical claims may be evaluated. If the struggle for existence was aided by following the claim, then it would be judged as ethical. The primary object of the struggle was not, however, the survival of the individual member of the species, although this had secondary importance, but, instead, the survival of the ongoing social unit. It is unclear whether Dewey would want to insist that it was because the caring for the old, the feeble and the sick contributed to habits of foresight, aided the development of war making skills, and thereby the struggle for survival, that these were judged ethical, but in establishing an evolutionary criterion for judging ethical claims, Dewey's argument could be taken as a muted echo of W. T. Harris' belief that the success of the conqueror is proof of his ethical superiority. Dewey did not explicitly carry his argument this far.

Part of the appeal of Dewey's argument lies in its philosophical ambiguity. For not everyone would agree that ethical behavior and evolutionary progress are the same thing or that the latter should serve as the criterion for the former. Some would even find peculiar the suggestion that our most cherished acts of altruism, such as caring for the old are best judged as preparations for war or other survival activity. If Dewey were putting forth only a factual claim, then all that could really be said is that at certain times in human history, there may be fortunate coincidences between ethical acts and evolutionary processes. But of course this watered down claim did not really suit his purposes and it was useful for him to leave the ambiguous quality alone. On the other hand, to suggest outright that evolutionary survival was to be the criterion for ethical activity would have been to provide some clear guidance as to how an ethical claim might be objectively judged. Yet precisely because such a criterion can be challenged on others grounds, it was again best for Dewey to allow the ambiguity to stand. However Dewey's claim does require some analysis.

Assuming that any adequate evaluation of the factual correlation between ethics and evolution would result in a significantly watered-down claim by Dewey, let's turn our attention to the idea that ethical claims are to be judged by evolutionary norms. And let us take as a case in point his example of the correlation between caring for the sick and developing habits of survival. The question to be asked is why (by what standard do we judge) the caring for the sick or enfeebled is considered to be an ethical act. If Dewey was proposing that ethical claims should be judged by evolutionary norms, then he would answer that the act is ethical because it contributes to the development of social habits that are important instruments for survival. Yet he offered this example as a *prima facie* instance of an ethical act, and then added that it also contributed to the survival of the group. But the *prima facie* quality of this example should lead us to suspect the criterion by which he eventually judged it. If someone were to ask a man in the street to explain why caring for a sick person is to be considered an ethical act, or even under what conditions it is to be considered ethical, a number of responses are likely, but it would be extraordinarily odd if the answer were, "Because it contributes to the survival of the person who is caring." He would be more likely to answer in the opposite vein saying that caring for a sick person who can make no direct and significant contribution to one's own well being is certainly to be considered an ethical act precisely because he is incapable of making such a contribution.

Given the *prima facie* quality of Dewey's example it would seem equally reasonable to suggest that caring for another is ethical because (or when) the act is designed primarily to aid the well-being of another instead of oneself, or even one's group. By avoiding questions of intent, Dewey was, of course, able to maintain that the ethical quality of an act was to be judged solely by its consequences. And, assuming that we have some idea of the object of the evolutionary process, then if we were to accept Dewey's argument, we should also be able to publicly exhibit the ethical nature of an act in a fairly objective fashion without appealing to some abstract standard. Moreover, if ethical acts could be reasonably determined in this fashion, then it would be also reasonable to *design* a set of institutions which assure with some reliability that people will *want* to act ethically. Of all institutions. Dewey observed, the school is best designed to carry out this task.

. . . by law and punishment, by social agitation and discussion, society can regulate and form itself in a more or less haphazard and chance way. But through education society can formulate its own purposes, can organize its own means and resources, and thus shape itself with definiteness and economy in the direction in which it wishes to move."[38]

## VIII. CONCLUSION

The shift from nineteenth- to twentieth-century educational theory involved a major overhaul in the relationship between science and ethics and in the concept of educational science itself. The nineteenth-century educator placed strict limits on the scope and insight of educational science confining them within the framework of ethical theories that usually saw man as a member of a unique species. The later theorists looked at morals and ethics within the framework of Darwinian evolutionary theory and argued that particular moral codes were to be judged as instruments for adaptation to the changing requirements brought about by growing industrial and technological needs.

Dewey provided the most articulate expression of this point of view. The problem of morality, he argued in *Human Nature and Conduct,* is one of mutual adjustment between the individual and his environment when old habits and customs no longer work. When the problem is looked at as one of adjustment, Dewey believed that the issue changed from one of moral laws and conscience to the techniques for engineering human and social change.[39]

To the reformer, questions concerning moral beliefs were very much questions of technique. Morals, like institutions were to be evalu-

[38] Dewey, "My Pedagogic Creed" in *Teacher's Manual: My Pedagogic Creed by Professor John Dewey and the Demands of Sociology Upon Pedagogy by Professor Albion W. Small, with an introduction by S. T. Dutton* (Chicago: A Flanagan Publication n.d.), p. 7.

[39] Dewey, *Human Nature and Conduct: An Introduction to Social Psychology* (New York: Modern Library), 1957, p. 10.

ated on a functional basis, and if they were found wanting, they were to be changed. By appealing to an evolutionary, biological model of man, all human elements could be objectified, examined for their functionality, and molded to meet more adequately the changing conditions of a social environment. To exemplify this process of objectification, consider the following: "Habit," wrote Dewey, "is energy organized in certain channels. When interfered with, it swells as resentment . . . Emotion is a pertubation from clash or failure of habit, and reflection . . . in the painful effort of disturbed habits to readjust themselves."[40] And "Morality is an endeavor to find for the manifestation of impulse in special situations an office of refreshment and renewal."[41]

With the human elements objectified in this way moral problems became the technical question of how best to change the character of another person. "The moral problem," wrote Dewey, "is that of modifying the factors which now influence future results. To change the working character or will of another we have to alter objective conditions which enter into his habits."[42] Because Dewey had objectified the feelings, emotions, and judgments of other people the question was not whether the deliberate alteration of another person's character presented any peculiarly moral issues. The moral problem was strictly one of design—how best to engineer such a change.

The impact of the reinterpretation and social application of evolutionary theory for educational reform was to shift the burden of proof from the new social and moral forms to the older one. Moreover evolutionary thought as reinterpreted established a functional standard against which different ethical norms could be judged, and by so doing it reversed the relationship between ethics and science that had existed in the nineteenth century. With this relationship altered the dominant concerns of education came to involve the questions of technique.

[40] Ibid., p. 76.
[41] Ibid., p. 169.
[42] Ibid., p. 19.

# CHAPTER TWO
# Objectivity and Ideology

## I. INTRODUCTION

Darwinian biology had a twofold influence on educational thought. First, it was used by people like Dewey and Mead to establish the viability of a functional analysis of human activity, including human values. Second, when it was merged with a positivistic orientation, it was used by others to support the claim that all aspects of human behavior could, when broken down into component parts, be quantified and measured. This particular claim was popular among many educational testers and administrators at the beginning of the twentieth century, but it was not wholeheartedly supported by other liberal educators.

In order to set the stage for an examination of the response of liberal progressive educational theorists to the requirements of technology, this chapter begins by looking at the arguments used to advance the educational testing and efficiency movements. While both the educational testing movement and the educational efficiency movement had a significant impact on educational practice and research, neither one met with universal approval. Walter Lippmann and John Dewey both wrote cogent articles in opposition to them, and their arguments set much of the tone for liberal and progressive educational thought during the 1920's and later. These articles often have been cited to show the progressive's opposition to the shortsighted expedient policies of others; they are looked at in this chapter, however, to show both the force and the limits of their functional analysis of American society.

## II. THE TESTING MOVEMENT

The impact of Darwin upon ethics and philosophy was not lost to students of psychology—the one field that many thought held the most promise for education. Darwin's work had prepared the way for the study of animal psychology and Darwin himself had initiated a comparison of animal and human emotions in his *Expressions of the Emotions in Man and Animals* (1872). John Romanes (1864-1894) extended the study of animal behavior to include studies of animal intelligence, speculating that a continuity in kind exists between animal and human intelligence. Galton's (1822-1911) work on individual differences and mental inheritance was another offshoot of evolutionary theory, and was followed with great interest by American psychologists.

American psychologists returning from visits to Wundt's laboratory at Leipzig were enthusiastic about experimental psychology blending into the German model a liberal sprinkling of Galton. Out of this mixture came a shift in emphasis from questions of generic mind to attempts to measure an individual's capacity to adjust to his environment.[1] Such people as James McKeen Cattell, Edward L. Thorndike, Lewis Terman, and Henry Goddard were instrumental in using the evolutionary theory to suggest new directions for psychology.

One of the most talented of the early students of the new psychology became one of the most influential educational scholars. Edward L. Thorndike (1874-1949) taught at [teacher's college] Columbia University for almost 40 years, where he influenced teachers, psychologists, and educational administrators.

The impact of evolutionary theory on Thorndike's ideas was twofold; first, he believed that evolution had established a significant connection between animal and human intelligence, and that an understanding of human learning was most easily gained by prior examination of animal behavior. Second, he saw learning to be the capacity of any organism to alter its response in light of changes in the environment, and thereby he argued that human intelligence could be measured objectively by tapping the individual's capacity to develop new responses.[2]

---

[1] Edwin G. Boring, *A History of Experimental Psychology* (New York: Appleton, Century, Crofts), 1957, p. 507.

[2] The dates of the testing movement cannot be pinpointed, but it is probably accurate to say that the interest of the professional psychologist in measuring the intelligence of human beings was strong in this country around

He believed that learning did not take place through the mediation of an idea, and that the view that one learns something by "keeping in mind" the *idea* of an object or a relationship was wrong. Instead, he found that learning occurred through a process of association whereby acts leading to satisfaction are stamped into the nervous system and acts lending to frustration are stamped out. He concluded that learning was a specific activity associated with specific stimuli and responses. If, for example, food was the object that would bring satisfaction, the animal did not form an abstract idea of a bone and then develop a plan for obtaining one—he merely acted in a way that in the past had resulted in his hunger being satisfied.[3] He did not form an idea of a causal connection between the act and the obtainment of food, he simply behaved and his behavior was directed by previous associations.

Thorndike's statement that learning was nothing more than the development of a series of specific associative responses, was used by himself and others to refute the claim made by defenders of the classical curriculum. The claim was that subjects such as Latin and Greek were

1900. It picked up government support just prior to and during World War I with the development of the Alpha and Beta tests, and that popular interest became keen in the early 1920s during the debates over immigration quotas. Some criticism was voiced early by people like Dewey and Lippmann and were heard more frequently in the 1940s and the 1950s. Psychologists then became more cautious about their claims. Nevertheless, the massive talent searches in the early 1960s and the Jensen debates later are indications of the continuing appeal of the movement.

[3] While Thorndike embraced most of the assumptions of positivism, he was not completely willing to write off some of the so-called invisible entities associated with mind. While he questioned, for example, the existence of ideas in lower animals, he believed that the variations in the learning curves of men (and of monkeys as well) indicates the presence of ideas. (For a more detailed discussion of this, see Geraldine Joncich, *The Sane Positivist: A Biography of Edward L. Thorndike,* Middletown, Connecticut: Wesleyan University Press, 1968, pp. 266-268.) Yet while he was not willing to deny the existence of things as ideas, he believed that they could be described in such a way so as to remove from them all elements of mystery.

The learning curve itself was one way of objectifying the existence of ideas without alluding to a mysterious, inner state to be known only by inference or introspection. Human intellect was to be seen as a complicated mechanism for adaptation. Ideas, rationality and the ability to draw inferences were viewed not as qualities unique to the human species but as the results of a highly complex physiology, a physiology that all other animals shared in a less complex form.

the best preparation for the tasks of later life even though their content may be unrelated to what the child was eventually to do. This claim was built upon the idea that the mind was divided into a number of faculties such as memory, attention, and sense discrimination and that these faculties when exercised, much in the same manner as a muscle, would be able to perform increasingly difficult tasks. Thus, even though the content of Latin and Greek may not be related to the child's future employment, it was believed that the faculties that they exercised were.

Thorndike believed that the argument for the classical curriculum could be understood as the claim that training in one area results in improvement in another, related area. It was this claim that his famous experiments on transferability of learning, performed with Robert Woodworth, was designed to test.

In order to measure the transferability of various faculties, such as quickness and accuracy, Thorndike and Woodworth set up a number of experiments. In the case of quickness and accuracy, for example, the subject would practice "marking every word containing the two letters *e* and *s* until he had attained a considerable improvement in speed and possibly in accuracy as well. Before and after this training he would be tested in marking words containing other combinations of letters."[4] From the results of these and other experiments, they concluded that it was misleading "to speak of sense discrimination, attention, memory, observation, accuracy, quickness, etc., as multitudinous separate individual functions . . . The mind is . . . a machine for making particular reactions to particular situations. The word *attention*, for example, can properly mean only the sum total of a lot of particular tendencies to attend to particular sorts of data."[5]

One implication of the view that learning consists of a series of associative neurological responses to external stimuli was that an individual's capacity to learn was neurologically determined, and that a score on an intelligence test corresponded to his neurological makeup. Thus, at least in theory, the study of human intelligence was thought to

[4] E. L. Thorndike and R. S. Woodworth, "The Influence of Improvement in One Mental Function Upon the Efficiency of Other Functions (III), Functions Involving Attention, Observation, and Discrimination," *The Psychological Review*, Vol. 8 (1901), p. 553.

[5] E. L. Thorndike and R. S. Woodworth, "The Influence of Improvement in One Mental Function Upon the Efficiency of Other Functions (I)," *The Psychological Review*, Vol. 8 (1901), pp. 249-250.

be as objective as any other science. It was grounded in the real world of nerve endings and tissue.

Thorndike observed that the human embryo already contains certain well-defined, natural tendencies. "What a man does throughout his life is a result of whatever constitution he has at the start and of all the forces that act upon it before and after birth."[6] All original tendencies are aimless, they seek no object, they have no purpose. They are exercised when a deficiency is felt and their activity ends when the deficiency is satisfied. "The animal does not originally run from a tiger because he intends to get away. He runs because of the tiger and because running in that situation is a satisfier to his neurons."[7]

Behavior was seen as rooted in the neurons, but while the original tendencies could not be changed, the objects that would satisfy them could be. This, to Thorndike, was one of the essential functions of teaching. In the last analysis, learning was to be explained by what took place in the neurons and in the various responses that lead to their satisfaction. The sensitivity of a neuron, or its capacity to be aroused by an external situation, was the precondition of learning while its essence was to be found in the neural connection made between the neurological awareness of a situation and the neurological response to it. Thorndike believed that whenever a response resulted in the satisfaction of a previously unsatisfied neuron a connection was established between that unsatisfied neuron and the specific neuron that triggered the response. The more often the response was made, assuming that it continued to provide satisfaction, the more likely that the response would be made again. Each response was rooted in a single neurological arrangement and in only that arrangement. For example, let us assume that a person who happens to be lonely at a particular moment hears the voice of his friend, John, and responds in an established way. This would mean that there had been a bond established between the neurological situation that is described by the term loneliness and the object (John) whose presence satisfies that situation.

It is possible to challenge Thorndike's model of intelligence and learning on a number of conceptual grounds, some which were offered by progressives like Dewey, but before looking at these challenges, we need to examine briefly another, closely related movement.

[6] E. L. Thorndike, *Educational Psychology: Briefer Course* (New York: Teachers College Press), 1919, p. 2.

[7] Ibid., p. 60.

## III. THE EFFICIENCY MOVEMENT

The testing movement was not an isolated phenomena in American educational history. If the testers saw their task as identifying specific levels of talent, many educational administrators saw their role as training each individual for his appropriate place in society. Many school administrators believed that their task began where the tester's left off. As the tester's role was to identify talent, the school administrator's was to supervise and guide its development.

The efficiency movement in education was modeled after Frederick W. Taylor's principles of scientific management which was designed to eliminate waste and promote efficiency in the factory. The job of the scientific manager was to analyze the process of production, to plan and control the details of the manufacturing process and to offer more efficient alternatives by examining the movements and time involved in performing a given task.[8]

The appeal to a science of education was not only an attempt to establish more effective modes of teaching, but was also a way of justifying the profession of education at a time when the expert was achieving more and more esteem. The progressive movement in politics, the alterations in the management of city government, and the development of a science of business administration were all consistent with the increasing cry for professionalization in the schools. As Raymond Callahan has pointed out, insofar as the practicing educators lacked a body of professional knowledge to which they could appeal, so too did they lack a way to justify themselves when their decisions were challenged. The inability of administrators at the turn of the century to defend themselves and their schools against the charges of waste and inefficiency resulted in short tenure for many superintendents and was one of the factors

---

[8] That problems were to occur in translating Taylor's system from the factory to the school might have been anticipated by passages such as the following:

Now one of the first requirements for a man who is fit to handle pig iron as a regular occupation is that he be so stupid and phlegmatic that he more nearly resembles in his mental make-up the ox than any other type. The man who is mentally alert and intelligent is for this very reason entirely unsuited to what would, for him be the trying monotony of work of this character. [Frederick Winslow Taylor, *The Principles of Scientific Management* (New York: The Norton Library), 1967, p. 59.]

involved in their turn to the efficiency movement.[9]

The efficiency movement (approximately 1910-1930) is illustrative of a turning away from consideration of ends to a preoccupation with means. With the business world held up to them as the model of efficiency, administrators were no longer to ask about the value of the task to be performed, but only about how best to perform it. Although the question of ends was to be avoided, the fact that the schools were involved in choosing some ends over others should have been obvious. The only question was *whose* ends were to be selected, and that question had already been answered by the administrator's response to the charge of waste and inefficiency—a response that made savings and efficiency the criterion of educational excellence. As one superintendent, Frank Spaulding, took up the banner of efficiency he asked:

Why is pupil recitation in English costing 7.2 cents in the vocational school while it costs only 5 cents in the technical school? Is the "vocational" English 44 percent superior to the "technical" English or 44 percent more difficult to secure? Why are we paying 80% more in the vocational than in the technical school for the same unit of instruction in mathematics? Why does a pupil-recitation in science cost from 55 percent to 67 percent more in the Newton High than in either of the other schools.[10]

Spaulding's respect for the techniques of cost analysis and his adoption of the values of the business community was carried to its extreme by Franklin Bobbitt, an instructor of education at the University of Chicago. Bobbitt proposed that the role of the school should be restricted to determining the most efficient means for reaching a preordained goal and that the efficiency of the "plant" is the responsibility of the school administrator who must see to it that teachers and methods conform to specification. The school administrator, like any manager, must enforce the standards, find the best methods for achieving them, control the quality of workmanship, and offer incentives for assuring that quality is reached. Yet, as in industry, the standards to be set are established from

---

[9] For a more detailed discussion of this problem, see Raymond E. Callahan, *Education and the Cult of Efficiency: A Study of the Social Forces that Have Shaped the Administration of the Public Schools* (Chicago: University of Chicago Press), 1962, pp. 52-64.

[10] Frank Spaulding, Superintendent of the Newton, Massachusetts School System, quoted in Callahan, *Education and the Cult of Efficiency*, p. 74, from 1913 *NEA Proceedings*.

outside. "A school system can no more find the standard of performance within itself than a steel plant can find the proper height or weight per yard of steel rails from the activities within the plant."[11] Bobbitt believed it was the duty of the business world to set standards for the school, to decide what kind of labor will be needed and the level of proficiency at which it will need to be performed.

The belief in science, the quest for objectivity, the turning away from the question of ends, and the concern for means were the driving forces behind *both* the testing and the efficiency movements. As the administrators were to find the best methods for processing the material of childhood, the psychologists were to measure its strength and test its tensility.

## IV. SOME PROBLEMS WITH THE "SCIENTIFIC" JUSTIFICATIONS OF THE TESTING MOVEMENT

Thorndike's view that intelligence described an unchangeable feature of individuals and that it could be objectively measured rested on a number of beliefs about the relationship between an individual's responses and the functioning of his nervous system. For example, he assumed that the nervous system was of such a nature that there could be only a single neurological response to the presentation of the same external situation and that once such a response was learned, it and only it would be triggered whenever the initial neurological situation was presented. This assumption was crucial to Thorndike for two different reasons. In the first place he believed that it was the most adequate explanation for his experimental findings that transfer was not a significant component of learning. And in the second place he believed that the only objective way to account for variations in individual performance on IQ exams was to attribute such variations to biological factors that, at least in theory, could be counted (such as the number or plasticity of an individual's nerve endings). Thus Thorndike claimed that

---

[11] Quoted in Callahan, p. 83, from Franklin Bobbitt, *The Supervision of City Schools: Some General Principles of Management Applied to the Problems of City School Systems*, "Twelfth Yearbook of the National Society for the Study of Education," Part I, Bloomington, Illinois, 1913, p. 35.

"the really same response is never made to different situations by the same organism."[12] Learning is specific because neurologic reactions are specific. In criticism of his view, it could easily be countered that all situations are different in some way, and that if Thorndike was, in fact, right about the nature of learning, then his whole argument is incomprehensible. For example, Fred comes in wearing a blue suit instead of the black one he wore previously. If we view these events as different situations, then the implication of Thorndike's argument is that learning is impossible.

Thorndike's responses to problems of this kind reveals that a basic circularity underlies his ideas about learning and intelligence. The fundamental question here involves the criterion by which sameness is to be recognized. The issue can be seen in the following way. Suppose we take Fred who is wearing a black suit and sitting in the kitchen as describing a certain situation; then are we to take Fred wearing a blue suit and sitting in the living room to describe that same situation or a different one? The question is whether sameness is to be determined by the external factors, or whether it is to be defined by the firing of the same set of neurons at two different times. Certainly there is a sense in which Fred wearing a blue suit and sitting in the living room is different from Fred wearing a black suit and sitting in the kitchen, but there seems to be another sense in which it is not. Thorndike *appeared* to recognize this difference and to incorporate it into his ideas about learning. He wrote: "To any new situation a man responds as he would to some situation like it, or it some element of it."[13] But to the question, how do we know that one situation is *like* another, Thorndike replies: "For situation $A$ to be like situation $B$ must be taken to mean . . . 'for $A$ to arouse in part the same action in the man's neurons as $B$ would.' "[14] Since the same neurological action leads to the same response, these statements, taken together, read: To any new situation a man will respond as he would to a like situation, and we know that one situation is like another when a man responds to each in the same way.[15]

Many of the difficulties inherent in Thorndike's theory of learning had been anticipated earlier by Dewey in his 1896 criticism of the

[12] Thorndike, *Educational Psychology*, p. 7.
[13] Ibid., p. 148.
[14] Ibid., p. 150.
[15] Ibid., p. 150.

reflex-arc theory, but Thorndike apparently failed to take these remarks into account in his own formulation.[16] Dewey's criticism was directed against the view that took the sensory stimulus (such as seeing a bright light) and the motor response (such as pulling one's hand away from a hot flame) as purely distinct acts. Instead he offered a view in which both were aspects of a co-ordinated experience.

Dewey's critique was directed specifically against earlier proponents of the reflex-arc theory, but it is relevant to Thorndike because it is directed against deterministic psychological views of human behavior. For example, Thorndike's difficulty in clearly stating what constitutes the "same situation" arose from his desire to establish human behavior as externally determined, so that for the presentation of each and every external situation there was established a single and identifiable neuro-logical response. The response *is determined* by the presentation of the external situation, and learning is nothing more than teaching an indi-vidual to respond in a certain way to a specifiable situation. Thorndike had to assume, however, that in some sense the nature of the external situation is what it is independently of the individual's response to it. If this were not the case then his model would break down since he would be unable to say definitely what the situation is to which one is respond-ing. Yet as we have seen, Thorndike had difficulty maintaining the radical distinction between the nature of the situation itself and the individual's neurological response to it.

In Dewey's argument against the reflex arc theory he criticized the view that the nature of the stimulus could be determined independently from the state of the person who receives it. Dewey wrote that:

Such an analysis is incomplete; it ignores the status prior to hearing the sound. Of course, if this status is irrelevant to what happens afterwards, such ignoring is quite legitimate. But is it irrelevant either to the quantity or to the quality of the stimulus?

If one is reading a book, if one is hunting, if one is watching in a dark place on a lonely night, if one is performing a chemical experiment, in each case, the noise has a very different mental value; it is a different experience.[17]

[16] John Dewey, "The Reflex Arc Concept in Psychology," *Psychological Review*, July 1896, III, pp. 357-370: Reprinted as "The Unit of Behavior" in John Dewey, *Philosophy and Civilization* (New York: Capricorn Books), 1963. Subsequent references are to the reprint.
[17] Ibid., pp. 237-238.

Dewey then proposed that "stimulus" and "response" should not be looked at as "distinctions of existence" but rather as "distinctions of functions," which have reference to the individual reaching for or attempting to maintain some end.[18] Dewey elaborated his point in a passage that is in direct conflict with Thorndike's notion that an individual learns not by forming an idea, but rather by association.

The conscious sensation of a stimulus is not a thing or existence by itself; it is that phase of a co-ordination requiring attention because, by reason of the conflict within the co-ordination it is uncertain how to complete it. Uncertainty as to the next act, whether to reach or not, gives the motive to examining the act. The end to follow is, in this sense, the stimulus. It furnishes the motivation to attend to what has just taken place; to define it more carefully. From this point of view the discovery of the "stimulus" is the "response" to the possible movement as "stimulus." We must have an anticipatory sensation, an image, of the movements that may occur, together with their respective values.[19]

The impact of Dewey's criticism was to emphasize the already established direction, the past experience and the present interest of the individual as determining both the nature of the stimulus and the response. This emphasis is a significant factor in distinguishing Dewey's views on education from those of Thorndike and others in the testing movement.

## V. SOME IDEOLOGICAL ASPECTS OF THE TESTING AND EFFICIENCY MOVEMENTS

Whatever the scientific merits of Thorndike's work may have been, his general theory of learning lent support to significant trends in American society. His attack on the classical curriculum, for example, in a period in which the nature of work was undergoing rapid change, criticized the claim that certain general subjects could best prepare youngsters for the world of work. In his *Educational Psychology: Briefer Course*, published in 1919 he cited, in order to refute them, the following typical claims made for the classical curriculum:

[18] Ibid., p. 242.
[19] Ibid., p. 245.

From Joseph Payne, *Lectures on Education,* Vol. I, "The study of the language itself does eminently discipline the faculties and secure to a greater degree than that of any other subject . . . the formation and growth of those mental qualities which are the best preparation for the business of life—whether that business is to consist in making fresh mental acquisitions or in directing the powers thus strengthened and matured, to professional or other pusuits."[20]

From H. M. MacCracken, Chancellor of New York University: "He will possess a better disciplined mind for whatever work of life he may turn his attention to."[21]

From Timothy Dwight, late President of Yale University: "Such an education is the best means of developing thought power in a young man."[22]

Whether or not such claims were reasonable would seem to depend as much upon the nature of the work that school youngsters might be expected to perform upon graduating as upon the nature of learning. The most significant point, however, is that the congruence between education and work had become the deciding factor in resolving disputes about the nature of the curriculum and moreover that other concerns such as the depth of human understanding provided by a certain curriculum had become, at least from Thorndike's point of view, of negligible significance.

It is little wonder that Thorndike's earlier experiments on the transfer of learning and the relations that he drew between human and animal learning received such widespread attention. The experiment (referred to earlier) to measure the transferability of quickness and accuracy from one set of data to another illustrates this point. To have subjects practice marking the letters *e* and *s* in a passage is indicative of the fact that Thorndike's view of learning involved the performance of a series of simple, rote, repetitive skills, much like many of the skills required by industrial society. Moreover given the nature of these *skills,* his views on the similarity between animal and human learning could certainly find support for at the point where the two do coincide tasks are indeed simple, rote, and repetitive.[23]

---

[20] Thorndike, *Educational Psychology,* p. 270.
[21] Ibid., p. 272.
[22] Ibid., p. 272.
[23] I am indebted to Ronald Szoke for this insight.

Thorndike's views on learning and transfer were totally consistent with attempts to associate education and schooling with the manpower needs of the society. However, Thorndike had not initiated this trend. As he had shown, even those who defended the classical subjects justified them on the grounds that they provided superior occupational training, and when Thorndike attacked their ideas he did so at precisely the point where they were most vulnerable, that is, where they claimed that the traditional curriculum was the best way to train a youngster for the world of work. His articles on the transfer of learning had ripped apart that justification for the general superiority of certain areas of study implying instead that the curriculum should be closely related to the task children were to perform in later life.

The influence of the testing and efficiency movement on education was a direct result of the increasing numbers of youngsters attending public schools and of the narrowing of other routes of entrance into the mainstream of American life. As urban centers were growing and the modern factory system developing, it was clear even in the later 1800s, as Cremin reports, that the apprentice system was breaking down "into a haphazard arrangement in which masters no longer cared to teach, in which boys were unready to accept long periods of indenture, and in which child labor had become exploitive rather than educative."[24] At different times both labor and management feared the other would gain control over apprentice programs and hence over the labor market, and each became somewhat reluctant advocates of vocational programs in the public schools.

The introduction of technically orientated vocational education was a response to many pressures. International competition, and the threat of war, the need to exercise wider control over the labor market, the increases in immigration were all factors in the rise of vocational programs. After 1917, the question became not whether vocational education was a legitimate course for the schools to pursue but, instead, how it was to be pursued and how it was to fit with the rest of the school's program. The larger problem involved the question of how to fit a program of schooling, established to meet certain predetermined national needs, into a society whose rhetoric emphasized democracy and self-determination.

[24] Lawrence Cremin, *The Transformation of the Schools,* New York: Vintage Books, Inc., 1961, p. 35.

To some of its advocates the testing movement was eminently designed to advance the causes of both manpower and democracy. It was argued that any democracy must have the happiness of its individual citizens as its ultimate goal and that the fulfillment of this goal demanded recognition of the fact that men are born different in ability and in aptitude and that the role of the school is to provide the opportunity for each person to rise to the level of status and authority that his talent would allow. The ideal expressed a commitment to equality of opportunity, a goal that had long been associated with the idea of a democratic society. Many in the testing movement, however, had a deep distrust of the masses and for them the idea of equal opportunity reflected a commitment to an expert elite. Thorndike spoke for many of the early testers when he wrote:

But in the long run it has paid the "masses" to be ruled by intelligence. Furthermore, the natural processes which gives power to men of ability to gain and to keep it are not, in their results, unmoral. Such men are, by and large, of superior intelligence, and consequently of somewhat superior justice and good-will. They act, in the long run, not against the interest of the world, but for it. What is true in science and government seems to hold good in general for manufacturing, trade, art, law, education, and religion. It seems entirely safe to predict that the world will get better treatment by trusting its fortunes to its 95- or 99-percentile intelligence than it would get by itself. The argument for democracy is not that it gives power to all men without distinction, but that it gives greater freedom for ability and talent to attain power.[25]

Moreover, "The abler persons in the long run are the more clean, decent, just, and kind."[26]

The use of the term "intelligence," as well as the allusion to the "95- or 99-percentile," were all technical references for Thorndike. They were statements of the objective information that intelligence tests could provide. "Intelligence" had a clear and objective reference indicating a score on an examination that subsequently measured a person's neurological potential. But it obviously meant more than that. It was a

[25] E. L. Thorndike, "Intelligence and Its Uses," Harper's Monthly, May 1922. For a more detailed discussion of the testing movement, see Clarence Karier's "Testing for Order and Control in The Corporate Liberal State" in C. Karier, P. Violas, and J. Spring, Roots of Crisis: American Education in the Twentieth Century (Chicago: Rand McNally and Co.), 1973.
[26] Thorndike, "Intelligence and Its Uses."

measure to Thorndike of character and responsibility and a statement as to the level of education and the type of job a person should be allowed to have. Even more, it was a statement of how society should be run and of how decisions in it should be made. "The man of amateurish semi-knowledge," wrote Thorndike "is a 'public danger' since he is likely to try to understand the specialist instead of obeying him and thus does not know his place intellectually."[27]

Fear of the masses was a great concern of many leaders of the testing movement. Goddard warned that "the disturbing fear is that the masses —the seventy or eighty-six million—will take matters into their own hands."[28] And he urged that the four million of very superior intelligence guide and direct the masses.

The distribution of wealth was believed to follow the distribution of intelligence and character, and it was warned that no society could ignore this fact. For Goddard, "the equal distribution of wealth in the world . . . is . . . absurd. The man of intelligence has spent his money wisely . . . while the man of low intelligence, no matter how much he would have earned, would have spent much of it foolishly."[29] Moreover, if a society was to be truly democratic it must be recognized that neither wealth nor position brings happiness, but only the proper coordination of both of these with talent, ability, and intelligence. After all, Thorndike wrote, "Probably three out of four chauffers would really much rather drive a car than live as the King of England does."[30]

Equality of opportunity was seen as a prerequisite of a democratic society, but the dominant concern was efficiency. The emphasis was not on increasing the freedom of the individual but on selecting and training him for the most appropriate social role. "Democracy" as the term was used was predicated on an individual's happiness rather than on his freedom or even on an understanding of his basic rights. And it was believed that his happiness was achieved when he occupied that station in life that best suited his intellectual capacity (as determined by objective procedures) and when he performed with diligence and loyalty the

---

[27] Ibid.

[28] Henry Goddard, *Human Efficiency and Levels of Intelligence,* Princeton, New Jersey: Princeton University Press, 1920, p. 97. I am indebted to Russell Marks for much of this material on the testers.

[29] Ibid., p. 101.

[30] Thorndike, "Intelligence. . . ."

duties that were accorded to that station. Virtually no consideration was given to the nature of the job the individual was expected to perform.

It is questionable whether the IQ examinations tested anything more than the student's ability to perform on that exam or to do well in schools that valued the same kinds of skills. It is also questionable whether the examinations mainly tested intellectual performance, or whether the major concern was to expose conformity to unexamined, but dominant social values. For example, the following items appeared on the World War I army Alpha and Beta tests suggest that intelligence was not the only item being measured. (The accepted answer is marked with "X".)

Form D.   10. Why should you not give money to beggars on the street? Because
it breaks up families
it makes it hard for the beggar to get work
it takes away the work of organized charities
X   it encourages living off of others

Form E.   1. If a man gets tired of his work, he should
throw it up
X   keep at it till the work is done
run away and loaf
make someone else do it

Form D.   6. If the grocer should give you too much money in making change, what is the thing to do?
take the money and hurry out
X   tell him of his mistake
buy some candy with it
give it to the next poor man you meet

Form C.   4. If a man knew he would die in two weeks, he should
blow all his money
X   make his will and straighten out his accounts
go dig his grave
start out on a sightseeing trip   [31]

Like the testing movement, the efficiency movement also supported the demand for technical vocational education in the curriculum. Each emphasized the need for a totally controlled educational environment in order to meet the practical and social requirements of industrial society.

[31] As quoted in Karier et al. *Roots of Crisis,* p. 13.

Even the traditional subjects were to be used to establish the proper frame of mind for the youngster's future vocational life.

This attitude is illustrated by David Snedden who served in a variety of academic and administrative posts from the early 1900s to the Depression, among them that of professor of educational administration at Teacher's College, Columbia University, and Commissioner of Education in Massachusetts[32] (1909-1916) where he was one of the most outspoken advocates of both vocational education and efficient management. Snedden not only illustrates the extreme to which the efficiency movement went, but he, perhaps more than the others, shows the extent to which the rhetoric of democracy and opportunity were subordinate to the efficient running of industrial society. A brief sketch of Snedden's views will help set the stage for an understanding of Dewey's views on education in an industrial age.

Snedden viewed the school as the primary instrument for social improvement and for social control, going so far in 1934 as to favorably single out Germany, among other states, as an example of the use of schooling for these purposes. A good deal of his attention was directed at youngsters whom he believed, whether for economic or intellectual reasons, could not profit from the usual academic curriculum. He therefore advocated that the school curriculum should be differentiated according to interest, capacity, and likely future career.[33] Snedden also declared that decisions regarding a child's course of study should be based upon the economic situation of his parents as well as his innate intelligence. He felt that only in this way could a realistic assessment of the child's future be obtained. His ideal school was one where every aspect of a child's development would be scientifically controlled. The school held primary responsibility for the child's moral education and this responsibility should guide every course of study. The reform school was cited as the outstanding model of education, because it controlled every aspect of the child's physical, spiritual, and vocational life. If the public school could achieve this kind of control, then Snedden believed that it would be relatively easy for it to offer each child the education appropriate for his social class.

---

[32] For a general description of the background surrounding Snedden's appointment, see Walter H. Drost, *David Snedden and Education for Social Efficiency* (Madison: University of Wisconsin Press), 1967, pp. 96-99.

[33] Ibid., p. 81.

In his belief that the school should provide an all inclusive environment, controlling every aspect of a child's behavior, Snedden offered a new rationale for the more traditional, nonvocational subjects. The vocation curriculum was but one side of the child's moral education. It developed habits and skills needed by the good producer who conscientiously served society. The other side was to be found in subjects such as history, literature, and social studies that would develop attitudes, such as conscientiousness, subordination, and commitment to service, demanded by a growing industrial nation. The ideal guiding the entire curriculum was to be that of social education, defined as "the effective control of native propensities and instincts . . . so as to produce . . . the habits, appreciations, knowledge and ideals" that are needed for worthwhile membership in society.[34]

Snedden reflected the views of many in the efficiency and the testing movements. Education could be scientific because it concerned only the question of means that, unlike ends, could be measured for economy, accuracy, and efficiency. The school was to train youngsters for their role in society, and the number of social roles were finite and identifiable. They were determined by the industrial needs of the community and the nation as those needs were enumerated by the business leaders. Others expressed the idea that the goal should be a meritocracy where a child would move up or down the social hierarchy according to his own capacity, as determined by the tests, without regard to economic or class background. However, the tests themselves were designed to the disadvantage of the lower class and immigrant child. They were the ultimate endorsement for the continuation of the existing ruling group, and it is not surprising that many educators concluded that the non-Protestant immigrant of Mediterranean origin was of inferior stock whose entry into the nation should be restricted. Snedden was more straightforward. He would simply determine the child's future role by the wealth and status of the parents as well as by the intelligence of the child.

Even in their most influential days the intellectual and social soundness of these movements were severely challenged by people like John Dewey and Walter Lippmann. At the time, the challenge was to

[34] As quoted in ibid., p. 83. Original in David Snedden, "History Study as an Instrument in the Social Education of Children," *J. Pedagogy*, Vol. 19 (June 1907), pp. 259-268.

reveal some of the more obvious shortcomings of these movements, but in rhetrospect, the challenge also reveals some questionable assumptions about schooling held even by its most liberal advocates.

## VI. THE LIBERAL PROGRESSIVE RESPONSE TO THE TESTING AND EFFICIENCY MOVEMENTS

Dewey and other liberals were aware of the possible misuse of educational science, and they often criticized the more blatant abuses. Ironically, Dewey's own views on evolution and ethics helped establish the groundwork for a positive science of education and his functional analysis had supported the view that ethical concerns were in fact subordinate to scientific ones. While Dewey challenged those who interpreted science in an overly *positivistic* way, his own views were consistent with the *optimistic* view of science held by many of his contemporaries. In general, he believed that the progress of science was linear and that its insights developed by incremental additions to the "storehouse of knowledge." Moreover, science was self-correcting so that less adequate theories were replaced by more adequate ones as additional information and procedures became available. Even though as early as 1906 Pierre Duhem, the French physicist, had pointed out that any so-called "crucial experiment" in science must remain logically inconclusive, Dewey continued to believe that the progress of science lay in the public character of its method and in the fact that anyone could repeat the procedures out of which a given conclusion was drawn.[35]

Dewey did warn against taking the findings of science with too much finality. In *The Quest for Certainty* he criticized the habit of mind that looks for absolute truths rather than for reasonable probabilities,

[35] Duhem's point is that any physical theory involves an intricate string of propositions. The crucial experiment involves predicting, on the basis of the theory, some happening. The traditional view is that if the prediction fails to come through, the theory under question is disproved. However, Duhem points out that because the hypothesis is generated from the string of propositions which compose the theory, it has only really been shown that some one proposition in that group has been condemned, but it has not shown which one [see Pierre Duhem, *The Aim and Structure of Physical Theory* (New York: Atheneum Publishers), 1962, pp. 183-190].

and he substituted the term "warranted assertability" for "truth." He thereby exhibited a caution towards the fixity of beliefs. Yet he also assumed that at any given time only one belief could be asserted with warranty and that only new evidence and experimentation could render the assertion unwarranted. Science was public, its evidence unambiguous, and, in the long run, it was self-corrective. While he was critical of much of what went on under the name of social and educational science, his views about ethics and evolution and the self-corrective nature of science were expressed in his conviction that desirable social change is a reflection of other changes in science and technology. His own views represent an advance over those of Snedden, but they were also limited by the attempt to formulate social and ethical norms in terms of the requirements of science and technology.

The narrow vocational emphasis of Snedden was sharply challenged by Dewey and others. Addressing himself to Snedden's proposals, Dewey objected to any vocational training that shortchanged the intellectual development of the worker as well as to those programs that were designed to "'adapt' workers to the existing industrial regime . . . Rather, one should work for a system of vocational education which would gradually 'alter' and 'ultimately transform' the existing industrial system."[36]

The testing movement came in for similar criticism from Walter Lippmann. In a series of articles written for the *New Republic* in 1922 and culminating in a bitter debate between himself and the psychologist Lewis M. Terman, Lippmann challenged the claim that the intelligence tests measured native intelligence. He argued that the claim was misleading because a clear and adequate definition of intelligence had yet to be formulated and because the results of different tests were inconsistent with each other. Moreover, if the tests were used without extreme caution they would support the false view that education is primarily a function of genetics and maturation. When interpreted in haste, Lippmann warned, the tests shift the burden of proof from the school to the child and hence excuse the school from its educative responsibility.[37]

Dewey expressed similar reservations. After arguing against the

[36] John Dewey, "Education Vs. Trade Training," *The New Republic,* Vol. 2, No. 27 (May 8, 1915), p. 42.
[37] See Walter Lippmann, "The Reliability of Intelligence Tests III," *The New Republic,* Vol. 33 (November 8, 1922), p. 277.

notion of a static industrial hierarchy, he outlined a concept of democratic leadership as an alternative. Dewey observed that the tester, pretending to have discovered the determinants of absolute superiority and of inferiority, had abstracted the individual from his concrete pursuits, and created an instrument that justified an industrial caste. He then reminded the reader that part of the purpose of education was not only to equip the student with some indispensable tools for livelihood but also to develop the qualitative uniqueness characteristic of individuality, a characteristic that he believed was threatened by industrial capitalism. He criticized the testing movement for classifying youngsters according to the dictates of the leaders of the industrial society and therefore for supporting "whatever education can do to perpetuate the present order."[38]

As Dewey expressed his reservations about the *status quo* and about the overly narrow identification of "democracy" with a specific social order, he also outlined a notion of democracy which he claimed was closer to the original intent of the founders of American society than the ill-conceived notions advocated by the leaders of the testing movement.

Democracy in its wider sense, he wrote "denotes a faith in individuality, in uniquely distinctive qualities in each normal human being . . . with willing acceptance of the modifications of the established order entailed by the release of individualized capacities."[39] He then argued that this faith made democracy the logical extension and the ultimate fulfillment of aristocracy. It is aristocracy "carried to its limits."[40] Whereas *the idea* of aristocracy proposed that those most fit to rule shall rule, *the fact* of aristocracy, Dewey observed, often diluted the idea and maintained a rigid and parochial system for selecting rulers. Nevertheless the idea in its purest form rejects and pre-established, numerically limited notion of classification. (Dewey here quotes John Adams approvingly: "An aristocrat is any man who can command two votes, one besides his own.") Its criterion of leadership was established in the concrete situation in which leadership is exercised. True democracy, Dewey argued, recognizes this same principle of leadership. Its natural

---

[38] John Dewey, "Individuality, Equality, and Superiority," *The New Republic,* Vol. 33 (December 13, 1922), p. 62.

[39] Ibid., p. 62.

[40] Ibid., p. 62.

enemy is any system that circumvents the concrete situation and limits the exercise of individuality. The idea of democracy differs from that of aristocracy only in its recognition that leadership has many aspects and is exercised in many different ways.

Democracy is a claim that every human being as an individual may be the best for some particular purpose and hence may be most fitted to rule, to lead, in that specific respect. The habit of fixed and numerically limited classification is the enemy alike of true aristocracy and true democracy.[41]

As harsh as these attacks on the testers were, they failed to challenge the idea that the school was to be the primary instrument to select and prepare people to carry on the tasks of society. For Lippmann, the issue was only whether intelligence tests were an adequate instrument for such selection. Denying that they were, he called on the psychologist to do better.

Just because the tests are so general, just because they are made so abstract in the vain effort to discount training and knowledge, the tests are by that much less useful for the practical needs of school administration and industry. Instead . . . of trying to find a test which will with equal success discover artillery officers, Methodist ministers, and branch managers for the rubber business, the psychologists would far better work out special and specific examinations for artillery officers, divinity school candidates and branch managers in the rubber business. On that line they may ultimately make a contribution to a civilization which is constantly searching for more successful ways of classifying people for specialized jobs.[42]

Dewey's challenge, based on an alternative concept of democratic leadership was vague and seriously threatened neither the selection process nor the distribution of work in industrial society. None of the testers would have disputed his idea that a democracy, like any other society, demands different kinds of skills. The only dispute was whether they, rather than some other agent, were best equipped to rank students according to such skills. And even if it was Dewey's intent to question the value and the necessity of ranking when he asserted that leadership is exercised by different people at different times, his argument is weak and easily challenged. The problem of leadership is not simply a ques-

---

[41] Ibid., p. 61.
[42] Walter Lippmann, "A Future for the Tests, IV" *The New Republic,* Vol. 33 (November 29, 1922), p. 10.

tion of who is best equipped to perform a given task, but, much more important, it is a question of how it is to be decided what particular task needs to be performed at any given time.[43]

## VII. THE LIMITS OF THE CHALLENGE

The criticism directed at the testing movement failed to challenge the selective function of the schools because the critics themselves had accepted the same process of industrialization as the testers and that acceptance meant that their proposals for humanizing schooling were to be located within the interstices of the larger concern of industrial efficiency. The reform sociologist William Fielding Ogburn stated this view most explicitly in his influential, 1922 volume *Social Change*.[44] He saw material-technological change to be relatively independent of others. The task of the reformer was to adjust social institutions and individual values to the lags created by a swiftly changing technology.

Dewey's rejection of the existing regime was directed against a *laissez-faire* society that was already in the process of being transformed. Criticizing the "economic anarchy" of *laissez-faire* capitalism for promoting rampant selfishness and insatiable individualism, he held up the values of individuality and uniqueness as alternatives. In the long run, he argued, *laissez-faire* individualism requires conformity to standardization and thereby destroys true individuality.

By directing his critique at *laissez-faire* capitalism and the tester's support of it, Dewey had located one important aspect of the problem, but he had missed another. For the way in which goods are produced in an industrial society is as much a factor in determining the limits of individuality and hence of schooling as is the way they are marketed. If individuality is more than a euphemism for greater planning in production and marketing, it means that a man's work is such that it allows him to express himself through it—that the execution is not divorced from the design and that mind and muscle work together as a coordinated effort of one and the same person. (This statement is compatible

---

[43] See Chapters Three and Four for a general discussion of the question of the selection function of schools.

[44] William Fielding Ogburn, *Social Change* (New York: Delta Books), 1966.

with Dewey's educational philosophy as an ideal.) But industrialization presupposes a sharp division of labor and a highly specialized process of production. If, in fact, we separate the concept of *laissez-faire* as simply descriptive of the marketing and consumption relations of a society from industrialization as descriptive of processes of production, it is as likely that individuality could be exercised at least as much in a *laissez-faire* setting as it could be in a different situation. Take as an example, a craft industry in which the craftsman has control over the design and production of the total product even though the object of his workmanship is sold in a *laissez-faire* market. As highs and lows occurred in the market, his prosperity would be affected, but except in the extreme situation where his livelihood was lost or severely stunted, he could still express himself through his work. However, as the division of labor sharpens with the development of highly mechanized modes of production, individuality becomes expressed less and less in the productive process. Capitalism, like war or international competition, may intensify the loss, but it does not initiate it. These considerations are necessary to an understanding of Dewey's views on vocational education and to an understanding of the limits of his challenge to the "existing industrial regime."

## VIII. DEWEY ON WORK AND EDUCATION

Dewey recognized some of the problems of industrialization and recognized some of the benefits of preindustrial society. He observed that in preindustrial society children are taught the skills of the older generation and thereby learn to avoid a good deal of the trial and much of the error of the past. In primitive societies the child is taught such skills not in any formal institution, but by watching and being tutored by an older member of the tribe. Moreover, as the child learns the skills needed to survive, he also learns the traditions and the customs which allow the tribe to act in unison and achieve a commonality of viewpoint and spirit. As the child learns the skills, customs and traditions of his society, he also comes to identify himself with that society. He understands that he is caught up in the same environment, subject to the same hazards and recipient of the same rewards as everyone else. The consequences of what he learns is rarely far removed from the situation in which they are learned. As the child learns to make a weapon for hunting, he is able to perceive the consequences of making a good weapon or a poor one. Dewey observed that for most preindustrial societies this close relationship between the learning situation and the consequences of learning is maintained. The child in the rural farm community sees an immediate relation between the act of caring for the animals and the sufferings and enjoyments of himself and the community. Dewey believed that in these situations there was not a large distinction between vocational and cultural education, for as a child learns a specific skill, he also learns, in an indirect fashion, the values and attitudes of his community. He used this characterization of preindustrial society to address some of the problems of industrial ones.

In industrialized society, Dewey noted, this relationship becomes more distant as the tasks to be performed become more specialized. In the first instance, specialization tends to remove the consequences of the act from the act itself as a large number of processes and people are required to produce a single object. Moreover, the number, complexity, and rapidly changing nature of such tasks makes the primitive method of informal education difficult to adopt. The difficulty is to be found first in the fact that the required social and intellectual skills are more complex and can no longer be taught by a master to an apprentice. Second, it is to be found in the disjunction that arises between the performing of industrial tasks and the setting of community life. The assembly line is simply not the place to learn the fundamental values of community. Therefore, Dewey noted, schools are established to do in a formal way what the communities once did informally.

Dewey warned that the change from the informal, community centered education to the formal school centered programs was accompanied by some risks. His primary concern was that the demand for efficiency and the need for specialization tended to support schools where specific skills were first abstracted from some real, concrete purpose and then taught in separation from any meaningful personal relationship. The result is a "purified" subject matter such as geography, which is then taught as if it had no significant relation to the way men live or think. When the child is confronted with a subject that has been so purified and removed from human experience, he is unable to see the concrete significance of the tasks that he must perform and as a result, the schools must develop an artificial system of rewards and punishments in an attempt to restore the motivation that once could be found in the concrete purposes of real communities. Dewey argued that by so separating motivation from skills, the school inhibits the child's expression of his own individuality and thereby hinders the development of a new concept of community. Individuality is threatened because the tasks to be performed are determined without consideration of the interests or inclinations of the child and thereby are held up as abstract aims that the child is to realize regardless of his own initial concerns. The development of community is hindered because the performance of the tasks and the learning of the skills occur apart from a consideration of their consequences either to one's self or to others. The only discernable consequences are found in the artificial systems of rewards and punishments that themselves engender a harmful spirit of competition.

It is in the context of the above point of view that Dewey's recommendations on vocational education are made. Specifically, Dewey rejected the idea that there was any real conflict between vocational education (in the true sense of the term) and cultural education. Modern societies may establish such a conflict, but this occurs in a setting where a division is made between the labor of the hand and the labor of the mind and in which the latter is given a higher status than the former. Dewey observed that a vocation is simply that which gives direction to life and organizes the various facets of an individual's existence. The opposite of vocation for Dewey was not culture or leisure but aimlessness and caprice.[45] The concept of vocation is not strictly limited to the occupation in which a man produces immediate, tangible commodities. Instead, each individual organizes his life around a variety of relations. [46] His membership in a family, a church, and his associations with friends are some of these relations. The fact that we usually name a person's vocation in terms of the one calling that distinguishes him from others in these relationships should not be allowed to conceal the fact that he is engaged in many callings each of which has a bearing on the one which we commonly and loosely term "his vocation." For example,

. . . as a man's vocation as an artist is but the emphatically specialized phase of his diverse and varigated vocation activities, so his efficiency in it,

---

[45] Dewey, *Democracy and Education* (New York: The Macmillan Company), 1916, Ch. 23, Sec. 1.
[46] Ibid.

in the humane sense of efficiency, is determined by its association with other callings.[47]

The danger for Dewey is that the distinctive activity may become dominant, thereby functioning to minimize other interests. When this occurs, Dewey warned that the significance of much of our daily activity is lost as we blindly follow the precedents of habit. The same danger exists in education whenever the schools begin to look on a vocational program as merely training for a gainful occupation. Given Dewey's enlightened concept of vocation, it is important to understand the extent and the limits of his challenge to an industrial society that was rendering such an ideal impossible for the vast majority of people.

Dewey's proposals for vocational education were designed to reduce the abstract, symbolic character of schooling while avoiding the narrowing tendencies of vocational training interpreted as gainful employment. His program for the elementary school is well known and need not be treated in detail. It is sufficient to say that, ideally, Dewey proposed that such programs should develop the habits of planning and foresight, should connect symbolic and manipulative skills, and should develop an understanding of the ways in which different skills interrelate in a communal setting. He believed that schools could use the concrete interests of children to develop an understanding of the relation between occupation and social need. In general, he did not believe that *elementary* school education should prepare the child for specific employment, and he warned against narrowing the child's field of choice too early.

His program for the secondary schools is less clear cut than that for the elementary one. Yet here too Dewey was opposed to any kind of vocational training which abstracted the student from the social context in which his work was performed. He believed that this would result in a loss of concrete meaning, individuality and community. Yet Dewey failed to challenge the industrial division of labor that was rendering education in his ideal sense so difficult. He also failed to see that the equal sharing of rewards and hardships which he believed to be essential to the community spirit of his idealized preindustrial society was more than just a *psychological* casualty of industrial society. It was a real fact of contemporary life, one which education alone could do little to address.

[47] Ibid.

## IX. DEWEY'S VIEWS
## IN A CONCRETE SETTING

Dewey's views on work and education are open to some interpretation. He was concerned to relate a person's vocation to his ongoing interests and to thereby establish the groundwork for the expression of individuality and the development of community. What is not clear, however, is the requirements that Dewey felt necessary in order to establish a meaningful relationship between a person's interests and his work. Specifically the question is whether he believed that such a relationship could be established merely through an intellectual understanding of the context in which a task was performed and through an awareness of the services that it rendered or whether he felt a fundamental change in the nature of work was necessary. Dewey's answer to this question appears ambiguous. He did believe that an understanding of the social context of work was essential for it to be meaningful. It is not nearly as clear that he also believed that a fundamental alteration in the nature of work (or in the way in which man related to both the machine and to the object of his production) was also a necessary ingredient in the establishment of meaningful work.

Dewey's writings on this subject have often been cited as an example of his more radical stance, yet they do not remove the basic ambiguity. In his chapter on the "Vocational Aspect of Education" in *Democracy and Education*,[48] for example, Dewey expressed the belief that vocational education when properly taught could have a revolutionizing effect on the world of work, but his meaning needs to be explained. In *Democracy and Education,* he noted a natural continuity between the play of the younger students and the work programs of the older. Both play and work when properly approached exhibit and develop skills of organization and habits of disciplining means to projected ends. He observed that the difference between the two is one of degree rather than kind with the ends of the work activity being more remote and distant than those of play. Like play, work "signifies purposeful activity and differs *not* in that activity is subordinated to an external result, but in the fact that a longer course of activity is occasioned by the idea of a result."[49] It is unclear whether this *idea* is occasioned merely by greater

---

[48] Ibid.
[49] Ibid., p. 204.

subjective insight into the interrelated aspects of production, or whether it should express a change in the objective conditions of production.

Dewey was also critical of the concept of work as it was expressed in the school and in the society at large. Here work is often identified as drudgery and play as some kind of release, an escape from the real business of life. It was precisely because he believed that the programs proposed by Snedden and others failed to do anything to correct this situation that he was critical of them. He believed that by changing the nature of vocational education, the meaning of work could also be altered, and he hoped for a society in which everyone would be engaged in some occupation that would enhance the lives of others, in which the barriers which divided people would be broken down, and where the ties that bind them would be more easily perceived.[50] And he argued that in order to further such a society, educators should refuse to abstract the task performed from the larger scientific and social context in which it occurred. The student should be taught to understand the scientific basis of the industrial age as well as the way in which his own work contributed to the work and to the satisfaction of others.[51]

Yet even given his view that a change in education would initiate a revolutionary change in the meaning of work, there is more evidence to suggest that he believed that such a "revolution" would arise out of an increased awareness of the social consequences of work, rather than from an alteration in the process of production and in the laborer's relation to the object of production. He wrote, for example, that

The ordinary worker in the factory is under too immediate economic pressure to have a chance to produce a knowledge like that of the worker in the laboratory. But in schools, association with machines and industrial processes may be had under conditions where the chief conscious concern of the students is insight.[52]

Insight is developed by understanding the full intellectual and social meaning of vocations and includes instruction in history, in science, in civics, and in politics. Yet as insight is developed in schools, the labor process in the factory remains essentially the same.

Because Dewey's educational philosophy is taken, perhaps rightfully, as one of the more humanizing statements on education to come

[50] Ibid., p. 316.
[51] Ibid., p. 314.
[52] Ibid., p. 315.

out of this century and because its influence is generally acknowledged, his ambiguity on the question of vocational education is significant. While Dewey firmly rejected the "anarchy of capitalist production," it was not as easy for him to assess the impact of technology on human values or to assess the harmful effects which technology in its broadest sense would have on the direction, initiative, and interrelations of people. The claim is not being made that Dewey was unaware of the harshest effects of industrial production, the long hours, and the poor working conditions. He was indeed aware of these and joined efforts to alleviate them. Many of these conditions could quite correctly be attributed to a capitalist economy, but technology itself, when allowed to develop an independent momentum, requires that certain values be translated into the institutional structure of things. Dewey was aware of some of these values, but he tended to accept them not as values, that it, not as objects of choice, but as part of the nature of things. As he accepted the increased role of formal schooling, for example, he also accepted the general decline of the role of the family in the education of the child. He did this, perhaps believing that in a technological, industrial society there simply was no other choice. He accepted, too, albeit implicitly, the infiltration of some industrial values into schooling. Punctuality, the subordination of contemplation to production, the identity of science and technology were some of the values that were incorporated into his proposals for the school.

The question of specialization and of the school's role in specialized education was an especially difficult problem for Dewey. Given the writings of Snedden, Bobbitt, Thorndike and others he was aware of the threat that specialization posed for a democratic community. Yet given his belief in the promise of technology, he seemed unwilling to tackle the more difficult aspects of the problem. Indeed, if we examine Dewey's reactions against capitalism and recognize that political, economic, and educational planning were to follow the lead established by industrial development, then his social and educational recommendations by implication require many more experts and specialists than *laissez-faire* capitalism. A new level of specialization has been added. Not only is specialization, skilled or unskilled, needed to run the machineries of industry and not only is some level of expertise needed to manage a given enterprise, but there is now a need for experts to coordinate the production and the relations among enterprises—to run the "machinery of government" (a favorite matephor of that period).

Dewey does discuss the need to involve workers in the planning process, but he is clear neither about the scope nor the mechanism of involvement. However, his recommendations about vocational education, his warnings against narrow training, and his demand that the scientific underpinnings as well as the historical background and social consequences of work be taught is best understood as much as an appeal for a planned economy as an attempt to develop individuality in the working process.

Whatever may have been Dewey's commitments in any ideal sense is less important for an understanding of liberal policy than the way his views were colored by the situations in which they were worked out. As the social context shifts from one social class to another the full implication of Dewey's pedagogy can be seen, and the way in which industrialization and his acceptance of it colored his educational philosophy can be better understood. In each of these different contexts there is common core that serves to identify the pedagogy as progressive. The teacher serves more as a facilitator orchestrating the learning environment rather than as a pedagogue cramming facts down the child's throat. There is a genuine attempt to relate the child's interest to that which he is expected to learn and therefore to unify play and work. Furthermore, there is an emphasis upon the mutually serving roles in modern society by making each school "into an embrionic community life, active with types of occupations that reflect the life of the larger society."[53] As this common core is applied to children of different social classes, however, it takes on very different meanings.

In part these differences can be explained by the various ways in which play was implicitly characterized as descriptive of the activities of different groups of youngsters. For example, in Dewey's laboratory school at the University of Chicago, activities such as weaving and carpentry were quite common and were seen as ways to engage the child's concrete interests. Here the activities were enjoyed for their own sake by the children and at the same time were used to establish manipulative skills, conceptual understandings, and communal values. More important, enjoyment of these activities did not depend on a child projecting himself into a future role as a carpenter or a weaver. This is under-

---

[53] Excerpted from SCHOOL AND SOCIETY: THE CHILD AND THE CURRICULUM, p. 29. Copyright © 1956 by The University of Chicago. Reprinted by permission.

standable given the fact that the children in Dewey's school were generally from the middle class, often with professional parents, and could be expected to assume middle-class, professional roles. However, these activities take on a different character when employed in classrooms of children from working-class homes.

Dewey's views on work and education are expressed in a general fashion in the following passage from *Schools of Tomorrow*, which Dewey wrote with his daughter Evelyn.

Work is essentially social in its character, for the occupations which people carry on are for human needs and ends. . . . Everything about this scheme is dependent upon the ability of people to work together successfully. If they can do this a well-balanced, happy, and prosperous society results. Without these occupations, which are essentially social life—that is human life—civilization cannot go on. The result is a sort of social education by necessity, since everyone must learn to adapt himself to other individuals and to whole communities. When it is left to circumstances this education, although necessary, is haphazard and only partial.[54]

This passage introduces the section on the Gary schools. It is interesting not because of the sentiment it expresses (it is certainly not unreasonable to want people to work together successfully or for society to be well-balanced and happy) but because the section provides insight into how this idea was translated when it came to the education of lower-class children.

Dewey was impressed by the Gary schools for two reasons. First he was impressed by the efficient use of the school plant, especially in light of Gary's average tax base, and second, he was impressed by the vocational education program. Dewey noted that the efficiency of the school is reflected in the fact that children attend it for the entire day, thus obtaining full use from an expensive plant and, even more importantly, reducing the pernicious effects of outside influences.[55] This concern is perfectly reasonable given the social climate that Dewey perceived existing outside of the school. Nevertheless, it is a comment that one does not find when Dewey is examining schools serving middle-class rather than working-class youngsters, and it suggests that Dewey only was willing to ameliorate the effects of industrial development. The

[54] From the book SCHOOLS OF TOMORROW by John and Evelyn Dewey. Copyright, 1915, by E. P. Dutton & Co., Inc. Renewal © 1962 by E. P. Dutton & Co., Inc., publishers, and used with their permission.

[55] See, for example, ibid., p. 131.

fact, for example, that Dewey did not question that in a town with a major industrial plant, the schools could depend on but an average tax base suggests again some of the limitations that he placed on his study. Allowing for this oversight, however, the Deweys' analysis of the vocational education programs in Gary reveals the different ways in which progressive programs were translated in middle- and working-class schools.

The authors observed, with some enthusiasm, that the children in Gary are not being trained for specific industrial roles but are developing a general understanding of shop work, of the scientific principles on which industrial labor rests, along with an awareness of the historical and social context in which the work is carried out. It is noted that one of the indexes of the success of the Gary school is the retention rate— fewer students leave school before the end of high school. As this point is elaborated, it becomes clear that success in this respect is due to other factors besides the innovative curriculum, and it becomes equally clear that the concept of interest as perceived in these working-class youngsters was not seen in the same light as that of the middle-class children from Dewey's laboratory school. The interest of working-class youngsters is met not only by the intrinsic value of the materials and activities of the school but also by encouraging them to project themselves into a variety of possible adult roles. As the authors explain the high retention rate, for example, it is noted that business men "come to the schools and tell the students what the chances for graduates and nongraduates are in their business and why they want better-educated employees."[56] Moreover:

Since the first day the Gary child began going to school he has seen boys and girls in their last year of high school still learning how to do the work that is being done where, perhaps, he expects ultimately to go to work. He knows that these pupils all have a tremendous advantage over him in the shop, that they will earn more, get a higher grade of work to do, and do it better. . . . He is familiar with the statistics of workers in that trade, knows the wages for the different degrees of skill and how far additional training can take a man. With all this information about, and outlook upon, his vocation it is not strange that so few, comparatively, of the pupils leave school.[57]

With so much of the school geared to developing work norms for these youngsters, the claim that "The industrial features . . . were not in-

[56] Ibid., p. 138
[57] Ibid., p. 190.

stituted to turn out good workers for the steel company, nor to save the factories the expense of training their own workers, but for the educational value of the work they involved"[58] sounds like wishful thinking at best.

The different ways in which a child's interest was perceived in middle- and working-class areas is not simply a reflection of the fact that middle- and working-class youngsters may have been interested in different objects. Rather the concept of *interest* was perceived in a different way. With middle-class children interest was orientated in the present, in the here and now value of the activity. With working-class youngsters, interest was programmed to be much more future oriented and, as with Gary, depended on the youngster projecting himself into an adult role.

This difference is expressed most significantly in the organization of *Schools of Tomorrow*. Each chapter begins with a description of the philosophy behind the school (primarily written by John Dewey) followed by a description of the school itself (primarily written by Evelyn Dewey). As we have seen, Dewey's educational philosophy was critical of any pedagogy that abstracted one aspect of human development as if it were the whole of education. This accounts for his criticism of the overly bookish learning of many of the schools of his time and his constant concern that the work of the mind be joined with the work of the hand. *Schools of Tomorrow* is a description of schools where attempts had been made to bridge the separation between mental, and manual activity and to deal with learning in a more integrated fashion. Nevertheless many different types of schools with students from many different backgrounds are described and in one important respect these differences are not acknowledged: each one of these schools had an activities curriculum of one kind or another. In the middle-class and rural schools the primary object of this curriculum was to develop motor, perceptual, and problem-solving skills along with a general awareness of different aspects of nature and life. However when the description turned to urban schools primarily for working-class children the activity curriculum took on a different meaning. Its goal was largely vocational designed to develop the work norms required for the modern factory and the basic attitudes associated with good citizenship.[59]

---

[58] Ibid., p. 129.

[59] It is instructive to contrast the chapters on "Play" with that entitled "Education Through Industry" in *Schools of Tomorrow*.

## X. SUMMARY

Dewey's response as an example of the liberal-progressive reaction to proposals embodied in the testing and efficiency movement can be seen from two different points of view. On the one side he may be seen as reacting against the impulse to guide educational reforms by narrowly interpreted industrial needs. He believed that the most severe problems of industrial growth were the progressive loss of community and individuality and that it was these problems that schools should address. His criticism was thus directed against the notion that schools should function *merely* to identify talent and then to train it according to some predetermined social roles. The more significant task was to recapture community and individuality in light of a growing industrial complex. Thus, as he wrote in explaining the rational behind the Gary plan:

It is just as valuable for the man who works with his brain to know how to do some of the things that the factory worker is doing, as it is for the latter to know how the patterns for the machine he is using were drawn, and the principles that govern the power supply in the factory.[60]

The other side is simply that when this goal was translated into educational programs for children who would eventually work in the factory, it was significantly different in aim and method than it was when applied to children who were eventually to work with their brains. Its effect was, in fact, to identify talent and to train it according to predetermined social roles.

That liberals and progressives did not often take note of this is explainable by their willingness to accept industrial growth not only as a fact of twentieth-century life but also as the context for all ethical deliberation.

[60] Ibid., p. 264.

# CHAPTER THREE
# The Democratic Ideal and Liberal Educational Policy

## I. INTRODUCTION

The ideal of equal opportunity has been a dominant theme of American ideology and has persisted through many different movements, such as the conquering of the frontier and the rise of free enterprise. It is, therefore, not surprising that it was used to justify the expansion and reform of public education. The belief that a person's background should not interfere with his achievement and eventual status was and is the dominant idea of liberal educational policy. Contemporary liberal educators felt that many of the traditional avenues of equality of opportunity were no longer adequate, and they proposed that the public school was the most appropriate agency to remedy this situation. Thus the ideal of equality of opportunity began to be transformed into the ideal of equality of educational opportunity.

This transformation was believed to be consistent with both the requirements of justice and those of a developing industrial society. It fulfilled the requirement of justice by demanding that accidental factors such as race, creed or family background not limit the individual's opportunity nor serve as a barrier to his achievement. It fulfilled the need of expanding industry by establishing provisions for drawing on a wider pool of talent and for developing new occupational skills and social attitudes that were thought difficult to maintain in the informal family and communal setting. Thus it was that the school became more attractive as an instrument for advancing the cause of equality of opportunity.

Perhaps because of the habit of viewing ideals in functional terms most liberals generally believed that the two sources of equality of opportunity were perfectly compatible. Yet the two are not necessarily compatible. The development of technology, may at times require, that traditional stereotypes not be challenged beyond a certain limit and that changes in a group's status be gradual and not disruptive to the production process. Justice, however, may require otherwise.

This chapter examines the response of liberal and progressive educators in their attempt to meet the requirements of both justice and technology in advancing the cause of equality of opportunity. It begins by looking at the social context of progressive educational theory and, using Dewey and Counts as the representative theorists, shows the extent that progressive theory was a response to technological demands. It then examines some specific cases in which the requirements of technology and the demands of justice seemed to be in tension and shows how the ideal of equality of opportunity was molded by these conflicts.

## II. THE SOCIAL
## CONTEXT OF PROGRESSIVE REFORM

Progressive education arose as a response to problems that technology and urbanization had created, and its theory included both a concept of education and a critique of schooling. Much of the theory of education was grounded in the philosophy of Dewey and in his belief that human knowledge was bound up with human experience. Knowledge was seen as the result of man's cultural and social history, and symbolic understanding was viewed functionally as the most effective means that man had found to analyze and resolve the problems that confronted him. The object of knowledge was dependent on the very process of knowing; ideas were not conceptual abstractions to be contemplated only as mental events. They were instruments allowing man, through symbolization, to project alternative paths when his experiencing was blocked and then to manipulate his environment according to his purpose.

Progressive educators like Dewey therefore believed that capturing the interest of the child was not simply a motivational gimmick to sugarcoat the distasteful task of learning. It was the way to teach the essential relationship between human knowledge and human experience. The child's interest was a necessary part of the learning process. By relating his interest to conceptual skills he could manipulate his environment and come to understand the way in which ideas were human instruments.

The progressives' critique of schooling was based upon these insights. Dewey argued that existing education rested upon an inadquate understanding of the relationship between the knower and the known. He thought that teaching was too often carried on as if the object of knowledge existed independently of the act of knowing, as if it did not matter *how* the child came to know but only *that* he did know. Thus the long sessions of recitation and memorization, so common in the schools of the time, were explained as resting on a general misunderstanding of the nature of knowledge.

Dewey, therefore, believed that the rigid nature of schooling was a perversion of the natural process of knowing, one where the knower was separated from the known. He thought that the reason for this development could be understood in terms of the pressures of specialization that taught symbolic and manipulative activities as two separate things, each one of which was divorced from the ongoing experience of the child. Together they reflected a society that was itself divided into those who worked with their heads and those who worked with their hands.

The progressive's critique of schooling was closely tied to a theory of education, but it is useful to separate them in order to understand the way in which the social context of the times guided progressive thought. It would be possible, for example, to accept the progressive educational theory while observing without concern rigid, mechanical schools, as long as one believed that schooling comprised only a minor part of a child's education. Dewey himself recognized that it was only because of circumstances unique to modern times that the progressive educational theory and its critique of schooling were brought together into a unified educational philosophy. In *School and Society,* written in 1900, Dewey reminded the reader that only a few generations before, the household was the place where all the typical forms of industrial occupation were carried on as people made their own cloth, grew and processed their own food, and built their own furniture. He reminded his readers that as children grew up in the household, they attained not only the skills to carry on those occupations but also the habits of industry, responsibility, and obligation.[1] In this situation, schools were of little importance for the great majority of people, and except for the rudiments of reading, writing, and arithmetic, they could cater to those who had more intellectual aspirations. However, industrialization and the changing pattern of family life meant that the school "must now supply that factor of training formally taken care of by the home."[2]

Dewey argued that the ideal of democracy was often perverted by the school because its program was drawn from an outdated educational theory and appealed only to the intellectual side of man. He wrote:

The result is that which we see about us everywhere—the division into "cultured" people and "workers," the separation of theory and practice. Hardly 1 per cent of the entire school population ever attains to what we call higher education; only 5 per cent to the grade of our high school; while much more than half leave on or before the completion of the fifth year of the elementary grade. The simple facts of the case are that in the great majority of human beings the distinctively intellectual interest is not dominant. They have the so-called practical impulse and disposition. In many of those in whom by nature intellectual interest is strong, social conditions prevent its adequate realization. Consequently by far the larger number of pupils leave school as soon as they have acquired the rudiments of learning, as soon as they have enough of the symbols of reading, writing, and calculating to be of practical use to them in getting a living. . . . If we were to conceive our educational end and aim in a less exclusive way, if we were to introduce into educational processes the activities which appeal to those whose dominant interest is to do and to make, we should find the hold of the school upon its members to be more vital, more prolonged, containing more culture.[3]

[1] John Dewey, *The Child and the Curriculum: The School and Society* (Chicago: University of Chicago Press), 1962, pp. 10-11.
[2] Ibid., p. 13.
[3] Ibid., p. 28.

Progressive education was therefore an attempt to address the problems that industrialization had wrought and for Dewey the place to begin was in the elementary grades where an active participation in man's vocational activity was to be an introduction to the cultural life of the human species.

These occupations . . . shall not be mere practiced devices or modes of routine employment, the gaining of better technical skill as cooks, seamstresses, or carpenters, but active centers of scientific insight into natural materials and processes, points of departure whence children shall be led out into a realization of the historic development of man.[4]

Moreover, "the scientific insight thus gained becomes an indispensable instrument of free and active participation in modern social life."[5]

Progressive education was seen as a way to close the gaps that industrialization had brought by reproducing the essential character education that previously had been carried on by the family. It was to teach youngsters about the interdependence of social roles and to provide an insight into the function of science in the modern age.

## III. THE CONFLICT BETWEEN TECHNOLOGICAL AND COMMUNAL VALUES IN PROGRESSIVE THOUGHT

Commentators on Dewey have pointed to the way in which his own thought was guided by the requirements generated by technology. Some like Kimball and McClellan believe that there was an inconsistency between his views on technology and his concern to resurrect community in industrial society. They write:

Dewey recognized that the basic dynamism of our day is found in expanding technology. On the other hand, . . . his vision of the future included communal control, through public agencies, of mass industries whose workers would not be mere appendages to machines but rather cooperating citizens in the control of their own destinies.

The inconsistency? Simply this: changing technology would no more spare the cooperative community of industrial workers than it had spared the New England village life from which Dewey's vision had sprung.[6]

---

[4] Ibid., p. 19.
[5] Ibid., p. 23.
[6] Solon T. Kimball and James E. McClellan, Jr., *Education and the New America* (New York: Vintage Press, 1962), p. 113.

Other commentators have argued that the inconsistency disappears once it is understood that Dewey's intent was to use schooling to reduce the alienation that otherwise would result from industrial life. Arthur Wirth expresses this point of view:

His point was that in the urban community individuals would be removed from direct participation in producing life's goods. In order to make sense of a world they could only experience in fragments, they would have to be helped to see it conceptually, and to understand that the intricate superstructure of specialized processes was an elaboration of means related to fundamental human needs. . . . The new complexity was the result of man's intellectual leap forward and the present task was to become thoroughly familiar with the intellectual skills, and with the content and habits of man that had transformed the banks of the Chicago River—and might eventually transform the face of the moon. The task of liberal education was to give the young an understanding of their place in the scheme of things. . . . Consequently they might avoid feeling alienated by the rush of the city's streets; they might feel that they could share in the processes that were contributing to the improvement of life.[7]

The difference between these two views is significant. The second view suggests that Dewey was less concerned about the active involvement of citizens and workers in decisions affecting their everyday life than is thought by some to be the case and that the intent of the new education was, instead, to teach youngsters to appreciate the promise of indusrial society. There are passages in Dewey that would lend support to both interpretations. The fact is, however, that Dewey did not see a conflict between the value of technology and the value of community because he simply did not view technology as a value; it was not an object of choice but a given fact of life around which all other forms of social activity were to be organized. Other forms of social life were adjustable to one degree or another, but the general contours of man-machine relations were not.

Because it was believed that technology held so much promise, the program of the progressive educator was designed to address the dislocations that it created. Industrialization meant specialization, but specialization threatened to destroy the unifying perspective which progressives felt to be essential for social harmony. Specialization was

[7] Arthur G. Wirth, *John Dewey as Educator: His Design for Work in Education, 1894-1904* (New York: Wiley, 1966), p. 292.

thought to be inevitable, but progressives argued that if youngsters could be taught to understand the interrelationship between diverse social roles, alienation could be blocked. To this end the progressive school emphasized science and the scientific method as the unifying agent of the new age. Science was seen as the foundation of modern industry that was based "upon machinery resulting from discoveries in mathematics, physics, chemistry, bacteriology, etc."[8] Thus the so-called vocational subjects were not to be taught for their practical value alone but also as vehicles for revealing some of the unifying aspects of the civilization that supported them.[9] In addition to an understanding of science as the underpinning of industrial society, youngsters were also to be taught that the scientific method could be applied to social affairs as a way to both clarify and resolve the source of conflicts. This accounts for much of the group work in progressives schools where children were to learn the appropriate methods for reconciling their own differences and where they would eventually learn the role of scientific procedures in resolving conflicts in the adult world.

The thrust of progressive reform was to provide the conceptual understanding that would allow industrial growth to continue without the side-effect of disruptive alienation. Yet within this general thrust, the idea of community did have its place. Both progressive and liberal educators have often advocated a more communal base for educational authority, one that was to place many decisions under the control of those immediately affected by them. Children were to have more say over the affairs of the classroom and parents and teachers over the work of the school. Such control was to be exercised within certain limits, of course, and often times the very same educators who advocated community-based authority on one level, advocated the need for central decision making on another. There is, however, no contradiction here. Central control was perceived to be a necessary aspect of expanding technology, but unless adequate room for local participation was provided, the likelihood of alienation and passive resistance would increase.[10]

[8] John Dewey, *Democracy and Education* (New York: The Macmillan Co.), 1961, p. 314.

[9] See ibid., p. 314 for an elaboration of this point.

[10] This can be seen most recently in the shift of the U. S. Office of Education and various foundations from the idea of consolidated schools in some areas to decentralized control in others.

## IV. THE DEMOCRATIC
## IDEAL AND EDUCATIONAL REFORM

Progressives often argued that there was a reciprocal relationship between a more nationally centered educational policy and the well-being of the individual. If schools could better serve industrial growth, they could also serve to break the bonds of social class and provide children the opportunity to transcend the boundaries of their local community. As Lawrence Cremin has noted:

On the basis of prudence alone, no modern industrial nation can fail to afford every one of its citizens a maximum opportunity for intellectual and moral development. And beyond prudence, there is justice.[11]

This, of course, expresses the ideal of equality of educational opportunity.

While the ideal of equality of opportunity was not unique to twentieth-century liberal reformers, the emphasis on schooling as the vehicle to achieve it was. The ideal itself was a carryover from a *laissez-faire* ideology that otherwise progressive liberals eschewed.

Before the rise of progressive education many conservative theorists recognized the value of equality of opportunity as a way to relieve social pressure that could arise from talented and discontented members of the lower class. However, twentieth-century industrialization required both new attitudes on the part of the population as a whole and new skills, especially for those who were to assume leadership roles. It was believed that the economic marketplace was swiftly becoming obsolete as an effective way to develop both the talent and the attitudes required by an increasingly complex society. The progressive educator George Counts expressed this point in 1929 in an address before the Department of Secondary School Principals of the National Education Association.

Counts observed that the extension of secondary education to almost half of the nation's adolescent youth must be seen first as an extension of an ideal that developed long before the rapid expansion of secondary education.

In response to a rare combination of life conditions our ancestors developed certain ideals regarding the nature of man and the place of the

---

[11] Lawrence A. Cremin, *The Genius of American Education* (New York: Vintage Books), 1965.

individual in society. Under the influence of the frontier and the simple farming community of pioneer origins, they threw off the artificial social distinctions which had characterized the older civilizations and evolved a theory of democracy suited to their mode of life. According to this theory the individual should be judged in terms of inherent worth and be permitted to achieve that station in society to which he is entitled by reason of his own talents, efforts, and character. While some may prefer to call this view of life individualism rather than democracy, the point which I wish to make is that it would seem to underlie our educational system and to have furnished the inspiration for the creation of the public high school as an upward extension of elementary education.[12]

Counts believed that the "democratic ideal" arose out of the nation's agrarian roots, but he perceived the use of the secondary schools to further the ideal as a direct consequence of industrialization. His statement that "industrialization has given birth to a society of enormous complexity"[13] was meant to emphasize the great expansion of different kinds of occupations and skills:

Back of this complex social mechanism, as back of the skyscraper, stands the supporting spiritual structure of science and technology. The knowledge and experience necessary for managing the old agrarian order could be gained for the most part through the ordinary process of living; the knowledge and experience necessary for managing industrial society must be gained increasingly through the more systematic methods of formally organized educational agencies.[14]

Yet the functional requirements of the new age also set limits on how far the school could go in achieving its ideal. As Counts noted:

Society sets definite limits to the task which we as specialists in secondary education may perform. In the large it would seem that the broad outlines of the secondary school are fixed by the social order. Within these boundaries we are free to work, but if we essay to pass beyond them our efforts are certain to be sterile. . . . Any defensible or sound theory of secondary education must be in essential harmony with the great social trends which characterize the age.[15]

---

[12] George S. Counts, "Selection as a Function of American Secondary Education," *National Education Association, Proceedings,* Vol. 67, Washington: The NEA Association, © 1929, p. 597.

[13] Ibid., p. 599.

[14] Ibid., p. 599.

[15] Ibid., p. 602.

To those familiar with Counts' writings in the 1930s,[16] the theme that the schools are fixed by the social order may seem a far cry from Counts' speech, "Dare the Schools Build a New Social Order," a speech in which he called upon progressive educators to serve the depressed classes. The seeming contradiction can be easily resolved once it is understood that Counts believed that the dominant social force was technology, and that it was the function of the school to bring other, subordinate forces into harmony with it. In his 1929 speech the message was that educators could not, no matter what their desires, return to an early age when the character of the high school was more selective. In his "Dare the Schools" talk the emphasis was on other factors in the social order which needed to be harmonized with technology, such as the attitudes that wedded sophisticated industry to the uncertainties of a *laissez-faire* market.

Counts' views on equality of opportunity reflected the general belief of liberal educators that the extent to which human values could be translated into institutions was determined by the independent force of technology. The growth of technology set limits to the expression of these values, but the implications for man's future was generally favorable.

## V. THE LIBERAL IDEAL
## AND ITS FUNCTIONAL LIMITS

Counts had articulated the democratic ideal as the belief that "the individual should be judged in terms of inherent worth and be permitted to achieve that station in society to which he is entitled by reason of his own talents, efforts, and character."[17] He believed that the limit to which this ideal could be realized was determined by certain characteristics of the social situation at any given time and that, because of a unique set of circumstances, associated with industrialization, the high school had become the major vehicle for the fulfillment of this ideal. The very functional requirements of technology demanded that justice be done.

Yet the democratic ideal, or the ideal of equality of opportunity, had two sources: an ethical and a prudential one. More often than not

[16] See Chapter Seven.
[17] See footnote 12.

the distinction between these two sources was blurred largely because of the liberal's belief that functional solutions were also ethical ones.[18] Nevertheless, it is certainly possible to separate the belief that justice requires that accidental factors such as a man's parents or social class should not be a barrier to his achievement, from the notion that technological growth requires the development of a certain level of talent. There may be times when the goals of justice and technological growth fortunately coincide and when therefore the distinction is merely academic. However, if the growth of technology requires things other than the development of talent, such as the recruitment of people into boring jobs, then it is not necessarily the case that the two goals always will be compatible. Insofar as the other requirements conflict with the demands of justice, then precisely to that extent will there be tension between the two goals.

Counts recognized that industrialization set limits to what the schools could do, but he did not perceive any potential conflict between justice and growth. Nevertheless, a fuller understanding of progressive reform can be aided by an analysis of its response to the conflicting requirements of justice and industrial growth. This can be achieved by examining the activity of progressive educators in situations where these two values did come into conflict.

## VI. DEWEY AND
## THE POLISH COMMUNITY

An example of the liberal's response to the conflicting demands of democracy and technology can be seen in Dewey's involvement in a study of the Polish community undertaken in 1917 when Albert C. Barnes, a millionaire industrialist and art critic, registered for one of Dewey's seminars at Columbia. At the end of the year Barnes suggested that the Polish community posed a counterexample to Dewey's ideas on community and he offered to support a project to find out why Polish groups in Philadelphia were not assimilating to American life. Believing the isolation of the Polish community to be a serious problem

---

[18] See Chapter Two.

for American society, Dewey accepted the proposal.[19] Barnes rented a house on the boundary of the Polish community for the members of the seminar and the project, with Dewey aboard, continued for three months. Out of it came a study of the churches of the community by Brand Blanshard, of the schools by Helen Bradshaw,[20] and of the political and organizational aspects of the community by Dewey. Dewey's study was printed in 1918 as a confidential report entitled "Conditions Among the Poles in the United States" and submitted, at the request of General Churchill, to the Military Intelligence Bureau of the federal government.

There is much in the report that could have been highly controversial to members of the Polish community who were engaged in a number of internal battles about organization, funding, and loyalty. The purpose of the study, Dewey wrote, "was to ascertain forces and conditions which operate against the development of a free and democratic life among the members of this group, to discover the influences which kept them under external oppression and control." Then, quoting approvingly from Barnes, Dewey continued: "The idea would be to work out a practical plan, based on firsthand knowledge, to eliminate forces alien to democratic internationalism and to promote American ideals in accordance with the principles announced by President Wilson in his various public communications."[21] Although there is a good deal in the study to suggest that there was much factionalism among Polish-American groups, and that there were different and varying degrees of sympathy to the Polish struggle abroad, there is virtually nothing of any substance to warrant Dewey's claim that such groups were under "external oppression and control." The worst that could be claimed is that some Poles maintained an identity and a loyalty to the homeland while resisting attempts at Americanization. Whether this loyalty was externally controlled or whether it was strictly volitional was not a serious article of study for the Dewey group.

[19] The phrase "cyst on American life" was originally used by Brand Blanshard, to describe Dewey's attitude towards the Poles during a telephone interview in the fall of 1970. However in a later interview (Dec. 1973) Blanshard expressed doubt whether this was Dewey's term, Barnes', or his own description of Dewey's point of view.

[20] This study could not be located.

[21] John Dewey, "Conditions Among The Poles in the United States: Confidential Report," Washington, 1918, p. 2.

In the study Dewey identified two major groups within the Polish community: those who feared and were opposed to Americanization and those who were not. Among the first group, which constituted by far the largest part of the study, was to be found most of the Polish clergy supported by the conservative financial elements led by Paderewski, the musician, and his wife. Dewey generally admitted that the clerics had the support of the majority of Poles, but he attributed this to disorganization among the people, to the absence of a Protestant middle group that he believed would somehow unify different factions, and to the manipulation of the majority of Poles by the priestly class. Little, if any information, was provided in the report, however, that could be construed as actual manipulation and while Dewey admitted that the conservative faction appeared to have more support than the one favoring Americanization, he yet described the priestly group as only "professing" to speak for the masses.

Dewey's major concern was not the manipulation of one group of Poles by another but the effect on the American war effort that such disunity might provoke. The report, Dewey wrote, is concerned with the conditions among the Poles "which have a bearing upon the disposition and morale of the Poles with respect to the war, in that they breed dissention and disturb the unity which is desirable for efficient prosecution of the war."[22]

Even more significant for a clarification of Dewey's own values and priorities was his identification at this time with American military and commercial interests. This identification presents another side of Dewey's social theory and his commitment to democracy. It reveals a fundamental commitment to a functionally organized society. Throughout the report Dewey implicitly questioned the loyalty of the Polish citizen, and in two specific places he proposed a concrete test of that loyalty. Both were related to the formation of an American commission to deal with Polish affairs, but the rhetoric of the proposal is of more than passing significance:

The willingness of the Poles to accept a distinctively American commission which should bring about a unity among the different factions of Poles, make a special study of the Polish question and get into relation with Polish conditions abroad, would seem a fair test of whether any Pole or group of Poles put foremost their personal or factional interest or their

[22] Ibid., p. 4.

desire for a free and independent Poland. . . . An American commission
would naturally co-operate with the Paris Committee (a prominent Polish
group in exile) and with all other Polish organized groups. The only thing
that an American commission would interfere with is the ambition of the
Paris Committee to become a provisional government for Poland and to be
its representative at the Peace Conference; and the desires and activities of
those Poles in America who are so afraid of Americanization that they
actually prefer allegiance to a group on foreign soil to an active interest
in the Polish question on the part of the United States embodied in a
distinctly American commission.[23]

Dewey clearly placed the burden of proof of loyalty and good
citizenship on the Polish-American people and their acceptance of such
a commission. He also suggested that their loyalty was to be determined by whether or not they were willing to accept the American government as representing the interest of the Polish nation instead of a
distinguished group of Polish citizens in exile. That such an issue might
not have been a question of loyalty at all, but rather a question of fact
about who could best represent the interests of the Polish nation never
seemed to have entered Dewey's mind.

Dewey felt so strongly about his proposed American commission
for Polish affairs that he suggested that reluctance of prominent Polish-
Americans to join it may be taken as *prima facie* evidence of disloyalty.
"Refusal of any faction or important Pole to join would indicate that he
put personal ambition or partisan interest before the cause of Poland, or
else that he put allegiance to some foreign group before his allegiance
to the United States."[24]

If industrialization requires more than equality of opportunity, then
so too does justice. Justice requires the recognition of civil rights as well,
and it should be evident that the loyalty test Dewey proposed was a
violation of that idea. But technological growth also requires more than
the development of a certain level of sophisticated skills and knowledge,
it requires a reasonable degree of industrial tranquility, and in this
respect the tasks that Dewey proposed be set before the commission
reveal his commitment in this matter. The commission was "to make
clear the active and directive influence of the United States in the Polish
problem, quieting German and Austrian propaganda and keeping the
Poles in Poland faithful to the cause of the allies"[25] and, furthermore to

---

[23] Ibid., pp. 46-47. Brackets added.
[24] Ibid., p. 79.
[25] Ibid., pp. 79-80.

"provide methods by which information from all Polish sources can be secured and organized and by which the cause of industrial unrest can be immediately detected and the unrest allayed."[26]

It is difficult, indeed it is almost impossible, to see in the report any major concern for democracy or equality of opportunity in the sense in which these are usually portrayed at liberal ideals of justice. Paramount in the report is a desire to keep the wheels of industry running, not only during the war, but after it was over as well. In the report, Dewey spoke to postwar concerns:

The great industrial importance of Polish labor in this country must be borne in mind and the fact that there will be a shortage of labor after the war and that there is already a movement under foot (which should be carefully looked into) to stimulate the return of Poles and others of foreign birth in Southeastern Europe to their native lands after the war. With the sharp commercial competition that will necessarily take place after the war, any tendency which on the one hand de-Americanizes and on the other hand strengthens the allegiance of those of foreign birth to the United States deserves careful attention.[27]

The passage about the continuing industrial importance of the Polish American follows somewhat after Dewey's description of the agrarian roots of the Polish-American and of the alienation and disorientation that occurs when he is forced into an urban-industrial center.

Dewey's concern to establish a new national identity among the Poles and his desire to keep the military and the industrial machinery running provides a somewhat different perspective on his views about democracy and education. One of Dewey's students, Helen Bradshaw, did a report on education in the Polish community. Unfortunately, this report has been lost. However, Brand Blanshard, who subsequently became Miss Bradshaw's husband and who served as Dewey's research assistant, did a work entitled *The Church and the Polish Community* that contained a short section on education that seems consistent with the recommendations of Dewey's own study. The fact that Dewey and Blanshard were in close communication when this report was researched and prepared also suggests that there was likely some influence of the older scholar upon his young graduate student. Blanshard's major concern was the control exercised by the church and the parochial school over the education of the Polish youth. The church, he observed, was

[26] Ibid., p. 79.
[27] Ibid., p. 73.

steeped in superstition and magic which it handed down through a monolithic theology to its youth. Like Dewey, he extolled the virtues of the Protestant religion seeing in it the virtues of diversity, tolerance and right thinking, and he concluded by proposing a drastic revision of the church.

Blanshard's report sheds additional light on the commitment of the liberal theorist to industrial growth. Regardless of whether one agrees or disagrees with Blanshard's description of the church, progressive reform had been justified as filling the gaps in family and community life that industrialization had created. However the relationship between the members of the Polish community and their church would indicate that no such gap existed and that indeed the church was serving to cement a community whose members might otherwise be traumatized by urban industrial life. Here then is a case where educational reform was being proposed not to fill a gap but to create one.

Ultimately one's view of the church's activity may make a difference in evaluating Dewey's proposals. If one is willing to overlook specific proposals that do violence to the notion of civil rights, then Dewey could be defended as attempting to break the parochialism of the church and integrate the child into American society. But before this defense could be accepted it is necessary to examine the priority that was given to integration as a liberal value.

## VII. DEWEY AND P.S. 26

Liberal educational reform has generally been known for its stress on integration as a crucial need of modern society. Counts articulated this need in the following way:

The integration of society makes necessary a widening of the intellectual and social horizon of the individual. Particularly does it require the bearing of heavier burdens in the realm of political and social life. The citizen is brought into a larger society, a society which in considerable part he can know only indirectly and from a distance. This means that he must come to depend less and less on immediate and unorganized personal experience and more and more upon various formal agencies of education....

The integration of society opens up to the individual occupational opportunities of the most diverse kind. Because of increased mobility he is no longer confined in his choice to the life of the narrow and limited geographical and social circle into which he was born. He therefore feels the need of being equipped to range far from home and family, to meet strange situations, and to control the course of his own life.[28]

Integration was clearly designed to serve the larger goal of equality of opportunity and it too had its support both in an idea of justice and in the perceived requirements of industrial society. Dewey's Polish study was, at least in part, an appeal for the integration of Polish people into the fabric of American life, but it was a request that issued from industrial concerns as well as from ethical ones.

Integration generally served the needs of industrial America but not always so. If the Polish study was an example of a push towards assimilation in the interest of national unity, Dewey's treatment of Negro education during this same time provided a somewhat different emphasis. Although his name was on the list of the founders of the NAACP, Dewey's vision was limited in his examination of Negro education. If the Polish study pushed for assimilation, his examination of Negro schools in the same period revealed a resigned attitude toward *de facto* segregated schools. Yet this resignation issued from the same source as his opposite concern for integration of the Poles. Dewey did not believe, as Gunnar Myrdal has said of Americans in general, that the Negro was a separate caste, unable to be assimilated into society. Yet he very well may have believed that the rest of American society believed this and until later in his career he was cautious in challenging this belief. To illustrate this point it is necessary to turn to a description of an all-Negro school that Dewey wrote with his daughter Evelyn Dewey in *Schools of Tomorrow* in 1916.

As we have seen, *Schools of Tomorrow* is a general survey of experimental schools and practices interspersed with statements about the theory behind the design of individual schools. For the most part, the book is descriptive, but it has been speculated that preferences are revealed by the order of the reporting with the descriptions of those schools that are more closely aligned to Dewey's theory coming in the latter parts.[29] This view seems correct. Dewey's comments are generally descriptive with certain aspects of the schools singled out for praise. He avoids making critical comments except in his treatment of the Montes-

---

[28] Counts, "Selection . . .", pp. 598-599.
[29] See Lawrence Cremin, *The Transformation of the Schools* (New York: Vintage Books), 1961, pp. 153-154.

sori school, but the exception is important. It indicates that the report was not simply descriptive.

One of the schools that Dewey reported on in the latter part of the book was P.S. 26 in Indianapolis. P.S. 26 was an all-black school in a poor black slum. In view of the condition of the families in the neighborhood and the poverty that Dewey described, the school was carrying on some worthwhile programs and was rightly included. Dewey mentioned that the school was located in "the crowded district of the city and has only colored pupils,"[30] and he observed that the school was not attempting to solve the race problem but that it was developing good citizens. If the experiment were to succeed, it would "mean a real step forward in solving the race problem."[31] Yet the program that Dewey then described was strictly a vocational program, albeit an excellent one where much of the school and the neighborhood served as a shop for the students. At a time when much black labor was unskilled or employed as farmhands, a program of skill development was an advance forward. Nevertheless, black boys learned how to cook and black girls how to sew.

It might be said in the context of the purpose of the Deweys' book that it is unfair to criticize Dewey for merely reporting on what was a splendid vocational program without commenting on the social conditions that made being a cook one of the highest aspirations of a Negro child. Yet in view of the somewhat mild, but nevertheless serious, criticism of Montessori, it would not have been too much to expect a comment on the implications of a strictly vocational program for black children. A more serious shadow is cast over Dewey's evaluation of the experiment as he suggests its greatest value to lie among the youngsters of Negro and immigrant parents. If it was realism that guided Dewey's attitude, it was realism of a peculiar kind, one that believed that the best way for a black man to cope with American society was to fit into it as best he could and as best as it would allow. Dewey's praise of the program for developing good citizens is of more than passing interest. Given the strictly vocational function of the school, his view of citizenship as it is presented here would do little to alter traditional stereotypes or to change the relations of power between groups. Dewey's

---

[30] John Dewey and Evelyn Dewey, *Schools of Tomorrow* (New York: E. P. Dutton and Co., 1915), p. 207.
[31] Ibid., p. 208.

endorsement of the activity of this school casts some light on the nature of the limits that Counts had in mind when he suggested that the schools must work within the contours established by the dominant society. From one point of view, it could be claimed that the school was serving the goal of equality of opportunity since it was providing a passage for some black youngsters into occupations that might otherwise have been closed to them. Moreover, in defense of the school's program it could be argued that training on a higher level might well have proved disfunctional even to the children themselves since the more advanced academic programs carried on in such places as law schools or medical schools were generally closed to blacks at this time. Thus it could be claimed that it was realistic to set the child's sights on the trades rather than on the professions and that because the school was functionally integrated into the norms of American society it was able to serve the goal of equality of opportunity without seriously threatening social stability.

Yet this defense highlights the problems as well as the merits of this approach, for clearly equality of opportunity was being served only in a restricted way. For if the ideal required that a person advance on his talent and effort alone, and that accidental factors such as birth or color not be a factor, then the ideal was being honored more in the breach than in the promise. Black children were indeed limited by their blackness alone. Had Dewey so chosen, the description of this school might have provided a suitable occasion to affirm equal opportunity as an ethical value and to analyze the social structure that made vocational education especially appropriate for black and immigrant children. That he did not is perhaps an indication of the limits of his own values and of the functionalist approach to social reform. Regardless of how one may appraise these events for an understanding of Dewey's point of view, they do reflect significant aspects of liberal educational policy in general.

## VIII. LIBERALS AND PROGRESSIVES ON NEGRO EDUCATION

One of the most significant features of the progressive education movement is to be found in the absence of any clear appraisal of Negro education until almost 1940. Until that time, the few analyses of black education, when not offered in support of the status quo, were offered as examples of a particular pedagogical reform. Dewey's treatment of P.S. 26 is only one example of this. Progressives, for the most part, addressed the Negro question within the context of an established national consensus.

By the time John Maynard Rice had written his series for *The Forum* in 1892 many Northern educators had long forgotten the idealism of the reconstruction era and were more than willing to allow Negro education in the South to be carried on by the Southern white patrician, supported by funds from northern industrialists.

By the 1890s educators had generally accepted two perceived facts about Southern and Negro education. The first was that reconstruction had failed and the second was that the South lagged behind every other region of the country in the development of public schools. A number of earlier educational documents had set the tone for what was to become a settled and accepted truth about schooling for almost half a century. An example of one such document is a report issued by the Bureau of Education in 1884 on illiteracy in the United States.

The report was written by Charles Warren with additional notes on National Aid to Education compiled by J. L. M. Curry (the general agent of the Peabody Education Fund). The report showed that there was a marked difference in the literacy rate in the South when compared to the Northeastern and the Pacific states. Illiteracy in the South was more than twice as high in the Pacific states and more than five times as high as that in the Northeastern states (given the native born white population). The Southern states were praised for the valiant efforts they had made in the development of public education, but the warning was sounded that their resources were slight and that therefore a significant infusion of federal funds was needed. Not far beneath the surface of the document, however, was an appeal that national strife must be put aside, that the North must reunite itself with the South and that in the process the control of Negro education should be placed in the hands of the South. In the projected unity between North and South, the Negro was seen as expendable. In a remarkable passage that essentially excused the South for slavery the author wrote:

Certainly the negroes, *per se,* are not a desirable population. Their original introduction was not of the South's choosing. If any desire to punish the South for clinging with too much tenacity to a system of labor forced upon her, surely the most revengeful may now well cry, "Hold, enough." In the well-being of the South the well-being of the union is involved. If "one member suffer, all the members suffer with it."[32]

The Negro, however, was considered to be outside of this membership.

There are, however, thousands of illiterate men and women of our own race, our own kith and kin, for whom our special sympathies are awakened and who make no special appeal to partisan or sectarian selfishness. The danger of the illiteracy of the black voter is perhaps no greater than the danger of illiterate white voters.[33]

By the 1890s the idea that the Negro was a race apart, and not (for the present) to be included within the national unity became significantly more prominant in the writings of educators. The conference of the National Education Association found the topic of Southern education to be a popular one. The message, rarely if ever challenged, was that a clear affinity existed between the whites of the North and the South and that for the sake of the unity and strength of the nation and its school system, the education of the black man should be guided by those who knew him best—the Southern white leadership.

It was a difficult message to dismiss given the direction of the nation both internally and externally. Northern educators were concerned more and more about immigration from southern Europe and they came to feel that the concerns that they were experiencing were similar to those expressed by their southern comrades over the education of the Negro race. Moreover, the excursions of the nation into the Pacific and areas south of the border made it significantly more difficult to chastise the South for failing to live up to the idea of equality and democracy. If conservatives like William Torrey Harris and progressives like Francis Parker were writing to justify our adventures into new lands arguing as they did that herein lay the moral responsibility of a superior civilization, then what could be said to decry the subordination of the Negro race at home?[34]

[32] Charles Warren, M.D., *Illiteracy in the United States in 1870 and 1880 with Appendix on National Aid to Education by J. L. M. Curry, LLD, General Agent of the Peabody Education Fund* (Washington: Government Printing Office, Circular of Information of the Bureau of Education), No. 3-1884, 10, 800 C. 13, p. 98.

[33] Ibid., p. 93.

[34] Harris did not argue as many others did that the black man was fit only for an industrial education. Instead, he argued that the need for leadership within the Negro race meant that at least some should be educated academically.

In 1898 a series of meetings were initiated at Capon Springs, West Virginia, between educational leaders from the North and the South to discuss the direction of Southern education. It was here that a model of Negro education was crystalized that would last well into the middle of the oncoming century. The key principle that guided the proposals regarding Negro education was "that his education should concern those fields available to him."[35] This principle helped set the stage for the expansion of a separate educational system that was to emphasize industrial training in both the lower and higher schools and to limit the aspiration of the black man to those fields "appropriate" for his caste. The decisions that developed at Capon Springs were indicative of the desire to foster sectional unity through the support of public education for the South and the consequence was to compromise the future status of the black man. Much of the early intellectual and organizational leadership of the conference at Capon Springs was provided by J. L. M. Curry who had emerged out of a Southern aristocratic, proslavery background to become one of the leading proponents of industrial education for the Negro. His ideas were given expression through his position as the general agent of the Peabody and Slater funds. In 1899 he sat as president of the conference of Capon Springs and his ideas on industrial education were to dominate the schooling of Negroes well into the middle of the next century.[36]

Much of Curry's influence came through the support he directed to schools such as Booker T. Washington's Tuskegee Institute during the 1880s and in his ability to establish the notion that such schools should serve as a model of Negro education at all levels. Curry was thereby praised by white and black alike as the great friend of the Negro. Curry's friendship, however, was not without its limits. He had once remarked to Booker T. Washington that he had been solidly opposed to "every movement that had been proposed to educate the Negro after the War," adding that only "after visiting several Negro schools" had he "become

[35] Henry Allen Bullock, *A History of Negro Education in the South: From 1619 to the Present* (Cambridge, Mass.: Harvard University Press), 1967, p. 102.

[36] For a detailed account of Curry's activities and his relationship to Booker T. Washington see James Anderson, *Education for Servitude. The Social Purposes of Schooling in the Black South, 1870-1930* (Urbana: Unpublished Ph.D. dissertation), 1972.

an advocate of the education of Negroes."[37] But what Curry had seen, speculated Horace Mann Bond, was the education of the Negro by the Northern missionary and what he proposed was that such education be the concern of "the white people of the South."[38] "Since it was to the best interests, both of the Negro and of the white man, that the Negro remain in an inferior position, education should be controlled and administered by Southerners."[39] Curry believed that the Northern missionary was imposing upon the Negro child a curriculum suitable for a more advanced race. The emphasis on Latin and Greek gave the Negro the mistaken impression that he was on the same plain as his former master. Curry therefore believed that the Southern white must retrieve the education of the Negro from the misguided Northern fanatic. If the white man of the South did not assume the responsibility of uplifting the Negro, Curry warned, he "will drag you down to hell."[40] The education of the Negro was part of the ransom property must pay "in order to guard against the perils of ignorance, agrarianism, nihilism, and dynamite."[41]

There is a direct relationship between Curry's ideas about Negro education and the support that Booker T. Washington was able to gain for his school at Tuskegee. To the large industrial and railroad interests of the North with whom Curry had significant connections, the aristocratic Southerner represented the stability required to establish their enterprises in the South. However, they were concerned least the Negro continue some of the overtures that had been made to the populist elements of Southern agriculture during reconstruction and establish a strong allegiance grounded on mutual economic interests.[42] Washington often took upon himself the role of defending the rich, and the industrial interests used the spectre of a black labor force to break up pending

---

[37] Horace Mann Bond, "The Influence of Personalities on the Public Education of Negroes in Alabama, I," *The Journal of Negro Education,* Vol. VI, No. 1, January, 1937, p. 21.

[38] Ibid., p. 21.

[39] Ibid., p. 23.

[40] Address before the Alabama General Assembly, quoted in ibid., p. 23, from the *Montgomery Advertiser,* December 23, 1908.

[41] Quoted in ibid., p. 22, from the Peabody Proceedings, III.

[42] For convincing support of this thesis, see James Anderson, *Education for Servitude.*

strikes. The vision of a black shadow labor force was able to keep Southern wages low for many years, and provided owners of Northern industry with a way to control labor by forecasting that increased wages would force them to relocate their business.[43] Washington himself was generally silent on the issue of the unionization of Negro workers, but on at least one occasion his silence lent implicit support to the strikebreaking efforts. Horace Mann Bond reports that in 1904 the effort to organize the Chicago Stockyards was eventually defeated by the importing of Negroes from the South. During the dispute the leaders of the union pleaded with Washington to address a mass meeting of black citizens and discourage them from working in the plant. Washington did not address the meeting and never issued the requested appeal. The strike was successfully broken. Moreover:

> In 1913 he published an article which by implication discouraged the unionization of Negro workers. Negroes generally, he said, looked to their employers as their friends, and did not understand or like "an organization which seemed to be founded on a sort of impersonal enmity to the man by whom he is employed."[44]

The sympathies provoked among liberal educators by Washington's views on black education might be explained from a number of different standpoints. Some like Eliot of Harvard were liberal with regard to their views on pedagogy but less enlightened about issues regarding race and sex. Others, such as Francis Parker, were receiving funds from sources that had interests similar to those supporting Tuskegee. And still others, seeing the major educational problem to be an overemphasis upon the classical subject matter, welcomed any experiment that introduced manual studies into the schools. But for many, the overriding issue was the need to bind the wounds of a war long over and to develop in the South a viable system of public education. In order to do this they were willing to accept the same institutional context and limitations that Washington was forced to accept.

Thus in the early part of the century, educational reformers even of the most democratic persuasion, tended to applaud the idea of industrial education seeing in it the opportunity to upgrade the public schools of

---

[43] See ibid., for a more elaborate treatment of this point.

[44] H. M. Bond, "The Influence of Personality on the Public Education of Negroes in Alabama, II" *The Journal of Negro Education,* Vol. VI, April, 1937, No. 2, p. 117.

the South while at the same time preparing the Negro for citizenship. Few expressed concern about whether the concept of industrial education was designed to break the binds of subordination. Given the traditional interpretation of Dewey's concept of democracy, for example, it is surprising that his description of P.S. 26 overlooked the most obvious fact about the school—that it was training black children for a role that had been cast down for them and that the uplifting at P.S. 26 was well within the boundaries of subordination. Dewey's active involvement in the formation of the National Association for the Advancement of Colored People is evidence that he was neither unaware of nor unsympathetic towards the problems of racial discrimination. Like others, however, his sympathies were bounded by what he felt the nation was willing to accept and by the degree of integration that he felt industrial progress could tolerate.

During the early part of the 1930s many educators who were later to become especially active over the struggle for Negro rights tended to overlook this as a specific issue seeing it instead in the wider context of the depression. One of the members of this circle, which had its center in New York, was William H. Kilpatrick, a disciple of Dewey's. Kilpatrick was later to speak out with some strength for the equality of the black man and expressed his discontent through his involvement in the Bureau of Intercultural Education.

Much like Dewey, Kilpatrick illustrates the mixture of justice and prudence to be found in liberal thought, and he illustrates the limits that prudence placed on justice. Although Kilpatrick was no radical, his analysis of the problem of the Negro had strong radical overtones, but his recommendations for social change were consistent with the liberal idea of gradualism.

Kilpatrick's memories of his boyhood in the south did not soften his perception of the injustice that was perpetrated upon the black man by American society. He observed that the Negro was no more free than any other colonized people. While slavery as an institution had ended three-quarters of a century earlier, the mores of a slave society still persisted. He wrote of his own personal awakening:

When I was very young I heard the word "master" in some of its variant forms used at times by former slaves as they addressed my father. And I came to understand that this had been the term expected of the slaves when they addressed any man of the master class. Many years later I studied conditions at first hand in India, Ceylon, and China. In India a man servant who went with us as we travelled over the country habitually called me "Sahib" and my wife "Mam Sa'b," and he spoke of the sahib as constituting a class. I took these as titles of respectful address, meaning little more than Sir and Madam do among us. But in Ceylon, where English is better established, I awoke as from a dream to hear myself addressed as "Master" and find myself in the master class. I saw as never before the history of my own early cultural surroundings. And I got further light as I came to understand better a certain tory attitude of superiority common among the foreign traders and lower officials whether in Calcutta or in Shanghai. This word "master" served as the key to unlock for me that distant past when somehow the European and colonial American got their moral consent to enslave the different colored peoples of the world to their own aggrandisement. In the effort to make this selfish advantage secure in their own conscience, they built . . . that supreme condescension and assumed superiority which as remnants still vex the world not only in India and the treaty ports of China but also in these United States.[45]

Kilpatrick also believed that the oppression of the black men was the result of a system that exploited both black and white. The poor white oppressed the black man in order to relieve his own sense of inferiority which resulted from his contact with the ex-slaveowning class.

Given the tone of Kilpatrick's analysis of the situation, one might expect his proposals to be equally hardheaded at the very least, calling for the use of any legitimate means to end the oppression of the black man. Such, however, was not the case. Beyond his description and analysis of the condition of the Southern Negro, Kilpatrick's radicalism ended and he retreated into a gradualism that W. G. Sumner would have appreciated. He believed that even an appeal to the courts to correct clear and obvious educational inequalities was an alternative that should be pursued with the utmost caution, and any procedure more daring than this was unthinkable. "The decision to resort to the courts should probably be made by the Southern Negroes and by these only after serious and frank discussion of the case with Southern white friends of Negroes."[46] Beyond this he was concerned that the situation not be used by other political groups, such as the Communists, for their own ends. "It appears to be true," he wrote,

[45] William H. Kilpatrick, "Resort to Courts by Negroes to Improve their Schools, a Conditional Alternative," *Journal of Negro Education,* Vol. 4, No. 3, July, 1935, pp. 414-15. Reprinted by permission.

[46] Ibid., p. 417.

"that a certain political-economic group, acting on a European psychologic analysis of society, hopes to find in the Negro the needed fertile soil for a program of so creating trouble as to bring about a violent revolutionary change in the social order." Their "fanatic zeal" if left unchecked would do great damage to "the peaceful solutions of interracial problems."[47] He then concluded with a statement of faith in those who he had seen to be the initiating cause of the master-slave relation. A peaceful solution would be brought about when the dominant class recognized its duty to interracial equality. Why he believed that they might recognize their duty was unclear, but the irony of his conclusion is not. The "European analysis" of society that he rejects is the belief that America is divided into distinct classes, a belief that on the surface at least seems eminently compatible with his observations about the oppression of blacks and poor whites alike.

With the coming of World War II, however, Kilpatrick found potent reasons for arguing against discrimination. He warned that the nonwhite races of the world would not be able to take the allies' claim to be fighting for equality and human dignity seriously if the policy of colonial oppression were continued. He saw the war as an occasion to reexamine the ideals of democracy and to extend them to areas where they had hithertofore been absent. And he saw too that his analysis of overseas colonization applied no less forcefully to the situation among the nonwhite races in America. He failed, however, to extend his earlier analysis and to see that economic as well as ideological interests were at stake, and he continued to believe that an ideological appeal to the dominant social groups would be sufficient to issue in an era of justice and good will.

Kilpatrick was not alone in his point of view. Even many black educational leaders expressed similar sentiments believing that equality must come gradually and through an integration of the black man into the dominant social and educational structure. During the 1930s W. E. B. Du Bois was one of the few black educational leaders to raise some fundamental questions regarding the type of unity that might be expected. Out of a frustration arising from the failure to achieve equality, he rejected the idea that black people could expect to convince hesitant white leaders that separate education ought to come to an end. Even if these leaders were forced to act against their own convictions

[47] Ibid., p. 418.

thereby bringing an end to segregation, Du Bois believed that the results would be harmful to the Negro child. Beyond frustration and fear, Du Bois seemed to be expressing annoyance at some of his own people whom he believed had come to accept the myth that a black child could be properly educated only in the presence of white youngsters. Believing this, they were willing to destroy their own sense of unity and nationhood as they accepted the white man's teachings about history, race, achievement, and progress. The problem, argued Du Bois, was not separation. The problem was that the black schools, from the kindergarten to the graduate school, were improperly financed. If as much energy had been spent in securing funds from state and federal agencies as was spent in breaking down the segregated facilities, there would be no inferior black schools. What the Negro needs "more than separate schools is a firm and unshakable belief that twelve million American Negroes have the inborn capacity to accomplish just as much as any nation of twelve million anywhere in the world ever accomplished; and that is not because they are Negro but because they are human."[48]

It is clear that Du Bois did not believe that the dominant white community could be trusted to advance the cause of equality. Had there been an actual debate between Du Bois and Kilpatrick, Du Bois could well have scored some points merely by pointing out that between 1876 and 1936 only 148 doctorate degrees had been conferred upon Negroes. Moreover, while Kilpatrick's own institution, Columbia, ranked second behind Chicago (tied with Harvard and Cornell) in these 60 years it had granted only 12 doctorate degrees to blacks or about one every five years.[49]

The evolution of black education in the United States and the liberal's response to it reveals a significant characteristic of liberal educational thought throughout this century. The failure of the liberal has been his failure to respond boldly to a situation that should have been so repugnant to his sense of justice that only a bold response would have been appropriate. The element of radical democracy that is sometimes attributed to the writings of Dewey and Kilpatrick is difficult to reconcile with the oversight and the caution that characterized their

[48] W. E. Burkhardt Du Bois, "Does the Negro Need Separate Schools?," *The Journal of Negro Education*, Vol. 4, No. 3, July, 1935, p. 333.
[49] See Harry W. Greene, "Sixty Years of Doctorates Conferred upon Negroes," *The Journal of Negro Education*, Vol. 6, No. 1, January, 1937, pp. 30-37.

responses to Negro schooling. Both, however, are understandable when seen in the context of their larger concern for orderly change under the imperative of industrial growth. To understand this larger context is to understand also why Kilpatrick was never able to develop a radical strategy from his radical analysis and why even an appeal to the courts was viewed as only a conditional alternative.

## IX. THE BUREAU OF INTERCULTURAL EDUCATION: THE RESPONSE OF LATER PROGRESSIVES TO THE PROBLEMS OF MINORITY GROUPS

Beginning in the middle of the 1930s, liberal educators became more aware of the problems of minority groups in American society and consciously directed energy and funds towards addressing those problems. Dewey's influence along with that of Horace Kallen and Kilpatrick can be seen in many of the programs that other progressives developed. On the ideal plane, progressives expressed a belief in cultural pluralism. Some criticized the ideal of the melting pot for the assumption that different cultural groups should all conform to a single model or give up their unique cultural traits. They argued instead that cultural uniqueness should be nourished, and that the schools should encourage a mutual respect for cultural differences. They believed that the consequences of cultural puralism would be a richer society and a higher level of culture.

In 1934 the progressive Bureau of Intercultural Education was founded by Rachael Du Bois to further the idea of cultural pluralism. Kilpatrick's ideas had a significant influence on the Bureau during its beginnings and in the late 1930s and throughout the 1940s, he maintained a formal relationship with it as one of its officers.

The Bureau's work was another attempt to fill a gap created by industrial America—its members wanted to reestablish a sense of community and hopefully of mutual respect of different communities for each other, and they believed that this could most effectively be done by working through the public schools. In all probability, the decision to strengthen ethnic communities by working through the public schools was not a deliberate one but simply reflected the generally optimistic climate in which the school was viewed as the major vehicle for democracy and opportunity. Nevertheless, this commitment generated responses that again reveal the limits that industrial goals placed on fundamental democratic values.

The rhetoric and the practice of the Bureau came as a reaction to the parochialism and restrictiveness of the melting pot ideology. Du Bois and those who worked with her in the early days of the Bureau's existence saw in "the melting pot" an ideology that demanded of immigrants a conformity to the Anglo-Saxon model of culture and society. Du Bois and her followers rejected the desirability of such conformity.

The rhetoric of the Bureau was representative of the most liberal aspects of progressive education. In it was expressed objections to the idea that the American culture had been fixed once and for all and to the belief that the newcomer had nothing to add to the culture but had only to absorb it. Diversity was seen as the key to cultural richness, to the blossoming of American art, music, and literature. It was also the necessary prerequisite for a continuing evaluation of the direction and priorities of the American nation.

Throughout the 1930s and the 1940s the Bureau staff worked with the public schools in the area of intercultural education. In the early years the largest part of this activity consisted in developing curriculum materials and in conducting in-service courses for public school teachers. As the Bureau grew in size and as changes in personnel occurred (Du Bois was replaced as director in 1939) its activity was redirected. Some of its projects became largely research oriented, and in cities where racial strife had been experienced its members took on other more active roles.

The work of the Bureau in extending the mutual understanding between ethnic groups continued to follow the basic ideas of Du Bois although those ideas were later refined and extended. Many of the techniques that were used show an innate sensitivity to the attitudes and feelings of minority cultures as well as a strong awareness of general insensitivity of the major institutions towards these cultures. Du Bois believed that it was important for the public school not to destroy a child's pride in his traditional cultures as she believed the insidious melting pot myth had done. She warned that the schools should not tear the child from his parents as often happened in the school in the name of Americanism.

Their daddy's may be Irish, German, Jew or Dutch, but if they're born
in Yankee land the rest don't count for much,

sang the young children of a school in a large eastern city. Instead, children were invited to share their holidays and festivals with each other, and teachers were provided with materials that would supplement or correct the deletions and distortions of the minority contributions by textbooks. Yet even in the early days of the Bureau, before it had succumbed to bureaucratic intrigue and while the humanitarian spirit of Du Bois was most strongly felt, there was special care taken to present the right image, the ideal type. Du Bois felt the world to be so torn by conflict, so alienating and so distorted by violence and hate that only by distorting a culture by a different light could children grow up to respect each other.

Not the Russian peasant, but Tolstoy, not the Indian Coolie but Mahatma Gandhi, not the drink-sodden denizen of the Glasgow slums but Sir Walter Scott are figures which the American child must visualize instantaneously when Russians, Indians, Scots are named if his reaction is to be appreciated in the highest sense.[50]

In order to achieve this understanding, adult members of different ethnic groups were to appear in the classroom, but it was important to invite only those members who could immediately counter the child's built-up stereotype. Visitations were to be restricted; only the articulate Negro, the athletic Jew, or the urbane Pole should be invited to engage the children in the classroom.

Certainly such techniques were built upon a false image of these groups and did little to address the more fundamental question of human rights that should be enjoyed even if one is not Mahatma Gandhi or Sir Walter Scott. Nevertheless, it seems unduly harsh to look too coldly upon Du Bois' dream of American society, for as dreams went, it was a good one. At the time when many saw ethnic cultures to be parasitic to American life, she believed them to be essential to its flourishment. At a time when some Negroes feared speaking in public of black culture and black pride, she was describing to Negro children the richness of their heritage and the extent of their contribution to American life. And while some were trying to escape the stigma that had been placed on them because of their background and culture, she was reminding others that the source of the stigma was only external.

[50] Bruno Lasker, *Race Attitudes in Children* (New York: Henry Holt & Co.), 1929, as quoted in Rachael Du Bois, *Adventures in Intercultural Education,* New York, unpublished D.Ed. dissertation, New York University, p. 125, n.d.

Yet Du Bois' dream, like Kilpatrick's, expressed as much faith in the willingness of the members of the dominant culture to open themselves up to influence from minority groups as it did in the value of the minority group culture itself. And it was perhaps because of this faith that she failed to approach the issue of power as it was needed to sustain uniqueness and cultural pride. Throughout its growth, its shifts in leadership and its various concerns, it was this faith that dominated the spirit and the operations of the Bureau of Intercultural Education.

The work of the Bureau is as significant for its style of operation as it is for its accomplishments. There is no need to minimize its accomplishments in order to illustrate this significance. Its work in curriculum, its sensitivity to the image of minority groups as pictured in school textbooks, and its workshops with teachers all revealed a sharp awareness of the problems minority group children might experience in the public schools. Yet when it faltered, as it sometimes did, it did so as a result of its willingness to trust the good will of the educational establishment and to serve it when trust was no longer warranted. And it faltered too because it was unwilling or unable to work directly with the minority groups that it was trying to help or to examine factors other than attitudes as the cause of ethnic conflict. The instincts of its members uniformly directed them to work through established channels even when those channels were obviously unwilling to advance the cause of the Bureau. As with Dewey, in the study of the Polish Community, it was perhaps inconceivable to the personnel of the Bureau that they might consider turning from those channels and serving directly the people they were attempting to help, nor was it conceivable that the basic conflicts were deeper than the attitudes of members of one group towards the members of another.

The most obvious and clear-cut failure of the Bureau in this regard came in its relationship with the Detroit public schools. During the 1940s the Bureau increased its operations with field offices in a number of cities, including Philadelphia, Gary, and Detroit. The work in Philadelphia was research oriented with some in-service training programs for teachers and administrators. Its work in Philadelphia and in Gary achieved some measure of success, but the program in Detroit, which lasted from the middle to the late 1940s, continued to falter as it ran into conflicts with the administrators of the public schools. By this time Du Bois was no longer director of the Bureau, and during this period a number of administrative changes took place. Nevertheless, the innate trust that she had expressed in the good will of school administrators and in their ability to translate that good will into programs of action persisted. The history of the Bureau's relations with Detroit presented some classic problems in intergroup relations.

The industrial development of the city of Detroit had spiraled its population of 285,000 in 1900 to 1,685,000 in 1945. In 1940, 20 percent of its population was of immigrant origins and another 9 percent was Negro. The city had its Polish section, its Negro section, its Hungarian and Italian areas, and as shifts in population occurred one group replaced another on the lower rung. During World War II, the Negro population of Detroit had increased considerably, but for the most part schools and housing remained substandard, and the Negro voice was inconspicuously absent from political affairs.

Throughout the depression, Detroit had often been an area of intergroup suspicion symbolized by the radio broadcasts of Father Coughlin and aggravated by the labor struggles. In the early summer of 1943, much of the strife that had existed between blacks and whites came to a head in the riots of June 20 and 21. With the war on, this was an especially difficult time. Subsequent efforts were made to uncover the causes of racial strife with part of these efforts undertaken by the schools as committees were formed on interracial understanding. In October, 1943, contacts were initiated with the Bureau of Intercultural Education and a large conference attended by 2000 Michigan teachers and administrators, sponsored by the Bureau, was held in March, 1944. During 1944 and 1945 the Detroit school system concentrated some energy in the area of intercultural education. Committees drew up intercultural policy statements; they emphasized equal employment and education and began to examine the intercultural aspects of the curriculum. During the same period, relations with the Bureau were established on a more formal basis, and by January, 1945, the Bureau had a staff developing a program with the Detroit school administrators.

There is no need to detail the methods and programs of the Bureau, but it should be sufficient to note that with the addition of some surveys and sociological research, many of the programs were similar to those initiated earlier by Du Bois. What is significant is the relationship sustained by the Bureau with the Detroit schools. In May, 1945, the superintendent of the Detroit schools, Warren Bow, died. Bow had initiated the contacts with the Bureau and in the eyes of its staff, had been sincerely active in the cause of intercultural education. Arthur

Dondineau was made acting superintendent and was appointed on a permanent basis in the fall of 1945. While Dondineau was still only acting superintendent, the Bureau staff sensed hesitation in his commitment to intercultural education, but attributed this to the confusion that accompanied the change in personnel. Nevertheless, by November, 1945, the "Bureau staff felt . . . that the Detroit people were unwilling to give much time and effort to carrying forward the program in the schools,"[51] and the superintendent had restricted his direct contact with the staff to occasional correspondence with the Bureau director.

Events occurring between December, 1945 and March, 1946 illustrate clearly the deterioration that had occurred between the Bureau staff and the school administrators. A memo written by the Bureau staff was submitted by Bureau Director Warren Giles to the school administrator in charge of intercultural programs. The memo listed suggestions for improving the intercultural program of the schools. It dealt with administration, teaching and with the control and selection of curriculum materials. The memorandum was submitted to the appropriate administrative committee and then suffered the following fate, as indicated by the minutes of the administrative committee meeting.

The memorandum of suggestions sent by the Bureau staff on the Administrative committee at our request was distributed. The members of the committee indicated their willingness to study this and discuss it in the next meeting.—From Administrative Committee minutes, February 15, 1946.

The memorandum from Dr. Giles and his staff on projected plans for Detroit was discussed briefly. It was decided that this was sufficiently important to deserve longer discussion at the next meeting.—From Administrative Committee minutes, March 7, 1946.

The memorandum from Dr. Giles . . . were to be carried over the next meeting.—From Administrative Committee minutes, March 28, 1946.

The records of the administrative committee did not give any hint that the matter was ever discussed again.[52]

---

[51] Edman field report to the Bureau of Intercultural Education, November 12-25, 1945.

[52] Information taken from a Bureau report written in 1949 as an overview and evaluation of its relations with the Detroit public schools to be hence referred to as Bureau Confidential Report on Detroit.

The relationship between the Bureau and the Detroit schools deteriorated from 1945 to 1949. While the reports of the Bureau personnel reveal that they were sensitive to this deterioration and to their own general impotence, they were unwilling to take any dramatic steps to remedy it. Indeed, their own confidential papers show them demoralized and frustrated but always willing to bite their tongue in public for the sake of continuing what was at best a marriage of convenience.

The reports of the Bureau were heavy with criticism of the super-intendent of schools and his top-level staff for their unwillingness to allow any significant research to take place about racial attitudes and practices in the public schools and for their failure to implement in any significant way the proposals of the Bureau. In one of the few statements of grievances that ever formally reached the superintendent, the Bureau staff documented the administration's unwillingness to follow its recom-mendations in a number of areas. Its suggestion that a citizens advisory board be established had been tabled. Its request that research be con-ducted regarding school boundary line, transfer policies and promotion practices with regard to minority groups had been ignored. No systematic effort had been undertaken to evaluate teaching materials and instruc-tional methods as they effect minority groups and no funds had been allocated for the problems of intergroup relations. The superintendent greeted the statement of grievance coolly and continued to do nothing about the recommendations.

For all the bitterness that was felt by the staff, they were as reluctant to leave Detroit as the administration of the schools was reluctant to have them leave. As ineffective as they were in improving the situation in the schools for Negroes and other minorities, they were still willing to have the public schools use them to quiet criticism. On February 7, 1949, shortly before the Bureau finally severed its relations with Detroit, the following was included in a statement by the school administration in a report entitled "Education for Democratic Human Relations in the Detroit Public Schools."

In a special survey of administrative practices sponsored by the Bureau for Intercultural Education in 1945, it is significant to note 94 of the 257 teachers appointed to the schools during the year 1945 were Negroes. Similarly, 148 of the 360 non-teaching employees appointed in 1945 were Negroes. In a quick check in 1948, there were reported 389 Negro educational employees and 546 non-educational employees.

The cooperative relationship of the Detroit Public Schools with the Bureau for Intercultural Education is another instance of administrative achievement. The Detroit Public Schools have had the advantage of working with both the field staff and special consultants of the Bureau since 1944.[53]

What the report failed to mention was that the survey was conducted the year of Warren Bow's death, and that the subsequent administration had repeatedly discouraged other surveys. (It is not clear who took the quick check in 1948.) Moreover, the fact that over one-third of the teachers hired in 1945 were Negro is not as impressive as its sounds considering the total number of Negro students and the ratio of black teachers to black students. In 1945, given a total student population of 222,391, 17 percent, or 38,529, were black, while out of 7,262 teachers only 286, or 4 percent were black. In 1945, 7 percent of the clerks and 10 percent of the janitors were black. Moreover, if the student population is broken down by age, there is evidence that the percentage of black school population was increasing at a consistent rate.[54] In 1945, 13 percent of the high school students, 16 percent of the junior high students, and 19 percent of the elementary students were black. Even more significant is the location of the black teacher with 6 percent in the elementary school, 2 percent in the intermediate grades, and 0.7 percent in the high school.[55] Negro teachers were generally restricted to schools that had a sizable black student population, and there were no black principals or supervisory personnel. (There was one black trouble-shooter who was sometimes sent to smooth over the ruffled feelings of black students and parents.)

The fact that the relationship between the Bureau staff and the school administration had become a marriage of convenience was clearly expressed in a conversation between the head of the Bureau's Detroit operation and a top-level Detroit administrator in a heated conversation shortly before the relationship was finally broken. The administrator is quoted as saying:

I think it would be most unfortunate for you, and for Detroit, if you leave Detroit. There are pressure groups in Detroit who will make it very hard for us. It would be bad for you because you will begin to get the reputation

---

[53] *Bureau Confidential Report on Detroit,* pp. 230-233.

[54] The evidence for this statement is not conclusive however given the usual increase in the dropout rate from elementary school to high school.

[55] Figures taken from Bureau's Confidential Report on Detroit.

of not being able to stick with something to its finish. We both need each other.[56]

While it was hard for the Bureau members to admit that such indeed was the nature of the relationship, the same conversation reveals the director of the Bureau asserting: "The Bureau has invested a lot of time and money in Detroit. We need to make reports to our board from time to time. Sometimes it is hard to report progress in Detroit at the same time that Dondineau won't invest a nickle in the program."[57] And it was the case that the Bureau made every attempt in its public reports to see progress where there was very little. The following are excerpts taken from the Bureau's report to the board (underneath the relevant passage of the public report is a relevant passage from the confidential one, in capital letters).

There was increased conscious adherence (in Detroit) to the principle that intercultural education should be integrated into all aspects of the curriculum and not isolated in separate courses, and greater emphasis on understanding basic human needs, human values, and social problems. "Human relations and education for democratic living have been the focus."[58]

SITUATION DEVELOPING TOWARD THE SEGREGATION OF NEGRO TEACHERS IN ALL NEGRO SCHOOLS.[59]

THE NUMBER OF ALL NEGRO SCHOOLS INCREASED FROM ONE IN 1943 TO SIXTEEN IN 1946.[60]

A program was begun for 4,000 "noncontract" employees. Activities included training in human relations for secretarial staff and for janitors, a campaign to encourage qualified Negro janitors to acquire training as building engineers, and greater attention to protecting the promotion rights of Negro employees.[61]

---

[56] Conversation between Paul Rankin, Assistant Superintendent, Detroit, and Fred G. Wale, Director of the Bureau, March, 1949, as reported in Bureau's Confidential Report on Detroit.

[57] As reported in Bureau's Confidential Report on Detroit.

[58] Bureau for Intercultural Education: A Report to the Board of the Year 1946-47, November 19, 1947, p. 10, "Detroit."

[59] B. I. E. Confidential Report on Detroit, excerpt taken from field report of November, 1946.

[60] Ibid., p. 131

[61] B. I. E. report to the board on the year 1946-1947, p. 11.

LARGE NUMBER OF NEGRO NON-CONTRACT EMPLOYEES
ENTITLED BY SENIORITY TO SUPERVISORY POSITIONS, BUT
ADMINISTRATORS ARE FEARFUL OF PLACING THEM AS
BOSSES OVER WHITE MEN. THE WHITE MEN WON'T
TAKE IT, THEY SAY.[62]

Reports of the Central Administrative Committee indicates a continuing
concern with the problems of evaluation, and committees are at work
investigating new techniques.[63]

DURGAN IS STILL OF THE OPINION THAT DONDINEAU IS
NOT GIVING SUPPORT IN THE INTERCULTURAL PROGRAM.[64]

SOME NEW ATTEMPTS AT GETTING EVALUATION PROCESSES
WERE STARTED, BUT DIDN'T BEAR GREAT FRUIT.[65]

Schools are continuing to work effectively with parent-teacher association
and other local organizations at the neighborhood level.[66]

C. COMMUNITY CONCERNS
OUR COMMUNITY CONTACT HAVE BEEN LIMITED UP TO
NOW. THESE CONCERNS THEREFORE ARE EXPRESSIONS . . . BY
THE FEW KEY PEOPLE WITH WHOM WE HAVE
CLOSE CONTACTS.
1. "THAT MORE COMPETENT SCHOOL ADMINISTRATORS BE
OBTAINED—SPECIFICALLY, THAT THE PRESENT
SUPERINTENDENT BE REMOVED." BASED ON A JUDGMENT
THAT HE IS NOT ONLY INADEQUATE BUT AN OBSTACLE TO
AN IMPROVED EDUCATIONAL PROGRAM. THERE
APPARENTLY IS INCREASING AGITATION FOR ORGANIZED
COMMUNITY PRESSURE FOR IMPROVING THE SCHOOLS.[67]

Yet the reported desire of the community to have the superintendent
removed was not a real issue for the Bureau staff. The very same report
in which the concern of the community is reported unchallenged con-
cludes by suggesting that the Bureau staff develop closer "working

---

[62] B. I. E. Confidential Report on Detroit, p. 131. Excerpt from November,
1946, field report.

[63] Report to the board for 1946-1947, p. 11.

[64] B. I. E. Confidential report, excerpt from May, 1947, field report.

[65] B. I. E. Confidential Report of Detroit, summary for year 1946-1947,
p. 137.

[66] Report to the board, 1946-1947, p. 12.

[67] Confidential Report, p. 198, from May 28, Field Staff Memorandum.

relations with the superintendent and his executive staff in order to attempt to get them sincerely committed to an effective program of improving human relations."[68]

The marriage between Detroit and the Bureau was a matter of convenience, but it was also a matter of selective perception whereby Bureau members believed that the only vehicle for effective change was the good will of the school administrators. The Bureau had committed itself to a concept of community, had accepted the value of group difference and had elevated the idea of diversity to a principle of explicit worth. Yet within its notion of community was an implicit commitment to unity of a certain kind. It was a unity in which ethnicity could be expressed for the sake of cultural richness but not as a vehicle of power. Whatever personal objections the members of the Bureau may have had to the superintendent of schools, however inadequate they felt his commitment to the improvement of intercultural education and to the protection of the rights of minority adults and children, they were still willing to serve him, to filter their information through him and to subordinate their interpretation of the facts to his. When criticism of the schools occasionally came from concerned quarters, they were there to be spotlighted for the moment until the furor died down. The ultimate commitment of the Bureau was to the public school system *and* to its administrative staff. When things went wrong, when it became clear that the administration was not supporting the intercultural program, the Bureau's response was to try and close a gap that they knew could not be closed. When they saw even their work with teachers becoming ineffective, the recommendation was to begin working more intensely with the principals and the supervisory staff. Thus as the weaknesses in the relationship became more and more obvious, the Bureau responded by attempting to ascend the bureaucratic ladder rather than by intensifying its work with teachers (an American Federation of Teachers chapter was assuming some leadership in Detroit) or establishing closer ties with the community itself.[69]

Neither the effects of the Bureau's work nor the limitations that possibly may have been imposed on it from outside need be overlooked

[68] Ibid., p. 199.

[69] Some members of the Bureau, such as Theodore Brameld, a consultant, gave favorable mention of the A.F.T. in public, but this was early in the relationship and the Detroit administration attempted to discourage the use of Brameld's services in Detroit.

in order to understand that its commitment to orderly procedure and bureaucratic legitimacy ran even deeper than its commitment to minority rights, equal opportunity or intercultural understanding. More importantly, the activity of the Bureau is consistent with the general direction taken by progressive educators throughout the century. Their concern for community was as much a plea for a functionally ordered society as it was for actual community participation in the decision-making process.

There is another respect in which the activity of the Bureau in Detroit is indicative of progressive education's response to industrialization. The ethnic and racial conflict that Detroit experienced was certainly partly the result of long standing stereotypes and prejudices, but it was a reflection of labor conflict as well. Only a few years before the ghetto exploded, police were beating strikers in Flint, Michigan. The long-standing espionage activities in which the auto companies would pay informers to identify union organizers contributed to a climate of suspicion throughout the city. The consistent use of blacks for the heaviest and dirtiest work in an industry built on heavy, dirty, and monotonous labor must have significantly contributed to the riot of 1943 and the problems thereafter. Yet the Bureau's analysis of the labor situation and of its contribution to the ethnic conflicts of the time was at best superficial. The problem was an attitudinal one, to be worked on in the school and the classroom. But from the point of view of industry, attitudes are a problem only when they manifest themselves in behavior that retards production. It may be safe to assume that the educational climate of Detroit was influenced to a large extent by the industrial climate. And whereas in 1943 ethnic antagonisms were indeed a serious threat to production, later they were not. Given this change, it is little wonder that the Bureau was frustrated and unsuccessful.

## X. SUMMARY

The liberal ideal of equality of opportunity issued from two sources. The first was a sense of justice and the belief that accidental factors such as race, religion or social class should not be a barrier to an individual's achievement. The second was the belief that industrial society required an expanded pool of talent from which it could draw to fill new occupational roles. While liberals and progressives recognized that industrialization placed certain limits on what schools could and could not do, they did not perceive any fundamental conflict between the two sources of this ideal. Therefore they looked to the school as the major instrument for its fulfillment. Nevertheless, the requirements of justice and the needs of technology were not always compatible and industrialization did indeed set limits to the degree that the ideal as an expression of justice could be realized. These limits were most clearly present in the schooling of black and immigrant children. The influence that industrialization had on progressive thought and the way it limited the notion of justice is best seen in its concrete activities and appraisal of existing programs. Dewey's Polish study, and his appraisal of P.S. 26 in Indianapolis, Kilpatrick's response to the problem of black education, and the activity of the Bureau of Intercultural Education in Detroit suggests that the demands of technology often had a higher priority than the requirements of justice.

# CHAPTER FOUR

# The Underlying Consistency of 20th Century Educational Reform

## I. INTRODUCTION:

Progressive education did not exist in a vacuum but was developed within the context of liberal principles concerning the growth of knowledge and access to opportunity. It was also developed in the context of political and social changes that influenced both its tone and its acceptability. In response to these changes, it shifted and altered its emphasis in the course of its 50-year history, but these changes were always within the limits of the accepted liberal principles.

Progressive education was by no means the only significant reform movement in American education; its proposals had to compete with others and in the long run it is questionable whether the major changes in American education could be characterized as progressive. Some reforms, such as increased federal aid to education or racial integration were advocated by some progressive educators and by some who opposed progressivism and cannot therefore be characterized as belonging to either camp. Progressive reform in the strict sense was addressed to a certain kind of classroom procedure and pedagogy. Regarding this concern, the two most obvious thrusts of educational reform have been the child-centered approach as represented by the progressive movement and the subject-matter or discipline-centered approach advanced by its critics. These conflicting approaches shared as a common focus of concern the structure of the classroom, but they differed about the most desirable approach to classroom procedure. The progressives emphasized the interests and activity of the child while their opponents put more stress on the structure of knowledge and what they considered to be the essential subject-matter areas.

Despite the differences that existed between the advocates of the child-centered classroom and the advocates of the subject-matter approach, each side represented different aspects of the same liberal reform. Each accepted the basic liberal principles about the growth of knowledge and the structure of opportunity, and each looked upon the school as the primary vehicle for realizing equality of opportunity. Moreover, each believed that schools could be instrumental in meeting the demands and smoothing over the dislocations caused by industrial society. The conflict between the two can be accounted for by the fact that each was reacting to different stresses of industrialization. Progressives, for example, often emphasized the need for youngsters to learn how to cope with technology by developing a sufficient understanding of its interrelated aspects so as to reduce alienation. Other reformers placed heavier emphasis on specific conceptual and vocational skills that the new technology required. Nevertheless, the fact that both sets of proposals were part of the same liberal educational policy meant that they were sharpened against one another making ready for the day when circumstances would dictate that one or the other was required.

This chapter highlights the liberal principles and the larger social changes within which the conflicts between the child-centered and the subject-matter educators took place, and it illustrates the ways in which both the child-centered and the subject-matter approach to education served the same end. Its primary focus is on educational reform since the second world war.

## II. LIBERAL POLICY AND
## THE DISTRIBUTION OF KNOWLEDGE

The liberal ideal of equality of educational opportunity was both a demand that artificial barriers to a person's achievement be removed and a statement about the allocation of educational resources. It was believed that beyond a stipulated minimum, a person's ability should ultimately determine his allotment of educational resources. Warner, Havinghurst, and Loeb, in their influential *Who Shall Be Educated* (published in 1944), expressed this belief as fundamental to the workings of democracy.

To make democracy work in our complex modern society it is essential that a high order of technical and civic competence exist at all social levels. Teaching such skills—technical, as well as social—is increasingly the responsibility of the schools. The individuals who exercise these skills should be the products of a superior native capacity, trained by highly competent instructors, and so placed after training that they can adequately employ their abilities. Wherever individuals with ability of one kind or another are found the schools must recognize their native endowments, train them and reward them. To do less invites filling critical positions in government and private organizations with incompetents who do not possess the skills necessary to do their job. Malfunctioning of the democratic order because of mere technical inadequacy is an important factor in arousing a questioning attitude toward democracy.[1]

This principle of allocation meant that the education system was to be "a system of election for positions of higher social and economic status," and thus it was advisable "to gear the selecting machinery to the demand and to the capacity of the social structure."[2]

Two factors were important in the selection process. The first was to strike the proper balance between training and placement and the second was to assure that education and mobility not become a threat to social stability. Warner and his associates stressed the importance of weighing these requirements in the following way:

If too few people are selected and promoted through the education system, the upper levels will be filled through other agencies and perhaps not

---

[1] W. Lloyd Warner, Robert J. Havighurst, and Martin B. Loeb, *Who Shall Be Educated: The Challenge of Unequal Opportunties* (New York, Harper and Bros.), 1944, p. 141.
[2] Ibid., p. 150.

filled with people as well equipped by skill and training for the positions. If too many people are selected and pushed up through the educational system, competition will become fierce for the higher-level jobs, and some people will have to take positions below the level for which they have been trained. Doctors will have to take jobs as laboratory technicians, engineers as factory workers, and teachers as clerks. This will cause feelings of dissatisfaction with the social order, and the social structure may be strained beyond its tolerance limit.[3]

The issue of social mobility was a complicated one. Within a certain limit social mobility increased the likelihood not only of industrial growth, but of social stability as well. Beyond a certain limit, however, mobility threatened stability and ultimately industrial development.[4] The line was a thin one. It was thought that when mobility allowed some talent to rise, discontent, which might otherwise become bottled up in the lower classes, would be dissipated. However, it was also believed that if the emphasis on mobility was too great, and the social structure not able to satisfy individual aspirations, the emphasis would actually generate discontent and social instability.

When the liberal concern for social stability is taken into account, another aspect of its standard for alloting educational resources is revealed, and this provides insight into the dual nature of liberal educational reform. As we have seen the principle of equality of educational opportunity directs society, beyond a certain minimum, to allocate educational resources according to talent. Ideally, other factors, such as birth or family background should not be considered in this allocation, but when they are it is only because not to do so would threaten social stability. This standard for allocating educational resources was promoted because it was believed that the general social good would be increased by allowing the most talented individuals to rise to positions of social responsibility.[5] Taken by itself, however, this principle of allocation entailed another, implicit threat to social stability. For by removing talented people from the lower classes and training them to assume positions of leadership, the distance between those minimally educated and the talented increased thus again creating the possibility for social instability. The problem for liberal educators in general was to devise

---

[3] Ibid., p. 150.
[4] See ibid., p. 158.
[5] See footnote 1.

a system that would allow talent to be properly trained and rewarded and that would reduce alienation among those who were only minimally educated. The different stresses of liberal educational policy can therefore be seen as attempts to deal with these two requirements.

## III. RITES OF PASSAGE
## AND EDUCATIONAL REFORM

Whatever the particular theory of pedagogy in vogue at a given time, twentieth-century education in America had one overriding concern: to use the schools to ameliorate the social and individual tensions caused by industrial development. Technology was a blessing, but if its promise was to be realized people had to learn to cope with many new situations. The guiding principle of technology was efficiency and adherence to this principle brought people and machines together in urban areas, accelerated physical mobility, altered the nature and place of work, and rendered the extended family obsolete. Twentieth-century educational reform developed as an extension of these events. The decline of the one-room schoolhouse was simply symbolic of the fact that the principle of efficiency was to govern education as well as industry.

Yet while the structures changed, many of the functions remained. Children still had to be brought up even though many reformers believed that the changing nature of work limited the extent to which this could be done by the family. They had to be inducted into the society even though the nature of that society was changing and the traditional socializing agencies were in a process of disintegration. Yet because technology was governed by the principle of efficiency, and was perceived to have an independent and dominant momentum, it was not believed that the traditional structures could be revived. Technology was not to be structured into existing communities but instead was to run its course with the school following behind, tending to the dislocations that it caused.

The most significant aspect of twentieth-century reform is to be found in the belief that the traditional agencies of socialization were no longer adequate and that the school should constitute the principle mode of entrance into the society. This belief explains the increase in compulsory attendance laws as well as the increase in the legal age for leaving school. It explains a number of other reforms as well.

As compulsory schooling attained nationwide acceptance,[6] the school population increased and the social-class background of the majority of students changed. Educators could no longer count on the motivational support of the parent to reinforce the traditional curriculum. They were thus forced to reconsider many of their accepted assumptions about schooling. The pedagogical reforms that subsequently occurred were developed within a framework where schooling was accepted as the primary avenue of access into society and as the major institution through which nationhood could be cemented and sustained.[7] The increasing importance of the school in meeting the dislocations of technology,[8] its increasing role as a socializing agency and the changing nature of the school population were the major factors influencing the subsequent ebb and flow of conflicting educational reforms.

Many specific educational reforms can be explained by the dual role of the school to identify and reward talent on the one hand and to socialize the young and assure stability on the other. For example, if in the process of training talent, the social distance between the talented and the minimally educated increased, then social solidarity would be threatened unless people believed that the process of selection was fair. As Warner and his colleagues noted:

The possibility of rising in the social scale in order to secure a larger share of the privileges of the society makes people willing to "stick together" and "play the game" as long as they believe it gives them a fair share.[9]

One of the reforms that can be explained by the new function of the school is the testing movement. The early acceptance of the testing movement among educators can be explained as a devise both to identify talent and to provide people with the assurance that the selection procedure was fair. Whether or not the tests were accurate in every detail was less significant than whether they enabled the school to carry out its selection function in a way that people believed to be fair. If people thought that science was properly invoked in support of the tests, then the tests were serving their function and when people began to doubt their validity, then some other procedure needed to be found.[10]

---

[6] By 1918 every state had a compulsory attendance law.
[7] See Chapter Three.
[8] See ibid.
[9] Warner et al., p. 157.
[10] See Chapter Seven.

In addition to the acceptance of intelligence tests among educators, the eventual acceptance of Thorndike's findings against the notion of the transferability of learning can also be explained by the increased emphasis on the school as a principle vehicle of socialization. Whatever problems the classical curriculum may have entailed, it is questionable whether Thorndike's experiments were a decisive refutation.[11] The traditional curriculum could certainly have been sustained for students whose families accepted its importance and believed it to be a proper vehicle for social status and position. For many reasons, however, this kind of education was thought to be dysfunctional by working-class parents many of whom possessed a different concept of work and leisure than their upper- and middle-class counterparts. With the increase in the school's role as an agent of socialization there came also a change in the composition of the upper grades and the high schools, and the classical curriculum was obviously not adequate to the school's new population. Many educators therefore believed that science only confirmed what common sense had already told them, and they gladly welcomed this support for their position.

## IV. SOCIAL TENSION AND THE RHYTHM OF EDUCATIONAL REFORM

The tone of educational rhetoric at any given time is related to the dual role of the school in identifying and training talent and maintaining social stability. In balancing these two functions, the school has had to consider larger social forces. Therefore, the degree that the child-centered or the subject-matter approach to educational reform is prominent at any given time is influenced by a constellation of social factors such as manpower requirements, migration patterns, and employment prospects. Prominent among such factors has been general beliefs about the primary source of social tension at any given time and whether such tension is perceived to be located internally within the nation or externally issuing from international competition. While the relationship between educational rhetoric and the perceived source of social tension is an indirect one and not sufficient to predict the tone that educational debate will take, it does illustrate the way in which

[11] See Chapter Two.

shifts in the emphasis of the schools follow other concerns. For a number of reasons, however, the correlation can only be suggestive. In the first place, even though the child-centered reform was more influential during some periods than others, the actual practice of schools seems to change more slowly than the rhetoric, and therefore it cannot be assumed that rhetoric is simultaneously reflected in practice. In the second place, as we shall see, there is a tendency for the advocates of a given reform to adjust their proposals to meet different kinds of tension and thus similar reasons are given for conflicting reforms.

Nevertheless when the major source of tension is perceived to be some kind of internal turbulence, the tendency is an increase in the child-centered rhetoric, but when it is perceived that the major threat to the nation is from an external power, the tendency is for the emphasis to shift to the subject-matter and discipline approach. In the first of these tendencies the emphasis is usually, but not exclusively, placed on the socializing role of the school and in the second on the sorting-and-training function. Other factors such as manpower needs and employment possibilities are also extremely influential, but often these too are related to the perceived source of tension.

These tendencies can be illustrated by the prominence of the efficiency movement and by the rise and support of progressive organizations. The efficiency movement, which emphasized the sorting and training function of the school, had its greatest appeal just prior to and during World War I. Although many of its proposals were incorporated into the ongoing activities of schools, progressive education began to achieve greater acceptance soon after the war ended. In 1919 the Progressive Education Association was formed with a heavy emphasis on centering classrooms around the interests of children. During the 1920s when many feared a breakdown in law and order and more so during the 1930s when the Depression presented a possible threat to the business and corporate structure of the nation, the child-centered approach gained in influence and stature. If the prominence of a movement can be judged by the financial support it receives, it is instructive to note that during the 1930s, the Progressive Education Association received a million and a half dollars from the Rockefeller-founded General Education Board and lesser amounts from the Carnegie Foundation.[12] As the

---

[12] This figure is from L. Cremin's *Transformation . . .* , p. 257.

war approached, progressive education itself came under growing attack, and foundations began to pull back their support, and after 1938 membership in the Progressive Education Association declined.[13]

## V. THE LIFE-ADJUSTMENT
## MOVEMENT AND ITS CRITICS

When educational debates are looked at as proposals for the allocation of educational resources, it is somewhat easier to see the influence that extra-educational concerns have had on educational policy and on the dual concerns of training and socialization. The different sides of liberal educational policy are apparent in the life-adjustment movement that arose in American education after World War II and in the subsequent debates that developed over it.

The life-adjustment movement marked a turning point in progressive reform. In the 1920s progressive education, as judged by the membership and activities of the Progressive Education Association, was basically a child-centered movement. The interest and activity of the child was emphasized; the structure of the curriculum was not. Later, in the 1930s the movement had a more radical flavor as its most prominent members proposed to use the schools to reconstruct society. The life-adjustment movement of the 1940s and 1950s was an attempt to use progressive techniques to help children cope with the forces and pressures of society as it existed. The life-adjustment movement indicated another turning point as well. The early phase of progressive education was centered in private schools for middle-class children. During the 1930s, its reforms were found acceptable by many public schools, but at that time the movement still had its greatest success among children from middle-class and upper-middle-class homes. The life-adjustment movement, however, was an attempt to use the public schools and progressive techniques to meet the needs of youngsters whom it was thought would neither go on to college or develop a skilled trade.[14]

[13] See ibid., p. 257.

[14] For a general history of the Progressive movement see Patricia Graham, *From Arcady to Academe: A History of the Progressive Education Association 1949-1955* (New York: Teachers College Press, Columbia University), 1967.

Early in 1944 a study by the U. S. Office of Education on the subject of "Vocational Education in the Years Ahead" was undertaken.[15] In a series of conferences that followed the study educators expressed the concern that the "overly bookish" nature of secondary education had to be supplemented if the high schools were to serve the needs of all youth. The spirit of this movement was articulated in a resolution offered by Charles A. Posser, the chairman of the final conference:

We believe "that the high school will continue to improve its offerings for those youth who are preparing to enter college." But, "In the United States the people have adopted the idea of secondary education for all youth. As this ideal is preached, the high school is called upon to serve an increasing number of youth for whom college preparation or training for skilled occupation is neither feasible nor appropriate. . . . We believe that secondary school administrators and teachers and vocational education leaders should work together to the end that the number of attempts being made in the secondary schools to meet this need will be greatly increased."[16]

The major concern of the life adjustment educators was for those youngsters who would not likely go on to college or be employed in a skilled vocation. Their curriculum stressed home and family life, getting along with others, health, physical fitness, and civic competence. This curriculum was remarkably similar in structure to one proposed in 1918 by the Commission on the Reorganization of Secondary Education in a document entitled *Cardinal Principles of Secondary Education.* That document advanced as the seven basic objectives of education health, command of fundamental processes, worthy home membership, vocational education, civic competence, worthy use of leisure time, and the development of ethical character. Conspicuously absent from this list was anything to suggest that the schools should be concerned with intellectual studies.

It is not too difficult to explain the attraction that the life-adjustment movement or the cardinal principles had for educators. The periods that followed them were both periods of urban expansion and urban

---

[15] For a discussion of the different commissions of the Life Adjustment Movement, see Cremin, *Transformation* . . . , pp. 332-338.

[16] "Posser Resolution" in Franklin R. Zeran, ed. *Life Adjustment Education in Action* (New York: Chartwell House, Inc.), 1953, p. 34.

immigration.[17] Moveover both movements came towards the end of a war when the social solidarity that had been achieved might be threatened by the absence of an external enemy.

The reaction to the life-adjustment movement began in the early 1950s and was typified by the affirmation of the importance of academic subjects in the curriculum. In general, the reaction failed to discriminate between two different aspects of the life-adjustment movement. The curriculum of the movement with its emphasis on psychological accommodation was the focus of the attack, but along with it went a rejection of the progressive pedagogy that of course need not be wedded to the life-adjustment curriculum. In their place stood a renewed emphasis on science, mathematics, and foreign languages and a recognition of the importance of external discipline and control.

The shift away from life adjustment and towards an emphasis on intellectual skills was an expression of the belief that the school's selection and training function should be primary and that the socialization of new groups should now be a secondary concern. The most obvious reason for the shift was the Cold War and especially the requirements for highly trained scientific and managerial manpower that accompanied it, but like the movement to which it was opposed, it too was justified as consistent with the requirements of a democratic society.

Among the most articulate critics of the life adjustment curriculum was Arthur Bestor, a professor of history at the University of Illinois.

---

[17] Between 1920 and 1930 approximately 15 million people moved from rural to urban areas, and for the first time more people lived in urban settings than in rural ones. Between 1940 and 1950 the migration into urban areas was significantly less, about 8 million, but the population of urban areas was about 40 million larger than that for rural areas. The migration pattern changed of course quite dramatically after 1924 with the restrictive immigration act. The pattern of migration is signficant. In 1881 almost five times the number immigrated to the United States from Great Britain than from Italy. (Britain was considered a desirable country, Italy was not.) Since 1891, and with the exception of 1919 immigration from Italy ran considerably higher than that from Great Britain. In 1921 222,260 came in from Italy and only 51,142 from Great Britain. The period from 1940-1950 shows significantly less foreign immigration, but it shows a significant rise in black migration from the rural south to the urban northeast. This migration had begun in the period 1920-1930, but had slowed significantly during the depression and increased again after 1940. For the figures on these movements see the Bureau of the Census, Historical Statistics of the United States, Colonial Times to 1957, p. 46, (25-73 and p. 56 C88-100).

Bestor's two major books on education, *Educational Wastelands* (1953) and *The Restoration of Learning* (1955), brought a severe challenge to progressive education which by this time was perceived as closely related to the life-adjustment movement.

A School that waters down its curriculum is not upholding but denying this time-honored ideal of democratic education, for it is in practice depriving our young men and women that abundant educational opportunity which democracy promised. A school that furnishes only a narrow vocational, workaday training to children of humble parentage is effectually denying the innate dignity of man—a doctrine which asserts that every individual, whatever his trade or his income is entitled to share in the high, humane tradition of the liberal arts and sciences. A school that puts the trivia of life adjustment on a par with rigorous study of the fundamental intellectual disciplines is not vindicating democracy but is doing its best to demonstrate that the opponents of democracy were right when they predicted that a democratic society would be a society without standards or values.[18]

Bestor argued that the traditional disciplines constituted the essence of human thinking and that they were therefore necessary for understanding, coping with and perhaps changing the world. As Bestor explained:

Consider how the disciplines of science and learning come into being. The world enters the consciousness of the individual—as a great tangle of confused perceptions. Before man could deal with it at all he had to differentiate one experience from another and to discover relationships among them. . . . Gradually he discovered that one kind of relationship could best be investigated in one way . . . and another in another way. . . . Thus the separate disciplines were born, not out of arbitrary invention but out of evolving experience. . . . The ability to face unprecedented situations by using the accumulated intellectual power of the race is mankind's most precious possession. And to transmit this power of thinking is the primary and inescapable responsibility of an educational system.[19]

He argued that the life-adjustment movement was, in consequence, anti-democratic advocating as it did that some students be trained in the disciplines and others in the ways of life or on how to get along in an industrial age.

[18] Arthur E. Bestor, *The Restoration of Learning* (New York: Alfred A. Knopf), 1955, p. 25.
[19] Ibid., p. 35.

In passing it is noted that both the curriculum proposals of Bestor and those of the life-adjustment movement were one-sided expressions of Dewey's pedagogy. Like Bestor, Dewey believed that the intellectual disciplines arose as historical statements of the methods by which men coped successfully with their world. In contrast to Bestor, however, Dewey believed that intellectual studies should be generated out of real problematic situations so that students could understand not only the subject matter itself but also the way it related to the everyday affairs of men. But if Bestor went too far in his emphasis on subject matter, many in the life-adjustment movement committed the opposite sin in their emphasis on the present everyday affairs of men. Bestor, was not concerned with the subtleties of Dewey's arguments, however, and dismissed the progressive pedagogy along with the life adjustment curriculum. He believed that what was important was the subject matter and not the method of teaching it, and he proposed a generally unified curriculum for all youngsters. His curriculum differed from the classical one of earlier times in its emphasis on science and modern language. He believed that only a few disciplines should comprise the curriculum, and that all youngsters in the elementary and the secondary schools should study the same subjects.

Students were to be sorted by standardized achievement and intelligence tests into various categories and then allowed to progress through the curriculum at a pace that was appropriate to their particular category. Within each category however, and especially at the highest, rigorous competition was to be the rule. For most youngsters, a high school diploma would be the terminal degree, but for those of exceptional talent who did go on to college, the competition would be evermore severe. Even the cost of their tuition would depend upon their grade point average.

Bestor's proposals were in serious conflict with the advocates of life adjustment education and they contained significantly different implications for schools. Nevertheless, in retrospect, the debate is significant not because of the differences, but because of the context that was shared by both sides.

Bestor and his opponents each believed that his own proposal was consistent with the cause of democracy and that the other was not. Those in the life-adjustment movement argued that they were furthering democracy by meeting the needs of the less academically inclined student, and they looked upon Bestor's proposals as elitist. Bestor believed that his proposals would allow all youngsters to partake of civilization's most cherished knowledge, and he saw the proposals of his opponents as discriminatory.

When these proposals are looked at in terms of the role of the school to train talent and maintain social stability at the same time, they are not however, in fundamental conflict. It must be recalled that the life adjustment movement was primarily advanced for youngsters who would not go on to college and that it was believed that the proposed curriculum would allow these youngsters to better cope with industrial society. The life adjustment educator did not challenge the school's role in identifying talented youngsters, and, more importantly, his proposals did not really speak to the issue of how they should be trained.

On the other side is Bestor emphasizing the selection and training function of the school and proposing a unified curriculum as a way to meet the requirements of democracy. But Bestor was not ignoring the socializing role of the school. As we have seen one of the prerequisites of social solidarity is the general belief that the selection procedures are fair and Bestor's emphasis on standardized tests and a unified curriculum spoke to this issue. The fact of the matter is that both sides had a good case against the other. The life-adjustment movement was discriminatory. It took youngsters where it found them and helped assure that they would not go much further. But Bestor wasn't much better. His unified curriculum was for some a training ground for the higher professions, but for others it was simply a way to socialize them into a world of professionals and experts. His unified curriculum was unified only in the sense that youngsters were to be exposed to the same subjects, but this exposure did not lead to the same outcomes. For some the knowledge gained would be an instrument for applying their own powers and manipulating their world, for others it was simply exposure, a vicarious way to enjoy the powers of others while believing that they were working to their benefit.[20] The similarities between Bestor and his opponents can be better understood by looking at their proposals in light of larger social concerns. Both were advanced in terms of the educational requirements of a democratic society, but there was another, equally important side to the debate. Bestor's thesis was a warning as well as an argument, and the warning was an echo of the earlier words

---

[20] See Chapter Seven for a more detailed argument against these general points of view.

of W. T. Harris that education must provide a way for labor to compete with other nations. As Bestor put it:

If the schools fail to do their part in this, the nation is threatened with the loss of intellectual strength and, as a direct consequence, the loss of industrial prosperity and military security.[21]

The curriculum was not simply a vehicle for human understanding and individual opportunity. It was also a weapon in the defense of the nation.

If we take education seriously, we can no more afford to gamble our safety upon inferior intellectual training in our school than upon inferior weapons in our armory.
. . . we propose to make American schools the world's finest . . .[22]

Considered as a weapon, we are able to understand why Bestor's "traditional" curriculum differed in content from the "traditional" classical curriculum and why, for example, he gave such little notice to artistic areas as a vehicle for human development and understanding. In arguing for his curriculum, he observed that:

It is a curiously ostrich-like way of meeting life needs to de-emphasize foreign language during a period of world war and post-war global tension, and to de-emphasize mathematics at precisely the time when the nation's security has come to depend on Einstein's equation $E = MC^2$.[23]

Bestor criticized the professional educator not only because of the "antidemocratic" nature of his programs, but also because he believed that his proposals were inadequate to the requirements of national defense. In issuing this criticism, Bestor directed his attack on the programs developed in a 1951 report entitled "The School and National Security." The report began with a statement of the requirements of national security drawn from an invitational conference of experts in various security fields after which the educators made some specific proposals about the way schools could serve these requirements. Bestor's criticism was unmerciful.

---

[21] Arthur E. Bestor, *Educational Wastelands: The Retreat from Learning in Our Public Schools* (Urbana, Illinois: The University of Illinois Press), p. 13.
[22] Ibid., p. 6.
[23] Ibid., p. 58.

"The first task of the social studies," the report begins is to "reduce the tensions and meet the *needs* of children and youth." Absent is any idea that the nation is in danger and that it may require of its future citizens some very hard thinking, not about personal problems first of all, but about the means of national survival.[24]

Bestor criticized the educators both for their naiveness in matters of national security and for their guilefulness in manipulating the security experts to their own end. The security experts were invited to the conference to talk about national security, but they were not asked to discuss education. As Bestor saw it:

"The panel was brought together under the chairmanship of a professional educationist, and its members were asked to discuss "the nature, dimensions, and requirements of the national security situation and the impact upon society of the measures that were likely to be adopted. The discussants, however, were distinctly forbidden to consider the implications for education: it should be noted that the purpose of this meeting was not to talk about education; this was to come later."[25]

Bestor's description of the meeting illustrates the intensity of feeling that this debate generated as he interpreted the statement that the purpose of the meeting *was not to talk* about education to read that the national security experts were *"distinctly forbidden"* to consider educational implications.[26] When the emotional elements are put aside however, and the content of the report examined, it is difficult to see any fundamental differences between its author's views and Bestor's about the basic purpose of the schools.

The very first paragraph of the foreword to the report begins:

The schools occupy a very strategic position in the national security program. They possess tremendous potential which, when properly developed, may contribute much to the military and productive powers of the nation.[27]

---

[24] Ibid., p. 99.

[25] Bestor, *The Restoration of Learning,* p. 174.

[26] It needs to be noted, too, that the participants were invited by the governor of Illinois and the state superintendent of public instruction and not simply by the professional educators. See "The School and National Security," (C. W. Sanford, H. C. Hand, W. B. Spaulding ed.) *Illinois Secondary School Curriculum Program,* Bulletin Number 16, May 1951, p. 1.

[27] Ibid., p. iii.

Moreover, it is carefully noted in the report that:

Over any extended period of crisis the improvement of education for all children and youth is basic to effective national security. It guarantees a continuous flow of competent soldiers, sailors, and airmen to man the weapons of modern war.[28]

Certainly there were specific programatic differences between Bestor and the authors of the report as would be expected. Nevertheless, the overriding concern that the schools be used as an effective weapon in military preparedness and national security was a shared one. It is true that the report stressed the interests of individual students to a degree that may seem foreign to one familiar with the requirements of military discipline at the time, but this stress was neither naive nor obviously incompatible with the requirements of national security. The report stated the urgent need to develop each child according to his maximum capacity and then it related this need to the current crisis in the following way:

Now, more than before, we should be certain that each child is developed to his maximum capacity. This is no time for an arbitrary program, arbitrary academic hurdles, and frozen attitudes toward children and youth that conceive them all as fodder to be molded into the same pattern.[29]

The responsibility to develop each child to his maximum capacity, meeting his interest and ability level, was believed to be of utmost importance for the requirements of national defense.

This is peculiarly necessary in time of crisis and mobility. The many forces tending to distract children and youth from their school work, and the many forces that literally tend to draw them out of the school, should be combated at both the intellectual and psychic levels. An educational offering which the individual child or youth will accept as worth his time and effort (again emotionally as well as intellectually) should be available to him.[30]

Bestor was correct in noting that the stress was on the interests of the child and on the need to develop a curriculum sufficiently flexible to meet the interests of many different children. But the point of the report was that only in this way would youngsters remain in school and

[28] Ibid., p. 38.
[29] Ibid., p. 40.
[30] Ibid., p. 41.

thereby develop the skills and attitudes important for military service, industrial growth, and national defense. As the writers of the report explained:

It must be recognized and reiterated that all of the foregoing is of no significance to the youth that do not remain in school. . . . Thus the curriculum, the guidance program, the community relations, and the service functions should all be under constant surveillance by the school staff for optimum contribution to the national security effort.[31]

In some respects, the report was significantly more comprehensive than Bestor's somewhat sketchy proposals. Even the aesthetic, recreational and artistic enterprises, which Bestor failed to consider, was recognized as potentially valuable to national security. The report proposed that "the great worth of these areas in building the inner resources necessary for this period of nerve-attrition should be re-emphasized."[32]

Even though Bestor and the advocates of the life-adustment movement came to share a common concern there were, of course, clear and important differences between them. These differences can be accounted for by the initial concerns and the evolution of the two. The life-adjustment movement had been initiated in anticipation of the end of a war as a way to cope with large-scale dislocation and the potential instability that peacetime industry was expected to bring. It was therefore initially conceived to serve the needs of marginal youngsters who were least likely to feel that they had a stake in the American system and who threatened to swell the ranks of an alienated urbanized population. As the life-adjustment movement evolved, much of this threat dissipated as the Cold War became a more significant factor in American life. Still concerned with the same student population, the life-adjustment educator began to adjust his goal to meet the new crisis addressing his curriculum proposals to provide these students with a place in national defense. Bestor's proposals were initiated after the Cold War had become an obvious and dominant fact of American life and with the understanding that many people of skill and talent would have to be brought into national service. The dispute between Bestor and advocates of life adjustment was not simply about the ultimate goal of education, but for all practical purposes, it was a debate over priorities, about where

[31] Ibid., p. 46.
[32] Ibid., p. 47.

funds should be spent, and over the children that should most "benefit" from them. Both recognized the importance of academic subjects in serving the national interest. Bestor, however, stressed the selective function of schools whereas those in the life adjustment movement argued that the first task of the school was to retain and socialize students even though their primary interest may not be academic.

## VI. LATER EDUCATIONAL REFORMS

The views expressed in the debate between Bestor and the life-adjustment educators are significant examples of the use of schools to meet the shifting demands of selection and socialization. These very same concerns are also present in the later proposals of James Bryant Conant who, like the life-adjustment educator, addressed the "needs" of the less talented student while at the same time proposing a system that, with Bestor, would train the academically talented in the "traditional" disciplines.[33] In two studies financed by the Carnegie corporation, Conant developed a set of educational proposals that he believed would assure the talent needed for international competition and would also calm any potential internal turbulence.

Conant began by classifying youngsters into two broad categories, the top 15 to 20 percent whom he identified as the academically talented, and the remainder whose interests and abilities he believed to be vocational in character. How he arrived at the classification and the percentages is somewhat of a mystery, but having done so he proposed that comprehensive high schools should be increased in number and should have sufficient breadth to service both groups. He wrote:

The three main objectives of a comprehensive high school are: first, to provide a general education for all the future citizens; second, to provide good elective programs for those who wish to use their acquired skills immediately on graduation; third, to provide satisfactory programs for

[33] Conant's career reflects a continuing interest and influence in both education and national policy. From 1933-1953 he was president of Harvard University. From 1947 through 1952 he was a member of the General Advisory Commitee of the Atomic Energy Commission. In 1953 he was appointed U. S. High Commissioner to West Germany and later, ambassador. The work under consideration in this chapter was financed by the Carnegie Corporation and administered by the Educational Testing Service.

those whose vocations will depend on their subsequent education in a college or university.[34]

Both of Conant's studies were praised for their timeliness. The first was written shortly after the Soviet Union had launched the first space satellite and in the midst of growing concern about America's capacity to compete in this area. This study was addressed to the needs of the academically talented student in the context of a comprehensive high school. He proposed that the academically talented should have rigorous training in science, mathematics, and foreign language and that other students should have a wide range of programs available to meet their stipulated interests and abilities.

Conant believed that one of the most important tasks for the schools at all levels was to prepare youngsters for future employment, both those who would end their education after high school and those who would go on. Equally as important as the preparation of youngsters was the accuracy with which schools communicated to future employers the level of employment for which a youngster was suited. This was not only to assure that the best people filled each job, but it was also a way to motivate youngsters while they were in high school. Thus, for example, Conant proposed that in addition to a high school diploma, which would assure employers that a youngster had satisfactorily completed his general education, each youngster was to carry "a durable record of the courses studied in four years and the grades obtained."[35] Conant went to some length suggesting how such a record would be of benefit to employers when interviewing applicants.

Conant's second report, *Slums and Suburbs,* was addressed largely to the issue of schooling in the black ghetto and to the way in which schools could be used to most effectively defuse the "social dynamite" that he saw there. Whereas his first report addressed the external threat from abroad, the second addressed the internal threat at home:

I do not have to remind the reader that the fate of freedom in the world hangs very much in balance. Our success against the spread of communism in no small measure depends upon the successful operation of our own free society. To my mind, there is no question that a healthy society requires a sound economy and high employment. Communism feeds upon

[34] James B. Conant, *The American High School Today* (New York: McGraw-Hill Book Co., Inc.), 1959, p. 17.

[35] Ibid., p. 50.

discontented, frustrated, unemployed people. As I write in June 1961, the unemployment rate nationwide is something over 7 percent for all age brackets, but unemployment among youth under twenty-one years of age is about 17 percent. . . . These young people are my chief concern, especially when they are pocketed together in large numbers within the confines of the big city slums. . . . With what kind of zeal and dedication can we expect them to withstand the relentless pressures of communism? How well prepared are they to face the struggle that shows no signs of abating?[36]

Conant's solution to the problem of slum schools was offered within the context of his general educational framework. Schools in the ghetto must better approach the needs and the interests of the young-sters, as he saw them, by offering a vocational curriculum that realisti-cally trained them for the jobs that they could get after graduation.

The significance of Conant's work for the liberal educational tra-dition can be best understood by placing it in context with earlier and later works. Conant's concern for the selection and training of the academically talented student was, for example, similar to the concern of Bestor, and both were developed in response to certain Cold War pressures. However in proposing a dual curriculum, one for the academ-ically talented and another for the majority of students, Conant was reflecting some of the concerns of the life-adjustment educator. Never-theless, his proposals for the education of the nonacademically talented student differed from the proposal of the life-adjustment educator in two specific ways. In the first place his curriculum placed a much heavier stress on marketable, vocational skills and in the second place, he believed that order and externally imposed discipline were imperatives and therefore did not give much credence to the progressive strategy of working through the expressed interests of the child.

One can only speculate about the reasons for these differences and about why one set of proposals or the other were acceptable at different times, but there are certain facts that are apparent. The role of the school for both Conant and the life-adjustment educator with regard to students classified as nonacademically talented was primarily a socializing one. Each believed, for example, that his own proposals would best assure domestic calm. The difference is to be found in part in the nature of the social structure that each believed the student would enter after leaving high school. The life adjustment movement grew in

---

[36] James B. Conant, *Slums and Suburbs: A Commentary on Schools In Metropolitan Areas* (New York: McGraw-Hill Book Company), 1961, p. 34.

popularity toward the end of and just after World War II at a time when many expected peace but also high unemployment. In its initial formulation, it was addressed to the needs of the marginally employable youngster in an attempt to provide some understanding of the forces that were  acting on him. To place a heavy emphasis on marketable vocational skills for these youngsters might have appeared overly optimistic and disfunctional. Conant wrote at a time of heavy unemployment, but there was generally more optimism about the prospects for the future and governmental programs were already underway to lessen the percentage of unemployed. In light of these different projections, both the earlier life-adjustment movement and Conant's proposals were clearly designed to provide these youngsters with the belief that they did have a stake in the system, and the differences are explainable by the expected fluctuations in the system itself.

Although both the life-adjustment movement and the Conant reports were significantly influential for a period of time, neither was without its critics. Shortly after the publication of *Slums and Suburbs,* for example, a number of perceptive commentators criticized Conant for proposals that they believed would have the effect of continuing the great disparity betwen the rich suburbs and the poor slums by stressing in the schools of the former an academic curriculum and in those of the latter a vocational one. These criticisms were addressed to a significant oversight in the Conant report and may have been instrumental in the subsequent support given to compensatory educational programs designed to allow talented ghetto youngsters the opportunity to compete with others. Nevertheless these arguments addressed an *oversight* in Conant's report, and they were therefore not inconsistent with the general rationale that he gave. It was pointed out that the need for trained talent was larger than the existing supply and that it was most important to provide every opportunity to the slum child who might otherwise be overlooked.[37] Recently, however, there has been a more intense reaction to the subject-matter approach to education expressed in the Conant reports, and the child-centered rhetoric is again accepable. This reaction is seen in the conflicting evaluations of classroom discipline and control to be found in Conant and his later critics.

---

[37] For an example of this point of view see John W. Gardner, *Excellence: Can We be Equal and Excellent Too* (New York: Harper Colophon Books), 1961.

One of the central differences between the child-centered rhetoric and the subject-matter approach to education is the conflicting ways in which external, teacher-imposed discipline is evaluated. The fact that those committed to a certain set subject matter are also those most likely to approve the external imposition of discipline is understandable given the emphasis on the selection and training functions of the school. If the child's progress is to be measured by how well he conforms to a fixed set of standards, then any reasonably straightforward technique to help him conform is acceptable. Moreover, given "reasonable" standards, the responsibility for educational failure tends to be placed outside of the school. The Conant reports expressed this point of view. Conant's description of the schools he visited, and especially of those located in the slums, was generally favorable. He reported seeing dedicated teachers often working overtime against impossible odds in order to improve the prospects of lower class children, and he praised the order and discipline that he found in many of these schools. For example, in an obvious reference to the more permissive educators, Conant noted one school where:

Many educators would doubtless be shocked by the practice of on-the-spot demotion of one full academic year, with no questions asked, for all participants in fights. In one junior high school I know of, a very able principal found so intolerable a situation that he established that very rule. As a consequence, there are fewer fights in his school. . . . In this school and in many others like it one finds the boys wearing ties and jackets to school. . . . When spoken to in the classroom, they rise to recite. . . .

In contrast to what one hears about "blackboard jungles," I think I am fairly safe in saying that the outward manifestation of discipline, order and formal dress are found to a greater degree in the well-run slum school of a city than they are in the wealthier sections of the same city.[38]

Conant's favorable appraisal of "the outward manifestations of discipline" followed naturally from his belief that the education of the slum child should be closely related to his employment prospects. The jobs available to these youngsters often require obedience to external authority and seemingly arbitrary rules and the schools were simply to train them for this experience. Yet Conant was not discriminating here. He believed that such discipline was good for all youngsters because he believed that educational standards are fixed at all levels.

---

[38] Conant, *Slums and Suburbs,* p. 22.

The later critics of Conant rejected his favorable evaluation of "the outward manifestations of discipline," but, as we shall see, they did not challenge the system of work on which it was based.

The influence of the Conant reports can be explained largely in terms of the need for trained manpower especially in light of the Cold War and as a response to the "social dynamite" of the ghetto. The return to the child-centered concerns of the last few years may also be explained as a reaction to events subsequent to 1961. A decade after the Conant reports were issued, Charles Silberman's book *Crisis in The Classroom: The Remaking of American Education* was published. Silberman's study drew on the research of the Swiss psychologist Jean Piaget and others as well as on the experience of the infant school in Great Britain, and it was designed to explain the benefits of the child-centered open classroom. While Silberman's proposals were developed within the framework of the child-centered rhetoric they did not reflect a return to the life-adjustment movement. He generally accepted the progressive pedagogy, but rejected the curriculum that became identified with that movement in the late 1940s.

Given the fact that Silberman, like Conant, was commissioned by the Carnegie foundation in order to find out what was wrong with American education and to develop proposals to correct it, the tone of these two works is remarkably different and on the surface, it would appear as if they simply canceled each other out. Like Conant, Silberman, too, toured the nation's schools, yet where Conant found order and discipline to be objects of praise, Silberman saw in them "mindless" repression, and where Conant proposed that schools should better prepare the young for future employment, Silberman cautions against a heavy and narrow vocational emphasis.[39] Silberman criticized Conant directly for suggesting that teachers in the slums should have different expectations for their students than teachers in the suburbs. He supported his criticism by pointing to the pernicious effect that the self-fulfilling prophecy can have on student's achievement.[40]

---

[39] See Charles E. Silberman, *Crisis in the Classroom: The Remaking of American Education* (New York: Random House), 1970, p. 67.

[40] Ibid., p. 86. The self-fulfilling prophecy has been pointed to by many educators to explain student's failure. The point is that students' performance tends to correlate to a teacher's expectations, and more significantly, that a teacher's expectations are causally related to the student's performance.

While Silberman is as optimistic as Conant about what the schools *can* accomplish, he takes special care to point out the shortcomings in what the school *has* accomplished.[41] He is critical of past education for "mindless" adherence to discipline, and for threatening the integrity of local culture. He denies that the schools have been even a significant vehicle of equality of opportunity for immigrants of the past and notes that for these immigrants, "middle-class status was achieved not through education but through politics and business, and to a considerable extent through crime."[42]

Although Silberman is willing to admit that the schools of the past were not everything they are cracked up to be, he believes that the schools of the future will be, given the adoption of his proposals. Silberman reports that employers are demanding more and more education from prospective employees and that therefore education "is becoming the gateway to the middle and upper reaches of society which means that the schools and colleges thereby become the gatekeepers of society."[43] The problem for education is to find a way that the schools can serve this function without discriminating against children from minority cultures, and Silberman simply does not believe that Conant's proposals are the answers. For him, the problem is not that the slum schools have failed to teach specific vocational skills, but rather that they have failed "to teach the intellectual and academic knowledge that students need if they are to be able to earn a decent living and to participate in the social and political life of the community."[44] Thus Silberman's curriculum is different from both that of Conant and the earlier life adjustment educator for he would place the stress on the humanization aspects of the curriculum while seemingly deemphasizing both vocational and practical concerns. He places a good deal of importance on what might be considered academic disciplines, but he is reluctant to identify any single set of courses as essential. Rather his concern is to demonstrate the structure of a discipline, to show the way that it holds together, and to teach students some general things about inquiry, evidence and culture.[45] Moreover, he believes that the best way to teach this is through informally structured classrooms and in

---

41 See ibid., p. 57-58.
42 Ibid., p. 56.
43 Ibid., p. 69.
44 Ibid., p. 62.
45 For Silberman's discussion of curriculum reform, see ibid., pp. 321-336.

schools where youngsters are allowed to pursue their own interests to fruitful ends. Thus, much like some earlier progressives, Silberman weds a child-centered pedagogy to an academic curriculum and suggests that this is the best and the fairest education for all children.

Given the close similarity between Silberman's claim and that of earlier progressives the experience of the latter can shed some light on the way open education might translate into actual practice. We have seen, for example, that earlier attempts to mold an academic curriculum around the interests of children actually was translated into radically different programs depending upon the class background of different youngsters.[46] The question is, therefore, whether any evidence exists to indicate that Silberman's proposals are subject to the same translation and are thereby likely to maintain the divisions that at least in some sense he wants to avoid. To answer this question we need, as with Conant and others, to put Silberman's writings in their social and political context.

*Crisis in the Classroom* was published almost a decade after *Slums and Suburbs* following a period when the "social dynamite" of the ghetto had exploded in intermittent bursts and when there was not only a crisis in the classroom but a crisis in the society as well. Yet during this same period, some of the factors that Conant had identified as most serious had been addressed by schools and other institutions. There was an adequate number of scientists and engineers, and in some areas there was an oversupply. The United States had surpassed the Soviet Union in space flights, and employment was higher both among the general population and among blacks. In 1958, the year after Conant's study was commissioned, the unemployment rate among blacks was 12.6 percent. By 1967, it had declined to a still high, but seemingly less dangerous, 8.2 percent. Moreover, by 1967 the unemployment rate among married black men was down to 3.2 percent.[47] Yet even with these advances many problems had intensified rather than abated, and 1967 was also a year that Detroit and other ghettos erupted in riot. Negro employment clearly left much to be desired. Yet if the ghetto had not exploded in 1958 or 1961 then unemployment was certainly not sufficient to explain the fact that it did explode in 1967.

[46] See Chapter Two.

[47] These figures are taken from *The Report of the National Advisory Commission on Civil Disorders* (New York: Bantam Books), 1968, p. 253.

By the time *Crisis in the Classroom* was published, it was obvious that Conant's approach to the problem of the ghetto was simplistic, and that employment alone was not sufficient to defuse "the social dynamite" that might erupt again at any time. The National Advisory Committee on Civil Disorders had (in 1968), provided some clue to the origins of the present problem when it described the typical black counterrioter as a resident who had achieved clear middle-class status in terms of income, education, and stable employment. Thus as Warner and his associates had earlier observed, the need was to provide people with the belief that they had a stake in the system. It was unlikely that many would be satisfied by a dead end education leading to a dead end job. Silberman clearly reflects the importance of this factor when he observes that:

What has produced such profound disappointment with the public school as an institution, and such burning anger at public school teachers and administrators, is the fact that recognition of the importance of education has coincided with a profound change in expectations, especially among Negro Americans, but now increasingly among Puerto Ricans, Mexican Americans, and Italian Americans as well. They are furious because the schools are not moving their children into the middle class rapidly enough.[48]

With this background, Silberman's case can better be appraised. Silberman is actually making two claims. The first is that with regard to the school as an agent of equal opportunity, the present is significantly different than the past. Whereas, he grants that the belief that schools *have* served equality of educational opportunity is false, he argues that now they can (and should) serve this ideal. His second claim is that open education is the most appropriate form of schooling for all youngsters, not only in some ideal sense, but also in terms of "the intellectual and academic knowledge that students need if they are able to earn a decent living."[49]

In order for both these claims to be supported, Silberman must show first that education is a major factor in the determination of income and status and second, that the traits he associated with open education, such as initiative and curiosity, are valued by prospective employers. Unfortunately much of the available evidence seems to indicate otherwise and Silberman is forced to come to grips with the discrepancies.

[48] Silberman, *Crisis in the Classroom,* p. 69.
[49] See footnote 45.

To begin with he acknowledges research suggesting that blacks will earn less than whites regardless of their educational attainments and that indeed factors other than intellectual achievement better explains the inability of some young adults to obtain suitable employment. Silberman cites the research of Duncan as an example of the type of study that has found that:

Negroes have received a substantially lower return than whites on an "investment" in education. At least one-third of the income gap between whites and blacks arises, Duncan writes, "because Negro and white men in the same line of work, with the same amount of formal schooling, with equal ability, from families of the same size and same socio-economic level, simply do not draw the same wages and salaries."[50]

Silberman is not willing to admit though that these findings represent a continuing trend, and he cites as evidence for his belief the experience of recent black college graduates whom he claims in many fields "command salaries equal to or higher than, those offered to whites."[51] Moreover he notes that the extremely good bargaining position of the Negro Ph.D. is also "good reason to believe . . . that the disparity in the 'return on education' may be narrowing."[52] Given this evidence, Silberman believes that the school is increasingly becoming a vehicle of equality of opportunity for blacks and other groups as well.

Putting aside for the moment Silberman's evidence for the increased role of the school as a vehicle for equality of opportunity, there is still the other issue. He must show that employers value schooling for its academic value and not for some other reason. Moreover, he must not only show that this is the case generally but also with regards to the specific jobs that lower-class minority students are likely to receive. Only if he does this can his claim be accepted that the academic curriculum will best serve the cause of equality of educational opportunity. In addition, given the many pressures on lower-class children to leave school and get a job, he must be able to show that the curriculum he proposes can meet these pressures without distorting the student centered pedagogy in the way that progressive education commonly did.[53] In other

[50] Ibid., p. 65.
[51] Ibid., p. 66.
[52] Ibid., p. 66.
[53] See Chapter Two.

words, he must explain why the open classroom will not become an education for initiative and leadership for one class while at the same time it becomes an education for accommodation and adjustment for another. And in order to do this, he must demonstrate that the pressure on lower-class youngsters to find a job can best be served by teaching them academic skills. Again the initial evidence is not very promising and Silberman turns to the work of Christopher Jencks to illustrate the other side.

"Despite much popular rhetoric," Professor Christopher Jencks of the Harvard Graduate School of Education writes, "there is little evidence that academic competence is critically important to adults in most walks of life. If you ask employers why they won't hire dropouts, for example, or why they promote certain kinds of people and not others, they seldom complain that dropouts can't read. Instead, they complain that dropouts don't get to work on time, can't be counted on to do a careful job, don't get along with others in the plant or office, can't be trusted to keep their hands out of the till and so on." Hence it is the school's failure to develop such " 'middle-class virtues' as self-discipline and self-respect" Jencks insists, and "not its failure to teach history or physics or verbal skills" that is the real problem.[54]

Silberman rejects Jenck's claim arguing that students are not likely to develop self-respect if they do not achieve academic competence,[55] and he proposes that:

Jencks is exaggerating . . . when he claims that dropouts' inability to read is not a factor in employers' reluctance to hire or promote them. Indeed, the contrary is true. A fair degree of literacy—for example, the ability to read the safety instructions on machinery, or the instruction manuals for repairing automobiles or other machines—is essential for even routine jobs on an assembly line or in an automobile repair shop, let alone an office.[56]

As we have seen Silberman is committed to developing two points. The first is that schooling can have a significant and favorable impact on the mobility of lower-class and minority-group youngsters. The second is that it can have this impact by emphasizing an academic curriculum for all youngsters and without forcing youngsters to learn in a

[54] Silberman, pp. 66-67.
[55] Ibid., p. 67.
[56] Ibid., p. 67.

dull, mechanical way. Unfortunately Silberman's evidence is weak and does not support his point. It is questionable, for example, just how much the employment prospects of a highly visible, articulate group, such as black Ph.D.'s can be taken as representing a trend for black employment in general.[57] It is further questionable whether the argument that a certain level of reading is required even for routine jobs, such as assembly line work, should be taken as a serious argument for open education or even for an academic curriculum.

Silberman is correct about one point: "children must have a sense of competence if they are to regard themselves as people of worth,"[58] and that the failure of a child in school negates his self-respect. Yet it is doubtful whether the kinds of jobs that are available to poor children require self-respect. With regard to some employment, the very nature of the job may cause the undesirable traits that Jencks mentioned for such traits are often simply manifestations of alienation and rebellion. When placed in this context it is unlikely that Silberman's proposals can avoid the fate of the earlier progressive schools when child-centered education became one thing for one class and quite a different thing for another class. If, as Silberman suggests, there are academic skills that are important for young adults to learn as human beings, that does not mean that anyone who learns those skills will also become an enthusiastic and willing worker. Whether or not that happens depends on the kind of work he will be doing and the principles that guide the distribution of the dull and routine tasks that a society requires to be performed. If, however, schooling is to be judged strictly by how well it relates to future employment then Conant's proposals are probably more adequate than Silberman's, and it should be no surprise that parents of poor and working-class youngsters, aware of what the world most likely holds in store for their children, are often the strongest advocates of external discipline and control.

Although there is no good reason to believe that Silberman's proposals would escape the fate of progressive reform and avoid becoming largely different for most lower class children than for middle class ones, his proposals are adequate for some of the purposes he has in mind. If he believes that the disorders of recent times have been caused

---

[57] It is perhaps significant that at this writing many of the economic advances made by blacks during the 1960s are on the decline as reported by Walter Cronkite in a CBS edition of the evening news on August 29, 1973.

[58] Silberman, p. 67.

by increasing expectations among minority groups, as he does, and that "they are furious because the schools are not moving their children into the middle class rapidly enough,"[59] then the open classroom, as Silberman describes it, can serve as an escape valve to pacify the discontent. To serve *this* function, however, the open classroom and the academic curriculum that Silberman attaches to it need not apply to all youngsters. If the major task of open education becomes simply to pacify discontent then the class characteristics of American schools and their curriculum is not really under challenge by open education. Implicitly, Silberman seems to grant this fact when, citing James Coleman, he pinpoints a major problem with Conant's proposals for the education of children in the slums.

"It is one thing to take as a given that approximately 70 percent of an entering high school freshman class will not attend college; but to assign a *particular child* to a curriculum designed for that 70 percent closes off for that child the opportunity to attend college."[60]

However in the original passage by Coleman the portion cited by Silberman is followed by "yet to assign all children to a curriculum designed for the 30 percent who will attend college creates inequality for those who, at the end of high school, fall among the 70 percent who do not attend college,"[61] a passage that in its totality, points out the dilemma of equality of educational opportunity as it is molded by the structure of American society.

When placed in the context of recent social and political events, Silberman's proposals can only be viewed as part of a continuing tradition of liberal educational reform and, therefore, as an attempt to use the schools to address the dislocations that are created by structures outside of them. As such these proposals can be evaluated both within the liberal tradition in terms of their effectiveness in meeting those conditions and outside of it in terms of the social context that molds liberal ideals.[62]

[59] See footnote 48.

[60] James S. Coleman, "The Concept of Equality of Educational Opportunity" in *Harvard Educational Review: Equal Educational Opportunity.* Harvard Press, 1969. Quoted in ibid., p. 86. (Original article is cited below.)

[61] James S. Coleman, "The Concept of Equality of Educational Opportunity" in *Harvard Educational Review,* Vol. 38, No. 1, 1968, p. 13.

[62] See Chapter Seven for the latter evaluation.

## VII. SUMMARY

Much of twentieth-century educational reform can be classified as belonging in one of two categories, reflecting either a child-centered or a subject-matter approach to the classroom. Despite the clear and obvious differences that exist between these two points of view, each represents a different side of liberal educational reform. Advocates of each accept the idea that the schools should be the primary instrument for achieving equality of educational opportunity, and they believe that the schools could be an effective instrument in smoothing over the dislocations caused by industrial society. The differences can be accounted for by noting the different needs that are stressed by the two. The subject-matter approach emphasizes the selection and training aspect of schooling and, as a consequence, places a greater emphasis on external control and discipline. The emphasis of the child-centered approach is more complex changing not only with stresses of the times but also according to the background and future prospects of the students. The significant aspect of the child-centered pedagogy is that it can be attached to different kinds of curricula. The tendency is to relate it to an academic curriculum when dealing with youngsters with middle-class aspirations and to thereby emphasize the development of academic skills and the habits of initiative and curiosity. With other youngsters, however, the tendency is to develop attitudes of adjustment and accommodation. In either case, the child-centered approach serves to reinforce the "social solidarity" that a heavy emphasis on selection and training may threaten. With marginal youngsters social solidarity is served by providing them with a generalized understanding of the forces acting on them and thereby increasing their tolerance for the strange and sometimes hostile world that confronts them. For talented youngsters with middle-class aspirations, the child-centered pedagogy coupled with an academic curriculum provides a way out of their situation and thereby relieves discontent that might otherwise disrupt the social order.

# CHAPTER FIVE
# The Image of Progress: History in the Service of Reform

## I. INTRODUCTION

One of the long-standing arguments for liberal reform has been that it is generally free of ideological bias. Dewey expressed this view in his lectures to the Chinese people during 1919-1920 when he warned that large ideologies should be avoided, and that social and political problems should be approached through the methods of science,[1] and in the late 1950s Daniel Bell heralded the liberal cause with a book entitled *The End of Ideology*. He proposed that mankind had entered a new era where political problems would be approached dispassionately through the methods of science and technology.

If one views the growth of technology as inevitable and as desirable on its own account, then the liberals' claim has merit, for within the limits of technological development liberal reform was flexible. If, however, one views liberal reform itself, as an essential element in the growth of modern technology, then the belief in the dispassionate

---

[1] John Dewey, *Lectures in China, 1919-1920,* trans. and eds. R. Clopton and Tsuin-Chen Ou (Honolulu: The University Press of Hawaii), 1973.

reformer-theorists becomes less plausible for then liberal reform itself will be understood as serving certain social and political developments which themselves must be evaluated on ethical terms.

If liberal reform is viewed in the context of a growing technology, then it becomes possible to understand some of the reformer's more fundamental commitments. We have seen that the belief in the inevitable growth of technology also entailed the belief that the direction of its growth must be guided by the principle of greater efficiency and this meant the centralization of people and resources in urban areas. Schools then had to address the dislocation that technology created. Among the needs to be served by the school was the selection and training of talent to fill the manpower requirements of the new technology. We have also seen that the school's role as a selection agency was limited by the requirements of social stability. Therefore, some individuals who, on considerations of talent alone, might have been candidates for high positions, were excluded from those positions by the requirements of social stability. Despite many problems, the belief persisted that the social good could be served best by allowing industrial growth to continue along the most efficient path, and that schools and other social agencies could resolve the problems that arose. The belief was implicit that by allowing talent to rise within the limits set by stability the social good would best be served. This belief will be examined more closely in the final chapter, but the purpose of this and the next chapter is to examine certain widely held images that allowed liberal theorists to cling to this view. This chapter looks at the liberal image of history as it is expressed in the idea of progress.

## II. THE INSPIRATIONAL
## SIDE OF LIBERAL THEORY

The major task of the liberal's view of history was to establish a perspective from which conflicting events and social forces could be judged while at the same time supporting the development of technology and the secondary institutions formed around it. Because the liberal historian believed that history, like other scholarly studies, should be pursued in a scientific manner, he claimed that questions about the overall direction and pattern of the past did not have empirical significance and were not worthy of serious study. He claimed that both liberal history and philosophy stood as a reaction to large ideas with religious overtones. To the liberal, the idea that the present could be understood through the recurring patterns of the past was misleading and artificial and much too simple for understanding the complexities of the present. Such views were dismissed as historicism. Yet liberal thought was not *just* scientific. It had its inspirational side too, and it was largely through this inspirational side that the liberal perspective was established and liberal judgments made. The inspirational component of liberal thought was expressed by a belief in progress that became the sustaining force behind many proposals for both educational change and social reform. However, this same belief shielded technology and the principle of greatest efficiency that guided its growth from careful consideration.

The liberal's belief in progress was not a simple one. Because liberal philosophy was presented as a reaction to large historical patterns, it was not the intent to substitute a new pattern for the older one. Thus progress was spoken of as possible but not as certain. The universe was open and amenable to man's will if he chose to exercise it intelligently. However, it was possible that man might do otherwise. Yet here was the inspirational message. Progress was analogous to God's grace. It was available to man, but only if man chose it. The belief in progress was an affirmation of the possibilities inherent in *this* life and in the efficacy of man's will and the ability of his reason to realize those possibilities. Like the ideologies it confronted, it too set a certain tone to human existence by providing a context with which to make sense out of human experience. Its appeal was found in its capacity to motivate and direct human striving within a continuing political and economic context by suggesting that the goals of man could be reached in this world through the ungirding of man's industrial potential.

## III. HISTORY IN THE
## SERVICE OF NATION AND SCHOOL

One of the reasons that liberal theorists rejected the view that the past revealed patterns that imposed themselves onto the present was because they believed that the American experience was unique and not subject to historical laws drawn from older nations. This belief was first expressed in terms of the American frontier, but it was later applied to the development of American institutions, such as the public schools. The theme of the historical uniqueness of the American experience tied a number of scholars together during and immediately after World War I. In 1917 Dewey expressed this theme by calling for the development of an explicitly American philosophy to be articulated out of the uniqueness of the American spirit. "Philosophy in America will be lost," he wrote, ". . . unless it can somehow bring to consciousness America's own needs and its own implicit principle of successful action."[2] And in an address before the National Education Association in 1916 he observed how the American nation, in distinction from all others, has minimized violent contact and hostility.[3] Even before World War I a group of young historians gained prominence by breaking with the older tradition of American historiography that emphasized the ties between Europe and the United States. These historians, led by Frederick Jackson Turner, were to build their work on what they saw to be the specific characteristics of the American experience.

Turner's 1893 paper on "The Significance of the Frontier in American History" was partially a reaction against what had been called the germ theory of American institutions. Turner believed that "Too exclusive attention has been paid by institutional students to the Germanic origins, too little to the American factors."[4] Turner argued that the frontier was the major factor in America's growth and in the development of her distinctive democratic institutions and national character. The frontier forced each generation of Americans to meet anew the conditions of primitive life, and as they set out to tame the wilderness, they were also tamed by it.

Turner described the frontier as the "gate of escape from the bondage of the past." It demanded a constantly new set of habits and the continued reformation of older institutional responses. Whereas the demand for space by peoples of other nations brought them into conflict with other people, the encounter of the frontiersman was thought to be with a physical environment.

Turner began his essay with the observation that the census of 1890 indicated that the era of the frontier had come to an end, and

---

[2] John Dewey, "The Need for a Recovery of Philosophy," in Bernstein (ed.), *Dewey: On Experience, Nature and Freedom* (New York: The Liberal Arts Press), 1960, p. 68.

[3] John Dewey, "Nationalizing Education," *The Journal of the National Education Association*, Vol. I, No. 2, October, 1916, pp. 183-189.

[4] Frederick J. Turner, "The Significance of the Frontier in American History," *The Bobbs-Merrill Reprint Series in History*, H-214, p. 201.

with it, "has closed the end of the first period of American history."[5] He believed the frontier was a uniquely American experience, and the major factor in explaining the American character. Into the frontier went immigrants of all nationalities to meet the same hardships and to forge a new civilization out of the primitive conditions that they encountered. Out of that experience was developed a composite national character. The frontiersmen were more like each other than they were like members of their parent civilization. Taking up Turner's thesis, many people came to believe that violence had been minimized in America[6] and that this was to be explained by the fact that national idiosyncrasies had been overcome by the Americanizing experience of the frontier. But if Turner were correct, the frontier period was quickly coming to an end. The wilderness was pocked with settlements.

The story of the frontier had many sides to it. Initially, it was invoked to lament the passing of the rugged frontier individual and to call for a return to basic American values, but it was soon used for other purposes. The liberal scholars who followed Turner accepted the idea of America's uniqueness and the vision that the hopes for civilized progress rested with the American nation. With Dewey, they minimized the scope of violence, and stressed the role of conflict. They did not, however, lament the passing of the rugged individual and saw the supposed absence of violence as a result of the peculiar character of American institutions. Against the conservatives, they argued that the closing of the frontier did not mean an end to national progress. As they saw it, the locus of progress was to be found not in a finite environment but in the nature of a set of developing institutions. Unlike the frontier, progress was infinite; it had no limits.

In view of these observations it is easy to see why the school took on such an important role in the century that was to follow. The public school was expected to begin where it was believed the frontier had left off. Just as the frontier had been pictured as taming people of different nationalities, forming out of them a similar character, now the school was to do the same thing. And just as it was believed the frontier had

---

[5] Ibid., p. 227.

[6] It is sobering to note Richard Hofstadter's comment: "We have a remarkable lack of memory where violence is concerned and have left most of our excesses a part of buried history." Richard Hofstadter and Michael Wallace, *American Violence: A Documentary History* (New York: Vintage Books), 1971, p. 3.

provided the nation with an escape valve whereby the discontent could move out to break new ground, now the school was to provide another kind of escape valve whereby the talented discontent could move up. In the same way that the frontier was believed to have minimized violent acts against the state and against other people, now it was felt that the school would serve the same function.

## IV. HISTORY AS AN
## INSTRUMENT OF REFORM

Morton White in his *Social Thought in America* has interpreted the writings of twentieth-century liberal scholars in America as a revolt against the intellectual formalism that prevailed in academic circles at the turn of the century. He views the work of the liberal scholar as directed against earlier scholarly themes that attempted to weave a theory of man and society from a single attribute that was then purported to describe all men or all societies at all times and places. Thus, in politics, liberal thought was a rejection of the idea that man was to be described only in terms of the quest for power; in economics it was a rejection of the view that men universally seek profit; and in psychology it was a reaction against the idea that man is basically passive and is moved to action only by the need to achieve pleasure or to avoid pain. Instead of trying to develop a universal theory of man, White depicts liberal scholars as attempting to understand man's present condition in light of factors that will aid in improving it. Among the scholars that White treats in some detail are the philosopher Dewey, the historian Charles Beard, and the historian-political scientist James Harvey Robinson. White emphasizes the fact that their beliefs are not similar in all important respects but that they are tied together in a familial relationship. Nevertheless the belief that ideas are to be judged as instruments for social change does run through their work as a central theme. As White describes their ideas:

Instrumentalism is Dewey's doctrine which holds that ideas are plans of action, and not mirrors of reality; . . . and that philosophy ought to free itself from metaphysics and devote itself to social engineering.

Beard's most serious contribution to the pattern is . . . the view that faction is the great problem of modern democratic society and that property is the source of faction. Beard, therefore, looks . . . with Madison for underlying economic forces that determine the acceleration of social life, and urges the historian to chart the process of civilization as a whole.

James Harvey Robinson . . . represented the view that history is not merely a chronicle of the past, but rather a pragmatic weapon for explaining the present and controlling the future.[7]

The implication of this point of view for liberal historians was that historical knowledge, like other forms, was ultimately to be judged as an instrument for human activity and for helping to realize the potential latent in the present state of affairs. Dewey provided the broad outline and the most articulate justification for this point of view while Beard and Robinson worked it out in their historical writings.

Dewey's denial of universality applied to the total range of knowledge from logic to jurisprudence and therefore to a wider area than simply the understanding of the past.[8] The significance of Dewey's point

---

[7] Morton White, *Social Thought in America: The Revolt Against Formalism* (Boston: Beacon Press), 1957, pp. 7-8.

[8] Stated in its most general form, Dewey believed that any proposition purported to have universal validity, holding true for all times and all places, is actually formed as a result of man's interaction with a specific range of experience and is therefore falsifiable. Such propositions are falsifiable because, as universals, they are asserted as applicable to all situations of a given type whereas in fact they have not been formulated under all possible situations of that type, but only under some of them. The implication of this view is that any claim, whether it is an ethical, legal, historical, or logical one, is conceivably subject to refutation, even though as Dewey observed, at any given point in time only a few are actually called into question. With regards to strictly factual propositions, few would have any quarrel with Dewey's view, but Dewey believed that his argument applied to analytic as well as empirical truths and thus he was making a very strong claim of falsifiability. The strength of this claim can be better understood by examining its implications for two fields, logic and jurisprudence. Logic is the one area that many philosophers might agree has a legitimate claim to universality. Traditionally logic has been held to be about the relationships between propositions and about the proper ordering of premises and conclusions. Its claim to universality arises from the fact that it does not have reference to an empirical subject matter, but instead to the variety of ways in which propositions can be validly ordered. For example, the validity of the statement, "If *A* then *B*, *A* therefore *B*" does not depend on the referent of A and B, but upon their formal relations. In an essay on logic and law Dewey attempted to refute the traditional view and to reduce even logic's claim to universality. He did this by looking not at the form of statements but at the process by which a reasoned decision is reached. Logic, he argued, is simply a statement of the procedures that have been successful

of view with regards to the revolt against formalism was to cut through the weight of older ideologies by affirming that developments in science and technology were so new and so significant to man's experience that they required a reinterpretation of human values and their institutional expressions.[9] Dewey's philosophy of history was therefore designed to

in arriving at reasoned judgments in the past, and it is possible that situations will arise in the future in which such procedures do not work. Thus even in the area of logical theory, Dewey was not willing to admit that universality was an appropriate notion.

Having made this point with regard to logic, Dewey went on to treat law in a similar way. Underlying his treatment of law is a concern to make the law more responsive to present conditions. To do this he argued that the primary concern of jurisprudence should not be that each ruling be spun out from the existing body of laws in an absolutely consistent manner. He admitted that there is a need to reduce the degree of arbitrariness pronouncements, but argued that there is an even greater need to recognize the contingencies of the present.

"There is, of course, every reason why rules of law should be as regular and as definite as possible. But the amount and kind of antecedent assurance which is actually attainable is a matter of fact, not of form. It is large whenever social conditions are pretty uniform, and when industry, commerce, transportation, etc., move in the channels of old customs. It is much less wherever invention is active and when new devices in business and communication bring about new forms of human relationship." (p. 138. See below for reference).

The thrust of his analysis was to bring the rulings of law into conformity with certain ongoing aspects of the present situation, in this case industry, commerce and transportation among others. See John Dewey, "Logical Method and Law," in Dewey, *Philosophy and Civilization* (New York: Capricorn Books), 1963, pp. 126-140. For a recent expression of a similar point of view see Stephen Toulmin, *Human Understanding: Vol. I* (Princeton: Princeton University Press), 1972.

[9] Once the strategic value of this approach is understood then a number of different evaluations are possible. The more traditional view has been to recognize the extent to which Dewey and others were fighting a rear-guard action in which technology was already raising havoc with traditional relationships and then to view their scholarship as providing support for efforts to adjust institutions to the changing times. Another way to view their approach is to emphasize the degree to which they accepted the lead of technology and then attempted to alter institutions and behavior in conformity with its thrust. The first evaluation proceeds by accepting the idea that the fundamental responsibility of the scholar is to aid the future adjustment of one part of the total system of human relationships to the others whereas the second is eventually committed to evaluating the principles expressed by the adjustment.

justify appraisals of historical scholarship on the basis of their effectiveness as instruments of reform and social progress.

Because it concerns the temporal flow and quality of human experience, the belief in progress is a belief about historical events. As a belief
about the past as well as the future, the belief in progress relates to the
question of how the past is to be known and how we are to choose
between conflicting views of the past. These issues constituted a central
part of Dewey's philosophy of history.

"History," Dewey pointed out, "has a two-fold meaning. History
is that which happened in the past and it is the intellectual reconstruction
of these happenings at a subsequent time."[10] This dual meaning was carried over into his own assertions about the openness of history. In the
first and most commonly expressed instance the statement expressed
Dewey's belief that the future is not absolutely determined by the past;
that there are no universal patterns guiding the unfolding of human
events. In the second instance Dewey meant that the writing of history
is open and that each new age produces its own written narrative of the
past, perceived from its point of view, with its own concerns uppermost
in the minds of its historians and generating its own consequences.
Although Dewey did not believe that there were any universal patterns
necessarily applicable to the past, present and future, he did believe that
the recent past had revealed to man the method for favorably manipulating the natural environment towards progressive ends. This belief,
interesting in its own right, highlights the element of judgment that
Dewey believed was so crucial in historical scholarship.

The historian, Dewey argued, does not simply capture the past as
it once happened. He reconstructs it by selecting out events, assigning
degrees of importance to evidence, and postulating a direction to change.
And he does so guided by problems that are foremost in the present.

---

The historical scholarship that White characterizes as the revolt against formalism was committed to the first response and the idea of progress that guided it
was an expression of the general direction of adjustment in American society.
It might be thought equally appropriate, however, for one to try first to be
clear about the nature of human values and then to try and limit technology
according to the requirement of certain ethical norms. (See Chapter Seven for
an attempt to do this.)

[10] John Dewey, *Logic: The Theory of Inquiry* (New York: Henry Holt &
Co.), 1938, p. 236.

Dewey's belief regarding the dominance of the present over the narratives of the past was not about the provincialism of historians but about the limits of historical knowledge in general. He made the point strongly: "All history is necessarily written from the standpoint of the present, and is, in an inescapable sense, the history not only of the present but of that which is contemporaneously judged to be important in the present."[11] And, at the same time, written history becomes an instrument "for moving the present into a certain kind of future."[12]

His message was not only that the present provides a context for interpreting the past but that the interpretation also has consequences for the future and, at least in part, is to be judged by those consequences. He granted that the past provided the material for its own interpretation (artifacts, documents, etc.), but he affirmed that the material exists in the present and is interpreted in light of the significance given to it today. In part this meant for Dewey that findings in other disciplines such as epigraphy, paleography, linguistics, and bibliography shed new and different lights on the "accepted" interpretations of historical events. But it also meant that the angle from which historical issues were addressed was largely determined by the problems that dominated the historian's present.

The urgency of the social problems which are now developing out of the forces of industrial production and distribution is the source of a new interest in history from the economic point of view. When current problems seem dominantly political, the political aspect of history is uppermost. A person who becomes deeply interested in climatic changes readily finds occasion to write history from the standpoint of great changes that have taken place over large areas in, say, the distribution of rainfall.[13]

In the trivial sense that the historian writes about the past from the standpoint of those interests which he has in the present, the above statement is obvious. The historian who, for example, writes primarily about climatic change is clearly looking at the past from his own present interests. Indeed we know that they are his interests by the way in which he writes about the past. But the implication is larger than this. It is that there are certain dominant changes which characterize a present period

[11] Ibid., p. 235.
[12] Ibid., p. 239.
[13] Ibid., p. 238.

of time, and that to a large extent history is to be judged by how well it reflects those changes by projecting them onto the past.

Changes going on in the present, giving a new turn to social problems, throw the significance of what happened in the past into a new perspective. They set new issues from the standpoint of which to rewrite the story of the past.[14]

It is in this sense that the present generation has the right to judge the past on its own terms. However, not every present standpoint is to count as equally valid.

Intelligent understanding of past history is to some extent a lever for moving the present into a certain kind of future . . . In using what has come to them as inheritance from the past they are compelled to modify it to meet their own needs.[15]

And implicitly the modification is to be judged by how well it allows the needs to be met. Concerning the matter of judging histories, Dewey was anything but neutral. An adequate account would give primary recognition to the development of industrialization and to man's ever increasing capacity, as he saw it, to intelligently control his environment through the development of democratic institution and scientific procedures.

Written history was open because the future had yet to be formed, and the way it was formed was influenced by the way people came to view their past. The historian's task was inspirational as well as academic, leading man into a new and hopefully better tomorrow. While Dewey elaborated the philosophy of history that provided the justification for progressive history, others, such as Charles Beard and James Harvey Robinson, reflected this philosophy in their interpretations of America's past.

## V. PROGRESSIVE HISTORY: CHARLES BEARD

Beard is most well-known for his economic interpretation of the U.S. Constitution and Robinson for his elaboration of the progressive

[14] Ibid., pp. 238-239.
[15] Ibid., p. 239.

stages of the human mind throughout the evolution of civilization. The inspirational side of progessive history is apparent in the works of each of these men, but they themselves chose to down play it and to stress instead the "scientific" character of their historical writings. Yet the works of these men illustrate not only the way progressive history was used to inspire social and educational reform but also the way historical interpretation effectively shielded the thrust of technology and the principle of greatest efficiency from a considered evaluation.

Both Beard and Robinson saw themselves as hard-headed, scientific historians and therefore in deemphasizing the inspirational qualities of their own writings, they constrasted their "scientific" histories with the literary history of earlier times that they claimed was written to comfort people and to strengthen their loyalty to established institutions.

In rejecting histories that were written to comfort, Beard gave special mention to the inspirational history of George Bancroft and quoted from Bancroft's *History of the Constitution of the United States* to illustrate the tone of the nonscientific, literary history he objected to.

By calm meditation and friendly councils, . . . they (the people) had prepared a constitution which, in the union of freedom with strength and order, excelled everyone known before . . . In the happy morning of their existence as one of the powers of the world, they had chosen justice for their guide; and while they proceeded on their way with well founded confidence and joy, all the friends of mankind invoked success on their endeavor as the only hope for renovating the life of the civilized world.[16]

In contrast, Beard's *Economic Interpretation of the Constitution* had shocked the conventional world by suggesting that the founding fathers had been motivated by economic rather than altruistic interests. In contrast to Bancroft, Beard observed that the phrase "We the people" in reality referred to a much smaller group of people than the totality of individuals who lived within the boundaries of the United States, and given this observation, he began to highlight the various economic interests of the framers of the Constitution.

Rather than viewing the Constitution as a divinely inspired document, he insisted on studying it as indirectly but profoundly related to property right. Most law, Beard asserted, is concerned with the property

[16] Charles Beard, *An Economic Interpretation of the Constitution* p. 10. Copyright 1913 by The Macmillan Company.

relations between men.[17] Constitutional law is concerned with "organs of government, the suffrage, administration."[18] "The primary object of government . . . is the making of rules which determine the property relations of members of society."[19] "Thus the dominant classes in society must, if they are to maintain their dominance, either obtain rules which are consistent with their own interest or else gain control of the organs of government."[20] "The social structure by which one type of legislation is secured and another prevented—that is, the Constitution— is a secondary or derivative feature arising from the nature of the economic groups seeking positive action and negative restraint."[21]

Beard's study reinforced his initial framework. He found that the movement for a Constitution was initiated by four groups that had been adversely affected by the loose structure existing under the articles of confederation: these groups were those whose wealth was tied to money, public securities, manufacturing, and trade. He emphasized the facts that no popular vote had been taken to call the Constitutional convention into session and that popular representation in both the framing and the ratification of the Constitution was severely limited. "The Constitution was ratified by a vote of probably not more than one-sixth of the adult males."[22] Moreover, "The members of the Phila-delphia Convention which drafted the Constitution were, with a few exceptions, immediately, directly, and personally interested in, and derived economic advantages from, the establishment of the new system."[23]

Much of Beard's reaction to earlier histories of American society was based on his aversion to explaining historical movements in terms of moral forces. Nevertheless, other mystical forces were implicit in Beard's interpretation. Instead of the forces of altruistic, divinely in-spired motives, they were the forces that guided personal motives to moral ends. Progress was the result of an invisible hand that worked out class and interpersonal conflicts towards worthwhile results. Even though the formation of the constitution was motivated by economic

[17] Ibid., p. 12.
[18] Ibid., p. 13.
[19] Ibid., p. 13.
[20] Ibid., p. 13.
[21] Ibid., p. 13.
[22] Ibid., p. 325.
[23] Ibid., p. 324.

interests and even though it was not representative of the immediate interests of the population, nevertheless it served the interests of the nation as a whole.

The Constitution was not created by "the whole people" as the jurists have said; neither was it created by "the states" as Southern nullifiers long contended; but it was the work of a consolidated group whose interests knew no state boundaries and were truly national in their scope.[24]

Beard's ideas on progress changed throughout various stages of his career, yet the belief in progress was an essential element of his new history. In the *Economic Interpretation of the Constitution*, progress was seen as a real and perhaps inevitable outcome of the clash of economic interests. "The whole theory of the economic interpretation of history rests upon the concept that social progress in general is the result of contending interests in society."[25] Before World War I, Beard seemed assured that progress was a real fact of America's history. Propelled by clashing interests the nation was moving towards a consensus and developing institutions that would minimize violence and resolve conflict through legal means. Sometime during the depression, his faith began to decline and self-doubt set in. The intensity of the doubt is highlighted in the different tone expressed in the concluding passages of *The Rise of American Civilization*, 1927, and then 1934. In 1927 Beard wrote with enthusiasm:

If the severality of opinion, as distinguished from that of the poignant specialist, was taken into account, there was no doubt about the nature of the future in America. The most common note of assurance was belief in unlimited progress—the continuous fulfillment of the historic idea which had slowly risen through the eighteenth and nineteenth century to a position of commanding authority. Concretely it meant an invulnerable faith in democracy, in the ability of the undistinguished masses, as contrasted with heroes and classes, to meet by reasonably competent methods the issues raised in the flow of time—a faith in that new and mysterious instrument of the modern mind, "the invention of invention," moving from one technological triumph to another, overcoming the exhaustion of crude natural resources and energies, effecting an ever wider distribution of the blessings of civilization—health, security, material goods, knowledge, leisure, and aesthetic appreciation and through the cumulating forces of

24 Ibid., p. 325.
25 Ibid., p. 19.

intellectual and artistic reactions, conjuring from the vasty deeps of the nameless and unknown imagination of the noblest order, subduing physical things to the empire of spirit—doubting not the capacity of the Power that had summoned into being all patterns of the past and present, living and dead, to fulfill its endless destiny.

If so, it is the dawn, not the dusk, of the gods.[26]

In 1934 enthusiasm had relaxed, disillusionment had set in and Beard chose to emphasize another side of America's past. Whereas previously the *voice of the common man* had been cited as the source of hope, now the response of the expert to the *winds of opinion* was the index of barren pursuits.

Even more than the world of education, the trade of letters was disturbed by the collapse of best sellers and security. Less fettered by tradition, more responsive to the winds of opinion, artists of the written word were quick to feel the shock of panic . . . In his *Fairwell to Reform,* John Chamberlain laid Theodore Roosevelt, Robert M. LaFollette, and Woodrow Wilson away in their tombs with Charles I, Louis XVI, and Nicholas II.

So, thought, weary Titan, continued to climb as for two thousand years the rugged crags between Ideology and Utopia.[27]

As Beard's faith in the ontological significance of progress waned, he re-established it as a pragmatic principle. Although such a belief was difficult to prove in reality, it was important because of the inspiration it provided the believer.

Hence the concept of continual progress furnished inspiration to countless thousands. . . . Nor could economic depression destroy it. It remains and will remain, a fundamental tenet of American society, and while vigor is left in the race it will operate with all the force of a dynamic idea rooted in purpose, will and opportunity.[28]

Until late in his career, Beard's writings were governed not only by a general view of progress, but also by the strong conviction that the

[26] Charles Beard, *The Rise of American Civilization* Vol. II, p. 800. Copyright 1927 by The Macmillan Company.

[27] Charles Beard, *The Rise of American Civilization,* one volume edition (New York: Macmillan), 1934, revised edition, pp. 836-837. I am indebted to Ronald Szoke for bringing these contrasting passages to my attention.

[28] Charles Beard's introduction to J. B. Bury, *The Idea of Progress: An Inquiry into its Growth and Origins* (New York: Dowes Publishers, Inc.), 1932 edition, 1955, p. xxxvii.

United States, and even more specifically, the federal government, was the key representative of democracy and progress throughout the world. The belief was subtle and articulated with discrimination. Beard did not, for example, applaud every act of the national government. He favored World War I but courageously opposed questionable decisions justified in the name of national unity. His voluntary departure from Columbia University over the firing of Cattell for pacifist activity is an illustration of this point. Moreover, he was an active opponent to the policies of imperialism and national expansion that occurred under McKinley and Roosevelt and as late as 1934 in a book entitled *The Idea of National Interest* he devoted considerable space to the arguments of the anti-imperialists while throwing an occasional barb at the moral proclamations of national leaders. "Allegedly to realize the precepts of moral obligation in action, all the engines of war, conquest, economic pressure, religious dogma, social control, and political power have been employed."[29]

More typically, however, he was to compare favorably the progressive thrust of American society to the retarded traditions of Europe. "The distinguishing characteristic of America lay in the fact that what was deemed unusual in Europe became the rule here."[30] Faith in democracy was the necessary condition for the continuation of democracy, and a strong belief in progress was the necessary condition for progressive development.

## VI. BEARD AND THE IDEA OF PROGRESS IN THE SCHOOL TEXTBOOKS

While Beard was critical of earlier historians for writings that tended to comfort rather than explain, his own view of progress was not without its comforting aspects. To highlight the economic interests of the framers of the Constitution was not to question the consequences of their acts, nor were the motives of other leaders at other times to detract from the beneficial consequences of their initiatives. Perhaps

---

[29] Charles A. Beard, *The Idea of National Interest* (New York: The Macmillan Co.), 1934, p. 406.

[30] Beard, introduction to Bury, pp. xxxii-xxxiii.

because of the initial shock of Beard's *An economic interpretation of the Constitution,* many other scholars have overemphasized his treatment of personal motive and underemphasized the general direction he believed manifested by the flow of America's past. Beard's view of the overall progressive direction of America's past was expressed in most of his scholarly works, but the clearest example of his views on this subject is to be found in the textbooks that he wrote for public school students. These texts provide an important example of the way in which progressive history was molded around the imperatives of reform. The image that most clearly comes across in these texts is one of conflict, and compromise resulting in increased strength and expanded democracy. In Beard and Beard (written with his wife), for example, the section treating the period of the Constitutional Convention is entitled "The American Republic Strengthens Its Foundations," and one of the subtitles is "Clashes of Opinions and Interests Lead to Compromises." The tone of the treatment that is afforded the framing and the ratification here is different from that of *An Economic Interpretation.* Little mention is given to the economic motives of the framers, but a great deal of attention is paid to the problems that developed out of the Articles of Confederation, although again the fact that such problems were felt by certain groups and not by others does not receive attention. The framers are described as eminent men with the national interest at heart, but the fact that they represented only a small percentage of the population is deemphasized. Regarding the revolution itself, there is one plate the caption of which—"The man who furnished money was as necessary to the patriot's cause as the fighter"[31]—sums up the treatment of this era by the text.

The Beard and Bagley textbook is written with a mission in mind: to assure the continuation of democracy in America and its flourishment elsewhere. "Such a story, if rightly told, must challenge the admiration and faith of those who believe that democracy is not to perish from the earth but to flourish and triumph everywhere."[32] The object of the text was not simply to challenge such faith, but to renew it, and to represent American Civilization as its guardian.

[31] Charles A. Beard and Mary R. Beard, *The Making of American Civilization* (New York: The Macmillan Co.), 1937, p. 167.
[32] Charles A. Beard and William C. Bagley, The History of the American People, second revised edition (New York: The Macmillan Co.), 1929, p. iii.

The fate of the nation in a very real sense lies in the hands of their sons and daughters who study its history in the public schools. They are to be the makers of history as well as the students of it, and this fact cannot be too often brought home to them. The achievements, traditions, ideals of the past—these are the sources of inspiration to those who hold the future in their hands. To help make these an open book to the coming generations is the underlying purpose of this volume.[33]

The theme of progress ran through many of Beard's scholarly works and it dominated his textbooks. The text written with Mary Beard, for example, stressed the ever growing spirit of democracy and national unity that they perceived developing as a result of numerous clashes of economic interests. There was also the strong suggestion that American history reveals consistent movement towards a time when all legitimate conflict would take place within the boundary of law. The same theme is found in Beard's introduction to Bury's volume on progress. Conflicts were viewed as becoming more and more conflicts of opinion rather than violence, and this itself was taken as a defining characteristic of American democracy.

Constitutional and democratic government is impossible unless the significance of ideas is recognized. It is founded on the assumption that all social conflicts will be fought out within the framework set by the fundamental law through the exchange of ideas. To government by opinion there is no other alternative except government by violence.[34]

One of the most important functions that the belief in progress served was to place the darker side of the American experience from exploitation to violence into a larger, more purposeful context, thereby maintaining faith in the basic soundness of the larger institutions from which reform would issue. One of the unstated implications of Beard's view of progress was that most, if not all previous conflicts, whether of a violent nature or otherwise, could be justified as having contributed to greater social justice and harmony. In the textbook written with Bagley, America is pictured as the spearhead of progressive civilization. Always reluctant to go to war and generally peaceful she intervenes on the side of right and never initiates her squabbles with others. World War I is pictured as a war between the peace-loving, democratic peoples of the

[33] Ibid., p. iv.
[34] Beard, introduction to Bury, *The Idea of Progress,* p. x.

United States against the ruthless, autocratic German Kaiser. Even the robber barons, the railroad builders, the land speculators, and the capitalists served their proper function in the development of this peace-loving nation.

Now we must try to picture to ourselves the work of the new groups created by the Industrial Revolution—businessmen, inventors, captains of industry, railway magnates, real estate speculators, and capitalists—hurrying to improve every kind of machine, establishing banks and raising money for industrial and railway enterprises, erecting factories, building railway lines through forests and over mountains. Under their daring leadership great cities rose, etc.[35]

Except for a brief mention in the preface of the book, there is little about the toil or the hardship of the laborer who built the railroads or who labored in the factories. Of course industrialization brought with it grave problems, but these were challenges for a democracy to solve. Faith in progress was the necessary condition for the improvement of American society and the purpose of the textbook was to reinforce that faith. Thus was established the primary criterion for inclusion and for exclusion and the major filter through which events were perceived. As explained by Beard and Bagley in what may have been the most striking example of exclusion:

The space given to the North American Indian has been materially reduced. They are interesting and picturesque, but they made no impression upon the civilization of the United States. In a history designed to explain the present rather than to gratify curiosity and entertain, Indian habits of life and Indian wars must have a very minor position.[36]

## VII. JAMES HARVEY ROBINSON
## AND THE PROGRESSIVE EVOLUTION
## OF THE HUMAN MIND

James Harvey Robinson was even more explicit than Beard about America's place on the cutting edge of civilization's development and about the job of the historian in furthering its progressive thrust. Pro-

---

[35] Beard and Bagley, p. 351.
[36] Ibid., pp. iii-iv.

gressive development was not simply an accident of history; it was an essential historical law manifesting itself in the development of the human mind as it moved from savagery to civilization.

Robinson believed that the essential course of man's development has been established and that man has followed it with only occasional deviations. Nevertheless, the job was not complete, thus leaving room for human initiative and direction. For in each stage of development remnants of the past were to be found, and the task was, therefore, to discard them. Man's reverence for authority and his willingness to let the traditions of the past tyrannize over him were believed to be remnants of a bygone era, no longer functional in an age of science. Man deludes himself into thinking that the dogmas received from the past represent the final word for the present and the future. Robinson therefore believed that the job of the historian was to help man cast off the vestiges of bygone days.

The mark of the modern age was that the common man had learned to hold the scientist above suspicion. Previously held in the light of suspicion by the clergy and the people, the present age finds "our scientific men carry on their work and report their results with little or no effective hostility on the part of the clergy or the schools."[37] Yet Robinson believed that same suspicion was now directed against the social scientist, and part of the historian's task was to free man's mind from the bondage of the past so that the common man would come to accept the work of the social scientist as he accepted that of the physical scientist.

Robinson believed that the job of history was to prepare the ground for the application of intelligence to social affairs. "Intelligence . . . is as yet an untested hope in its application to the regulation of human relations."[38] Someday, however, its application to social relations would prove as successful as had its application to physical ones.

With Beard, Robinson also criticizes the older histories for serving a particular cause. They were unscientific histories because the historians who wrote them had a particular purpose in mind, to serve state or church, Protestant or Catholic, etc. The older histories were also un-

[37] James Harvey Robinson, *The Mind in the Making* (New York: Harper and Bros.), 1921, p. 11.
[38] Ibid., p. 24.

scientific because they were often written with literary style as the primary concern. They were designed sometimes to entertain, sometimes to comfort.

Like Beard, Robinson believed that the new history was scientific. Historians were becoming more conscious of the source and validity of their data, were re-examining the evidence used by past historians, finding much of it questionable. They had developed more sophisticated methods of cataloging and had intensified their search procedures. Robinson believed that history had reached the stage of a science not only because of more sophisticated methods, but also because historians had finally uncovered a major and lasting historical truth. They had discovered the idea of progress expressed in every aspect of human affairs. "Every generally accepted idea, every important invention, is but the summation of long lines of progress."[39] The continuity of history is a scientific truth and the historian's "attempt to trace the slow process of change is a scientific problem."[40] And "the discovery and application of this law . . . has raised (history) to the dignity of a science."[41]

The outstanding discovery of the new history Robinson proclaimed was the progressive development of the species and this discovery marked the new history off from the old. The discovery of progress brought present historians to the point of seeking the cause for the new in the old, of tracing modern inventions and ideas back to older ones, and of recognizing the remnants of the past which remain but are yet dysfunctional for the present.

Robinson, perhaps because of his criticism of business, or because he traced some of his intellectual roots to Karl Marx, was frequently depicted, along with Beard, as one of the radical historians. Yet no less than Beard, his writing was designed to sing the praise of America by acknowledging its place on the cutting edge of civilized progress. He wrote, for example,

In no other country is morality more highly prized or stoutly defended. Woman is held in her proper esteem and the institution of the family

---

[39] James Harvey Robinson, *The New History: Essays Illustrating the Modern Historical Outlook* (New York: The Macmillan Co.), 1922, p. 64.

[40] Ibid., p. 64.

[41] Ibid., p. 65, parentheses added.

everywhere recognized as fundamental. We are singularly free from the vices which disgrace the capitals of Europe, not excepting London.

In no other country is the schoolhouse so assuredly acknowledged to be the corner stone of democracy and liberty. . . .

We are an ingenious people in the realm of invention and in the boldness of our business enterprise. We have the sturdy virtues of the pioneer. We are an honest people, keeping our contracts and giving fair measure. We are a tireless people in the patient attention to business and the laudable resolve to rise in the world. Many of our richest men began on the farm or as office boys. Success depends in our country almost exclusively on native capacity, which is rewarded here with a prompt and cheerful recognition which is rare in other lands. . . . No alert American can visit any foreign land without noting innumerable examples of stupid adherence to outworn and cumbersome methods of industry, commerce, and transportation.[42]

## VIII. HISTORY IN THE
## SERVICE OF THE COMMON MAN

Robinson was critical of older historians for their unscientific methods and for their attempt to comfort rather than enlighten. Their works were written not to establish objective, scientific historical truths but to secure the loyalty of the reader to a specific authority. Yet aspects of Robinson's views on the new history were strikingly similar to aspects of the old that he criticized. Robinson did not really rule out service to a particular cause, only now he claimed that rather than serve a specific institution, history was to turn its efforts to the service of the common man. Robinson believed that when history taught the common man to respect the authority of science instead of the authority of some institutional order, that the common man would be serving his own end. In order to do this, Robinson proposed that the mission of the historian could best be accomplished by developing a special history to be taught to the children of the industrial worker.

In proposing such a history, Robinson argued that education continued to harbor a bias against the manual laborer and favored the man of leisure by its liberal arts curriculum. History itself perpetuated the

[42] Robinson, *The Mind in the Making,* pp. 184-185.

bias with its emphasis on the exploits of men from the upper reaches of society. He believed that as the study of the past, history has no single and right subject matter, and each age has the right "to select from the annals of mankind those facts that seem to have a particular bearing on the matters that it has at heart."[43] The problem, as he saw it, with the history books of his day was that they were filled with facts that were not worth the attention of the modern-day youngster, and they omitted other facts that were. Robinson then elaborated the considerations that should be uppermost in the selection process.

In elaborating these considerations, Robinson provided a clear example of the way progressive historians molded their works around the imperatives of reform and the requirements of the industrial age. These considerations also reveal some of the ways the ideas of progress and reform were used to pacify the potential dissonance to be found in the industrial class. Indeed, it is ironical that Robinson criticized the older histories for their attempts to comfort the masses for his own history was designed to do precisely the very same thing. In order to meet the needs of the children of the industrial worker, Robinson wrote that the historian needs first to ask:

What, considering the needs, capacity, interest and future career of the boys and girls in industrial school, is most necessary for them to know of the past in order to be as intelligent, efficient, and happy as possible in the life they must lead and *the work they must do?*[44]

The framing of this question provided an ample clue to the way in which Robinson was to answer it. He began by asserting as an undeniable fact that the relationship between the classes will remain constant for a long period of time, as will the relation between man and machines. From this it followed that there will continue to be a "very large class of boys and girls who must take up the burden of life prematurely and who must look forward to earning their livelihood by the work of their hands."[45] Contrary to what one might expect from a history that was purportedly designed to improve the welfare of the industrial worker, Robinson did not suggest that the social conditions of the machine age should be highlighted so that workers could make intelli-

---

[43] Robinson, *The New History,* p. 135.
[44] Ibid., p. 139. (Emphasis mine.)
[45] Ibid., pp. 132-133.

gent decisions about their own fate. He mentioned that these conditions have in fact "left the mass of workers whose lives are passed in factories in almost a worse plight than that of Greek and Roman Slaves,"[46] but this remark was meant for the writers of history, not the consumers of it. Instead of highlighting the real conditions of industrial life, history was to deal with the attitudes of working-class children and to teach them "to see the significance of their humble part in carrying on the world's work, to appreciate the possibilities of their position and to view it in as hopeful a light as circumstances will permit."[47] The goal of history for the child of the industrial class was to teach him to become "influential in bettering the lot of himself and his fellow workers without seriously diminishing the output."[48] It may be unkind but it is accurate to summarize Robinson's position as one that would use history to teach the children of the working class to trust the social scientist so that these children could come to appreciate and tolerate a plight that left them worse off than the Greek and Roman slaves.

Robinson's views supported the thrust of liberal reform in general. The proposals of the liberal educator were frequently justified in terms of democracy, equality and progress, yet his proposals were developed in the context of an ungirded technology. The reformer was unable to challenge many of the objective conditions of alienating labor without also challenging the principle under which rewards and drudgery were distributed, and this he was generally unwilling to do. Thus, he often directed his energies towards changing attitudes as they reflected the alienating process. Alienation was treated as a subjective condition, not an objective fact and schooling was designed to change attitudes not to alter the process that created them. The belief in progress served the reform movement by allowing it to minimize the hardships of industrial labor seeing such hardships as moments in a larger movement that was to bring economic prosperity and security to all. Progress was an important aspect of the reformer's world view helping to condition his social-political perceptions by selecting out as insignificant those aspects of American life that, while seemingly essential to developing industrialization, were difficult to subsume under the belief in a democratic America.

---

[46] Ibid., p. 151.
[47] Ibid., p. 140.
[48] Ibid., p. 142.

## IX. THE IDEA OF PROGRESS EVALUATED

There are a number of possible meanings to the assertion that the recent history of civilization reveals a progressive development of man, and each of these meanings was acceptable to Beard and Robinson at one stage or another of their career. Robinson's view that "Every generally accepted idea, every important invention, is but the summation of long lines of progress"[49] implicitly associated progress with the idea of continuity and is better rendered in the following way: given any artifact, idea or institution, its origins can be developmentally traced to artifacts, ideas or institutions of the past. Furthermore, implicit in Robinson's notion of continuity is the idea of a necessary sequence whereby, because of increasing complexity the earlier forms must *necessarily* come into being prior to the latter ones. Thus the sequence of development was not only viewed as chronological, it was also seen as logical. Where technology was concerned not only was the sequence of development logical, it was also inevitable. Beard and Robinson both assumed that regarding technological inventions, if *A* and *B* were necessary for the invention of *C*, and if *A* and *B* were in fact available, then *C* would be invented by someone.[50] While Beard and Robinson attributed an inevitability to inventions in the technological realm, they did not attribute the same quality to institutional and social development. In this area, they felt obliged to call for the willful exercise of human intelligence to bring about the requisite social forms but only within the limits that technology itself had ordained.

More than Beard, Robinson was to confound the notion of continuity with the idea of progress. Robinson's confusion can be expressed as follows: the continuity of history has been established as an objective, scientific truth. We call this continuity progress. Progress implies the continued improvement of the human species. Therefore the continuous improvement of the human species has been established as a scientific proof. Thus by labeling continuity as progress and by then adding some qualities associated with progress but not necessarily with continuity, Robinson could assert that the continuing improvement of the human species is an objective, scientific fact.

---

[49] Ibid., p. 64.

[50] The inevitability of technological development was articulated as an explicit part of W. F. Ogburn's sociology. See William Fielding Ogburn, *Social Change* (New York: Delta Books), 1966 (originally published in 1922).

A second meaning of "progress" is found in the belief that human development and social institutions exhibit a consistent movement towards a goal and that this goal, when expressed in terms of a standard, is judged to be good. Both Beard and Robinson at different times and to differing degrees also accepted this meaning, but they were vague about the specific standard to which they were appealing. While they clearly envisaged an eventual end to the traditional ills of man, such as hunger, disease, and inadequate shelter, they addressed the issue primarily as one of industrial growth and development, not in terms of a standard of distribution. Their assumption seemed to be that if social institutions could be arranged so as to free the production potential of industry, the problems of distribution would automatically be cared for. It was of course reasonable to assume that there was a connection between growth and distribution, for in order to maintain reasonable stability, some minimum individual shares probably needed to be guaranteed. However, there is little reason to believe, even given a minimum share, that continued industrial growth necessarily results in a fair distribution. Without addressing the principle of distribution, this belief was simply a matter of faith.

Eventually Beard was to abandon the position that there was any valid way to measure progress, but instead of abandoning his belief in progress itself, he proposed that the belief should be held for pragmatic reasons alone. As a pragmatic belief, Beard's claim was not that progress could be proven as a fact but that the facticity of the idea is a result of people believing in it. Thus Beard came to argue that those who believed in progress would act in a progressive way. Instead of resigning themselves to the hardships of the world, they would attempt to overcome them, both for themselves and for others. This particular view of progress was accepted by Beard during the 1930s when it was difficult to accept the idea of progress as a fact, and it was also an implicit aspect of Robinson's ideas about the affinity between the new history and social reform.

The validity of the claim to progress depends a great deal on the meaning that is applied at a particular time. Certainly the idea of continuity has the weight of common sense behind it, although it might be countered that there are many leaps whereby a total invention is conceived and then some of the links that are not available in the existing repertory of invention are supplied. The concept of continuity becomes considerably weaker, however, when the idea of logical necessity is attached to it. It may be the case, given the invention of the wheel and the combustion engine, that the automobile was *destined* to be developed, but it may not be the case. Perhaps all that can legitimately be said is that the automobile *was* invented and that these other inventions were invented prior to it. It is not inconceivable, for example, that a certain society because of its moral system would prohibit inventors and technicians from exploring developments of certain kinds, although admittedly, this has been rare in modern Western society. Whether or not this kind of restriction should be advocated is a difficult question to decide with arguments on both sides of the issue. To raise the question, however, is to remove it from the realm of a scientific assertion and place it in the area of moral consideration where it belongs. Neither Robinson or Beard chose to do this. Instead, accepting as inevitable the direction of technological development, they wrote a history that would aid the reformer in adjusting human institutions and attitudes to meet the perceived requirements of the new age.

When Beard abandoned the view that progress could be objectively assessed and began to argue for the pragmatic value of the belief, he raised a number of conceptual problems. Beard abandoned the position that progress could be measured in any objective fashion because he no longer believed that such measurement was possible. Yet he affirmed the value of a belief in progress on the grounds that the belief itself sustains progressive activity. Given the fact that Beard had denied the possibility of measuring progress in an objective fashion, it is difficult to assess his pragmatic argument. For the progressive nature of an activity involves, at least in part, its consequences in the real world. In fact it is the odds and the consequences that help distinguish progressive activity from other, well-intentioned behavior that would be described as Quixotic floundering. In a strict sense, however, when Beard denied that progress could be measured in an objective way, then he implicitly raised some questions about an argument that claims that a belief in progress will lead to progressive activity, and presumably progressive consequences (which cannot, in reality, be measured).

Adopting a looser method of evaluation, however, and assuming with Beard that there are certain obvious facts of human life about which the terms "better" or "worse" can usually be applied, it is not clear just how much a belief in progress supports progressive activity. Beard's treatment of the Indians, Robinson's proposals for the children of the industrial workers indicates that a belief in progress was sometimes joined by a moral complacency that was buoyed by a faith that time and changing conditions would resolve an injustice or end oppression. Often the belief in progress served as a refuge from personal responsibility encouraging the view that the world would eventually catch up to the problem.

More important, the failure to identify a clear-cut standard for evaluating human progress and to rely instead on the functional adjustment of attitudes to the requirements set by industrial growth diverted the liberal analysis from what should have been the obvious implication of Beard's critique of the Constitution—an examination of the relative distribution of power, influence and wealth in the light of some principle of fairness. Instead, however, scholars and policy makers became more satisfied to measure the size of industrial growth and output.

## X. PROGRESS IN LATER SCHOOL TEXTS

Historians have subsequently taken issue with many of the themes and analyses developed by Turner, Beard, and Robinson, but the pervasive and continuing influence of these men has been felt throughout the twentieth century. One exception has been Louis Hartz, who laments the fact that American historians have worked in the shadow of Beard, picking him apart on this or that issue, but never challenging the fundamental categories of historical analysis. One of these categories, as Hartz notes, was the purity of the American nation. "The nation never really sinned: only its inferior self did, its particular will."[51] Another was progress. "There was amidst all the smoke and flame of progressive historical scholarship a continuous note of reassurance. A new Jefferson would arise as he always had before. The reactionaries would be laid low again."[52] With the presence of such faith, there was no need to deeply analyze what might have been structural deficiencies of American society.

Nowhere has greater pain been taken to express the idea of progress than in the public schools. The history textbooks have been the major transmitters of the American faith. Some of these texts such as that written by Ralph V. Harlow were written or revised during wartime and unbashfully expressed their mission:

[51] Louis Hartz, *The Liberal Tradition in America* (New York: Harcourt, Brace and Co.), 1955, p. 31.
[52] Ibid., p. 32.

Today, when the basic principles of our civilization are ridiculed and challenged by barbarians abroad, an understanding of our past has become essential. This knowledge, properly appraised, affords ample ground for pride in our record; it also provides abundant justification for the present war against aggression.[53]

Harlow's text is significant not only in its expression of America's mission, but also as a sample of a treatment of Negro Americans that later came under heavy criticism by civil rights groups. For example, Harlow reports that many slave owners dealt with unrest by treating their slaves with ever more kindness, sometimes cooking them a sumptuous meal, and then he concluded by noting that "it was a rare Negro who could resist the appeal of a good barbeque."[54]

Not all the textbooks written or revised in the 1940s and used in the early 1960s (Harlow's text was revised in 1943 and used into the late 1950s) were quite as vivid as Harlow in their treatment of the Negro, but the theme of progress and mission were almost universal. The widely read Nevins and Commager, for example, acclaimed the unique mission of American society:

From its earliest beginnings, its people have been conscious of a peculiar destiny, because upon it have been fastened the hopes and aspirations of the human race, and because it has not failed to fulfill that destiny or to justify those hopes.[55]

With the advent of the civil rights movement, significant changes were made in the way history and other textbooks treated black Americans, but the theme of progress continues to dominate these texts, and changes have been guided as much by political pressures as by scholarly consensus. The result generally has been that changes have been made only in areas under specific attack while the larger background remains relatively stable. Thus, while the treatment of the black American has improved, the question of violence as part of the American experience is downplayed, and there is still a strong tendency to disparage those, such as certain abolitionists and other reformers, who spoke with "too much" passion against the moral climate of their times.

[53] Ralph Volney Harlow, *The Growth of the United States: Volume I: The Establishment of the Nation Through the Civil War* (rev. ed.) (New York: Henry Holt & Company), 1943, p. v.

[54] Ibid., p. 320.

[55] Allan Nevins and Henry Steele Commager, *The Pocket History of the United States* (New York: Pocket Books), 1956, p. v.

Similar tendencies are also carried over into non-history textbooks. Basic readers now picture black faces, but any cultural distinctions are downplayed, hair is short-cropped, and dress is almost always conventional and middle-class. Marital patterns, whether black or white, consist of the conventional pattern and rarely are single parent households depicted. Moreover, father goes out to work while mother stays home to clean house.[56]

## XI. THE IDEA OF PROGRESS AND EDUCATIONAL HISTORIES

Besides the view communicated by the textbooks, the belief in progress had another relation to schooling. It is to be found, implicitly or explicitly, in the writings of almost all educational historians, whether of conservative or liberal persuasion.[57] If historians accepted the idea of a national mission in the cause of civilization, many educational historians believed that the schools were the primary instrument for carrying out that mission. Ellwood P. Cubberley, influential for his books on educational practice and history, as well as in his position as Head and Dean of the College of Education at Stanford University from 1898 to 1933, saw in American education the wisdom of the protestant mind at work preparing the ground in the nineteenth century for the resolution of problems that the nation was to encounter in the twentieth. Cubberley's image of the immigrant was no more flattering than that held by many in the testing movement. The new immigrants from southern and eastern Europe, in contrast to the older ones from England, Scotland, Germany, and Scandinavia, were seen as undemocratic, selfish, of low intelligence, and, in general, a serious problem for the political institutions of democracy to cope with. It was precisely in anticipation of such problems, Cubberley wrote, that the early educational leaders fought the battles to establish free public schooling. The national salvation

[56] For a more detailed treatment of the way basic readers treat social themes see the faculty and students in HP Ed 304, "The Teacher and His Material," *The Elementary School Journal,* Vol. 73, No. 7, April, 1973, pp. 347-353.

[57] Some recent exceptions to this view may be the historians Edward Krug, Clarence Karier, Paul Violas, and Michael Katz.

rested on the public schools and those associated with it; the superinten-dents, principals, and professors of education (conspicuously absent from this list, much to their credit, are teachers) were doing more for the national welfare than any other single group.[58] Cubberley had no doubt that given a scientific policy of restrictive immigration, the public school could carry on its mission.

Although Cubberley's image of the immigrant was especially in-sulting, the notion that the public schools were established to carry out a specific mission was a common theme among educational historians throughout the twentieth century. The battles that took place during the nineteenth century for free public education were seen often as conflicts between the forces of progress against those of "indifference, selfishness and conservatism."[59]

Many educational historians were to see the educational develop-ments of this century as representing the increasing realization of the nation's commitment to equality. Little research was performed in order to discover just how much equality occurred as a result of such things as increased school attendance. Also overlooked was the question of whether mobility could be best accounted for by openings at the top or by new groups coming in at the bottom. Recently, educational historians have seen an increasing movement towards equality and have often traced it to the moral requirements demanded by the nation's leadership in the fight against international communism and to the need to con-vince others of our sincerity.[60]

A belief in progress continues as the dominant assumption behind the writings of most contemporary educational historians. Cremin,[61] in a work on the evolution of the common school, expressed the belief that the philosophy of Thomas Jefferson provided the outline for the subse-quent development of American education. Jefferson "embraced the complimentary commitment of a free society to equality and to excel-

---

[58] Ellwood P. Cubberley, *An Introduction to the Study of Education and to Teaching* (Boston: Houghton Mifflin Co.), 1925, p. 29.

[59] Edward H. Reisner, *The Evolution of the Common School* (New York: The Macmillan Co.), 1935, p. 320.

[60] This was one of the themes for example of Merle Curti's new introduc-tion, "The Last Twenty-Fve Years," to his *Social Ideas of American Educators,* rev. ed. (Patterson, New Jersey: Littlefield, Adams and Co.), 1961.

[61] See Chapter Three.

lence, guaranteeing a minimum education to all citizens and offering further education to those who desire it and who qualify."[62] Subsequent to Jefferson, Cremin suggests that the remainder of American education can be seen as the working out of one side or another of his idea. The school is thereby pictured as the source of social mobility increasingly offering to people the chance to develop their talents on an equal basis with others. The image is not false, but it is likely distorted because it fails to examine other factors. It is not necessarily the case that because upward mobility has occurred and because most of those people that have been upwardly mobile have also had some public schooling, that the latter is the cause of the former. Indeed, recent research seems to suggest that the causal relationship is less than usually supposed.[63] The other side of this picture is the extent to which the public schools have been used not primarily as vehicles for either freedom or equality, but for controlling potentially dissonant elements. Freedom and equality have had their place as elements in the function of control, but in this function the belief in mobility was more important than the fact. Nor, of course, has much serious attention been given to an evaluation of the ideal of equality of opportunity as a guiding principle for education.[64]

Even in those areas where equality has obviously not been the case, educational historians have tended to see the primary direction of schooling as a progressive development towards freedom and equality. In some instances, this development is viewed as an inevitable movement, taking place independently and often times in spite of the actual decisions of educational leaders. Henry Allen Bullock's recent synoptic history of Negro education[65] is a case in point. Unlike many who evaluate the post-reconstruction education of the black man in terms of its adequacy as a response to existing situations and attitudes, Bullock reveals the fact that such education was designed to establish inferior

[62] Lawrence A. Cremin, *The Genius of American Education* (New York: Vintage Books), 1965, p. 40.

[63] For a recent challenge to traditional ideas of equality of opportunity see Colin Greer, *The Great School Legend* (New York: Basic Books), 1972. Also see Chapter Seven of this book for a critique of Greer's point of view.

[64] See Chapter Seven for a critique of the idea of equality of educational opportunity.

[65] Henry Allen Bullock, *A History of Negro Education in the South, From 1619 to the Present* (Cambridge: Harvard University Press), 1967.

training and to reinforce an inferior status. Nevertheless, he believes that the primary direction of black education has been towards freedom and equality, a direction that had been set during reconstruction by the northern missionaries who established schools in the south. Keeping his faith in progress alive, Bullock describes the more than 80-year period in which industrial and separate education marked the instruction of the black man as "the great detour," suggesting that history sometimes leaves the main road, but, in spite of the intentions and the acts of men, it eventually gets back on course. The development of the civil rights movement, the point at which Bullock believes Negro education began again to approach the main road, is but the unintended, yet seemingly inevitable result of the system of industrial education. In the work of both Cremin and Bullock as in that of Beard and Robinson there is a strong hint of a necessary historical movement that proceeds in a zigzag but consistent path towards freedom, equality, and progress. And in these hints they carry forth a tradition that is to be found in most other educational historians throughout this century.

## XII. SUMMARY

Of all who expressed a belief in progress during this century, few stated it as strongly as James Harvey Robinson. Robinson believed that progress was not only an inevitable aspect of human civilization and an objective, scientific fact, it was also the pivotal point for the scientific study of history. Progressive development was the brute fact with which historical inquiry began and the historian's task was to unfold its component parts and accelerate its development. Few expressed their belief quite this strongly, but most followed Robinson's guidelines. It was believed that the schools obviously represented the most progressive development of freedom and equality and with this as their starting point, educational historians had only to trace the roots of this wise and collective enterprise. Yet there was a good deal of ambiguity in the meaning of "progress" and in only one sense—the notion of continuity —could progress be taken as an objective, even if not a universal fact. Obviously, to restrict the notion of progress to that of a continuity of parts without also agreeing that that continuity has somehow contributed significantly to the well being of the human species was not satisfactory for most of the people we have discussed in this chapter.

Nevertheless, it is a sobering thought to think of the wars that have been fought this century, the carnage and ruin, and the destruction of peoples and cultures before lauding too highly our role as the leader of civilization in the twentieth century. The point is not that we were totally responsible for all of the wars fought and the destruction that resulted from them. It is merely that we must come to accept a great deal as fixed and determined before we can come to the point now of believing that this century has shown man the best possible life.

It must be admitted with Beard that a belief in progress is a powerful weapon in directing the actions of men. And, perhaps, it is a weapon, not as an assertion of fact, that it is best judged. Beard felt that a belief in progress was a force for progressive action, and there is some truth to this. If men are certain that their actions will bear little fruit, they are perhaps less prone to act than if they believe otherwise. At least this is so if they also believe that intelligent *moral* action must carry with it any guarantee of success. But a belief in progress has been a two-edged sword. If it has motivated people to act on some issues, it has dictated patience on other, equally important ones. And if it has led men to address fundamental social problems in some areas, it has also inhibited them from asking fundamental questions in others.

# CHAPTER SIX
# The Liberal's Image of Society:
## Intelligence at the Service of Power

## I. INTRODUCTION

One of the consistent threads of liberal ideology has been the belief that social progress could best be accomplished by working through the accepted avenues of authority. This was one very important reason why schools were such attractive vehicles for liberal reform, and we have cited instances such as Dewey's Polish study, the work of the Bureau of Intercultural Education, where this ideology was translated into liberal practice. Yet there have been many times when liberal reformers themselves would admit that their efforts have been subverted by the established channels, thus suggesting that the responsibility for social problems is not to be found in the liberal idea itself. In this way, some liberal reformers have been able to maintain a somewhat radical tone, as they "pushed" the power structure to its limits.

Many think of progressive reform as the radical wing of education and indeed some of the most penetrating analyses of the relationship between school and society were written by progressive educators during the 1920s and 1930s when they argued that the hand of the business establishment rested too heavily on American policy. Early in the 1920s, for example, Dewey came out for restrictive immigration legislation on the unorthodox ground that an unchecked flow of immigrants would allow the capitalists to manipulate labor to its own advantage, and in the early 1930s he advised that blacks should support a socialist political alternative.[1] In 1928 Counts published his penetrating study of the Chicago schools[2] which showed the influence of the business interests in determining curriculum. In some of these critiques was to be found a strong hint that America, in the traditional Marxian sense, is a class society in which the owners or managers dominate the secondary institutions, including the schools.

Yet the radical element of liberal and progressive education must be viewed within the context of the times and within the larger framework of more general views about society. The class analysis offered by some during the twenties and thirties was never really acceptable to most educators who viewed themselves as progressive, and as the United States moved out of the depression with the power of the federal government significantly increased, the tone of even the "radical" progressive commentary shifted to a more acceptable interest group analysis of American society. This is understandable given the wider intellectual context of progressive thought. Progressive and liberal educational reform arose as a reaction to a traditional distrust of large and powerful government and it was developed by men who believed that the unfettering of technology required changes in the location of power and in people's attitude towards its exercise by big government. Thus it was not tactical considerations alone which led liberal reformers to work through established political structures in effecting their reforms, for their own ideology set the limits of reform within those very structures.

With these considerations in mind, this chapter examines the "radical" edge of progressive reform within the context of larger

---

[1] See John Dewey, "Racial Prejudice and Friction," *Chinese Social and Political Science Review,* VI, 1921, 1-17. I am indebted to Ronald Goodenow for bringing this article to my attention.

[2] George S. Counts, *School and Society in Chicago* (New York: Harcourt, Brace and Co.), 1928.

ideological concerns. The central focus is on the progressives' image of society and the liberal's belief about the proper role of the intellectual within the social order.

The progressives' image of society served a function similar to their image of history and the idea of progress which governed it. Both allowed reformers to place certain events in a larger context and thereby to maintain their faith in key social institutions and in the belief that most social problems could eventually be resolved through the educational institutions. However, there is an important difference between their image of history and their image of society. The idea of progress with American society on the cutting edge of civilization's advance was in general an uncriticized assumption of progressive thought, one which they did not feel the need to argue at great length. The liberal view of society, however, was challenged from a number of fronts. Marxists felt that it misrepresented the nature of American society, while traditional conservatives balked because of the expanded governmental power which it implied. Thus reform theorists were forced to argue more explicitly for their position. These arguments span many years and it is only in the later stages, during the 1950's, that their full implication is revealed. Thus in examining the image of society, this chapter traces the arguments that were used to support the liberal view and in doing so highlights the limits that were placed on the reform ideology.

## II. MARXISM IN RETREAT

In 1932 Counts is said to have shocked the Progressive Education Association with a speech entitled "Dare the Schools Build a New Social Order" and ever since the progressive movement had been identified as a radical force in American education. Unfortunately the subsequent answer to Counts' challenge was no, neither progresive educators nor the schools dared to build a new social order. Nevertheless, in the eyes of its critics, from the American Legion and Joseph McCarthy through Dwight Eisenhower, Admiral Rickover, and Ronald Reagan and despite numerous denials to the contrary, progressive education has been depicted as peopled by untamed radicals intent on corrupting America's young, and redistributing her vast wealth to the "less resourceful" elements of the population. The reasonableness of such a program is not at issue here, but the accuracy of the image is. Counts' career, although somewhat to the left of the mainstream of the movement, is a generally accurate mirror of its progression. He began the 1930's with a call to educators to build a new social order; he ended them by combatting Communist influence in the teacher's union. By the late 1940s just as most progressive reformers were turning their attention to life adjustment programs, Counts joined forces with the cold warriors of the educational and political establishment with a series of works comparing the promise of America to the oppression of the Soviet Union.

Although Counts maintained the validity of the class analysis longer than most, his career is a muted reflection of the conservative drift of progressive education. Because Counts is viewed as one of the more radical progressive educators, the changes in tone and emphasis in his writings can illustrate the general direction of the progressive ideas.

During the late 1920s and early 1930s Counts' writing is clearly the most radical.[3] During this period two themes recur again and again. The first is the need for large scale planning, and the second is an apparent demand for some redistribution of wealth. Regarding the first of these themes, Counts wrote in 1934:

American society is not planned: it grows in response to the drive of internal forces and within the limits set by external circumstances and the interaction of its various members. . . . Although the individual commonwealth and the federal union have both gradually increased the scope of their activities, yet it remains substantially true that American society possesses neither the will nor the means for planning the general evolution of the social structure.[4]

The theme of social planning remained consistent throughout Counts' writings, but the call to redistribute national wealth was expressed

---

[3] To some extent Lawrence Cremin in *The Transformation of the School* emphasizes the radical Marxian elements in Counts although he is careful to separate Counts from the Marxists. Gerald L. Gutek in *The Educational Theory of George S. Counts* (Columbus: University of Ohio Press), 1970 deemphasizes the Marxian aspect of Counts' thought. Given the total span of Counts' career, Gutek's view is probably the more accurate of the two, but in view of Counts' most conspicuous period during the early and middle 1930s, it is quite reasonable to read his works in a Marxist light. It also is the case that as Counts' position towards the Soviet Union hardened he read his later views back into his earlier works.

[4] George S. Counts, *American Road to Culture* (New York: The John Day Co., Inc.), 1930, pp. 174-175.

less emphatically after 1935. Commenting on the Soviet five-year plan in 1932, for example, Counts emphasized both the need for planning and for the redistribution of wealth. A similar five-year plan in America, noted Counts,

Would be very unlike the Soviet plan. Our industrial plant has been constructed. The need for sacrifice, like that demanded in Russia, would not exist. Our problem would be one of utilizing the facilities which we already possess and of *distributing economic goods to the population.*[5]

While the need for state planning remained a major theme throughout Counts' writings, the call for a redistribution of wealth was later muted and replaced by a somewhat more conservative appeal. In 1934, for example, Counts provided a typically Marxian analysis of American government:

It (American government) has commonly been the tool of powerful groups devoted to the attainment of special ends. . . . Class control of the state would seem to be securely rooted in the institutions of capitalistic society.[6]

By 1938 a different emphasis and a different picture of American institutions was presented.

Let the experiment with free institutions fail here and men and women in all lands will lose faith in the possibility of organizing a society of, by and for the many. It may be said today, as it was said by Washington, that the destiny of free institutions is "justly considered . . . as stated in the experiment intrusted to the American people."[7]

The new emphasis had implications for the school. Instead of building "a new social order," the school, said Counts,

Should seek to enlist the energies and talents of the rising generation in the realization of a program dedicated to the purpose of conserving and re-enforcing the great cultural pattern of democracy.[8]

---

[5] George S. Counts, "Soviet Planing and the Five Year Plan," in Counts, Villart, Rorty and Baker, *Bolshevism, Fascism and Capitalism* (New Haven: Yale University Press), p. 53. Emphasis mine.

[6] Counts, *Social Foundations of Education* (New York: Charles Scribner's Sons), 1934, pp. 524-525. Parentheses mine.

[7] Counts, *Prospects of American Democracy* (New York: The John Day Co.), 1938, pp. 359-360.

[8] Counts, *The School Can Teach Democracy* (New York: The John Day Co., Inc.), 1939, p. 32.

Even Counts' class analysis of American society changed over the years as he moved closer to the view that America was comprised of different and conflicting groups, each pressuring a relatively flexible government to accommodate itself to its particular interest. In 1926 Counts expressed a radical view of American society in commenting on the capitalist's control of education:

Except for the district and county boards on which the farming population is strongly represented, these boards are composed for the most part of members of the favored economic classes. . . . The control of education rests in the hands of the capitalists and closely associated class.[9]

Again, the projection for education was quite clear. "Until capitalism or political democracy begins to crumble, the school will probably be used as an institution for supporting it."[10] By 1932, when Counts delivered his "Dare the Schools Build a New Social Order," he expressed more optimism about the role of education in social change, but the analysis still had a radical tone. By 1938, Counts was retreating from his class analysis of American society. Although he still held to the belief that America contained an economic aristocracy, he more firmly eschewed class violence,[11] thus highlighting the already present differences between himself and the Marxists—differences that were previously deemphasized. More important, he expressed the belief that the plurality of groups in America could hold the line against an aristocracy that he saw in retreat. While still adhering to an economic interpretation of social organizations, Counts no longer saw the aristocracy in control, and wrote as if the essential battle had been won.

The natural and most basic pattern of popular organization in contemporary society follows the lines of production. Already this type of combination either in industrial or craft form is well advanced through labor unions, farmer organizations, and numerous bodies of technical and professional workers. The experience of both Europe and America demonstrates fully that these organizations, and particularly the unions of manual workers, are the democratic clubs of the present day, the defenders of popular rights, the foes of aristocracy, the most powerful bulwark against the resurgence of autocracy.[12]

[9] Counts, "Place of the School in the Social Order," in National Education Association, *Addresses and Proceedings,* 1926, Vol. 64, p. 313.
[10] Ibid., p. 315.
[11] See *Prospects for American Democracy,* p. 530.
[12] Ibid., pp. 181-182.

Often, he was simply to affirm that the battle could be fought and won through established channels. "An informed, determined and united popular will cannot be thwarted long at the polls."[13] By the late 1940s Counts was thoroughly convinced of the soundness of American society. And in the late 1950s he joined the chorus of concern over the Soviet's Sputnik hoping only that American society and education was not so decentralized as to fail to meet the challenge.[14]

## III. THE PROGRESSIVE
## IDEAL OF MANAGEMENT

Dewey, Counts, and other progressives achieved their radical reputation during the late 1920s and the early 1930s largely because of their limited flirtation with Marxist philosophy. It was also during this time that they were attracted to the political and educational experiments being carried out in the Soviet Union. What attracted them to Marxism and to the Soviet Union was not only the attempt to close the gap between wealth and poverty (although this was a factor) but also the promise that they believed such experiments held for controlling the activities of a large population towards a common end. Dewey's description of the relationship between education and propaganda in the Soviet Union reveals part of the appeal that the experiment had for him:

Nowhere else in the world is employment of it (propaganda) as a tool of control so constant, consistent, and systematic as in Russia at present. Indeed, it has taken on such importance and social dignity that the word propaganda hardly carries, in another social medium, the correct meaning. For we instinctively associate propaganda with the accomplishing of some specific ends, more or less private to a particular class or group and correspondingly concealed from others. But in Russia the propaganda is in behalf of a burning public faith. One may believe that the leaders are wholly mistaken in the object of their faith, but their sincerity is beyond question. To them the end for which propaganda is employed is not a private or even a class gain, but is the universal good of universal humanity.

[13] Ibid., p. 67.
[14] See Counts' introduction to George S. Counts, *Khrushchev and the Central Committee Speak on Education* (Pittsburgh: University of Pittsburgh Press), 1959.

In consequence propaganda is education and education is propaganda. They are more than confounded; they are identical.[15]

Counts expressed a similar sentiment a few years later:

If progressive education is to be genuinely progressive, it must emancipate itself from the influence of this (middle) class, face squarely and courageously every social issue, come to grips with life in all its stark reality, establish an organic relation with community, develop a realistic and comprehensive theory of welfare, fashion a compelling and challenging vision of human destiny, *and become less frightened than it is today at the bogeys of imposition and indoctrination.*[16]

The appeal that the early phases of the Soviet experiment held for these educators was as much an indication of their essentially managerial philosophy as it was an expression of their ideas on social justice. Because they were never very clear about the requirements of justice for the distribution of national wealth, the managerial ideas of industrial growth and planning became ever more attractive as cures for poverty and social instability.

The managerial side of progressive thought is perhaps more obviously apparent in the thought of progressive political scientists such as Charles Merriam (1874-1953)[17] about schooling than it is in the writings of the educational progressives. Merriam's interest in schooling developed from his belief that the rapidity of technological change threatened the stability of societies everywhere and that internal peace depended upon the establishment of a common national allegiance.[18] He was concerned about the potentially disruptive antagonisms that existed among different nationality and ethnic groups within the nation,

---

[15] John Dewey, *Character and Events,* Vol. 1 (New York: Henry Holt & Co.), 1929, p. 399. Reprinted with the permission of the *Center for Dewey Studies,* Southern Illinois University at Carbondale.

[16] Counts, *Dare the Schools Build a New Social Order,* mimeographed copy, parentheses and emphasis mine.

[17] Merriam spent the major part of his professional life as a professor of political science at the University of Chicago, but he was an influential figure in educational circles as well as in political ones. He ran for mayor of Chicago in 1911 and served on a number of significant national committees during the Hoover and Roosevelt administrations.

[18] Cf. George Z. F. Bereday's introduction to Charles E. Merriam's *The Making of Citizens* (New York: Teacher's College Press), 1966, especially p. 4.

and he saw in the school a way to resolve these antagonisms. The schools' function was first to create a citizenry that was responsive to technological changes and second to shift primary allegiance from local groups and symbols to national ones. Social science, which he described as an essentially neutral instrument, was an important means to alter attitudes and manipulate loyalties. As Merriam observed, "the question of how much economic pressure, or ethnic pressure, or religious or cultural pressure is necessary to induce the patriot to change his allegiance has never been intensively studied and the whole field remains for the most part a *terra incognita*, inviting the attention of the student of government disposed to wander from the more professional or usual subject of inquiry."[19] He rejected the cruder instruments of indoctrination for the more sophisticated one of behavior modification in the hope that "no one escapes the formal educational system with a disintegrated, disordered, or unbalanced personality, or a type that will obstruct the process of orderly human relations in the field of politics."[20] Although Merriam is identified more with the political than the educational progressive his writings anticipated much of the direction of subsequent progressive educational thought.

Dewey shared with Merriam the belief that the function of the school was to shift loyalties from one group to another. The Deweys' descriptive citation of the Gary School in *Schools of Tomorrow* provides some idea of the techniques that were available for this purpose.

They (the immigrant parents) are naturally suspicious of Government and social authority . . . and it is very important that their children should have some real knowledge on which to base a sounder judgment. Besides giving them this, the schools try to teach American standards of living to the pupils and so to their parents. On entering school every pupil gives the school office, besides the usual name, age, and address, certain information about his family, its size, its resources, and the character of the home he lives in. This record is kept in the school and transferred if the child moves out of the school district. . . . By comparing these with any family record, it is a simple matter to tell if the family are living under proper moral and hygienic conditions. . . . If bad conditions are due to ignorance or poverty, the teacher finds out what can be done to remedy them, and sees to it that the family learns how they can better themselves. *If conditions are very bad,*

---

[19] Merriam, *The Making of Citizens*, p. 42.
[20] Ibid., p. 380.

*neighborhood public opinion is worked up through the children on the block.*[21]

The managerial concerns of progressive thought and the use of the schools to shift loyalties from local to national groups was consistent with the larger framework that Dewey had established in his *Human Nature and Conduct* where the moral problem was to "change the character or will of another."[22] Yet there was more to it than this, for there was also the belief that the larger structure to which loyalties were to be directed was basically sound. It was at this point that the progressive image of society played a key role.

## IV. CONFLICTING CLASSES OR PRESSURING GROUPS

The radical image of progressive education arose largely because of the attitude of people like Dewey, Counts, and others towards the experiments of the Soviet Union during the 1920s, but it arose too because of the later debates that took place regarding the merits of a class analysis of American society. A few progressives, such as Counts, and John Childs, were especially taken with the class analysis of American society and at least during the early and middle 1930s, argued that many of the difficulties of the American nation resulted from the wide discrepancy in wealth. Much of their analysis, however, centered only upon the so-called business establishment, and except for some harsh words about the Hoover administration and some disenchantment with the early phases of the Roosevelt administration, after 1936 there was little analysis of the relation between business and government, and of the possible interrelationships between the two. Indeed throughout this era there was a strong hint that the problems created by business could be solved if more power were given to the government.

Nevertheless, during the 1930s some progressives adopted a class analysis of American society arguing that teachers would find their most

---

[21] John and Evelyn Dewey, *Schools of Tomorrow*, pp. 147-148. Copyright, 1915, by E. P. Dutton and Company, Inc. Renewal, 1943 John Dewey and Evelyn Dewey. Renewal © 1962 by E. P. Dutton & Co., Inc. Publishers, and used with their permission.

[22] See Chapter One of this book.

natural alliance with the working class of the American nation. During these years a loose coalition was formed between the more radical members of the progressive education movement (centered at Columbia University) such as George Counts, John Childs, Theodore Brameld, and, to a lesser extent, John Dewey, Harold Rugg, and W. H. Kilpatrick with people from other areas of academic life such as Sidney Hook, Charles Beard, and Merle Curti. The members of this coalition were committed to the development of what was loosely and vaguely called democratic collectivism. Issues such as the proper relationship between teachers and workers, the appropriateness of indoctrination, and others were debated in the pages of the *Social Frontier* magazine. In the course of these debates two conflicting analyses of American society were put forth.

The November, 1935, issue of *The Social Frontier* contained an article by Theodore Brameld entitled "Karl Marx and the American Teacher" in which Brameld, without explicitly advocating the Marxist position, sympathetically explicated it. An editorial in the same issue proposed that it was part of the teacher's role to dispel the myth that Americans live in a classless society and to reveal instead the vast discrepancies in wealth that persisted in American society. The editors further argued that a sharp class distinction existed between those in America who own the wealth and those who create it and that teachers, as creators of wealth, should find their natural alliance with the working-class population. While the details of such an alliance were not spelled out, at the very least it was proposed that teachers should give their support to the teacher's union and that they should find a way in their classrooms to provide a more sympathetic treatment of collectivist alternatives. The debate that followed in subsequent issues of *The Social Frontier* has been often cited as evidence of the radical flavor of progressive education, but the debate was short-lived, because it went outside the acceptable limits of progressive ideology. Evidence that the editors had ventured outside of the mainstream of the movement is apparent even from the early depression writings of Dewey. In his 1929 *Individualism: Old and New*, for example, Dewey had put forth as a "socialist" alternative to American *laissez-faire* capitalism only such ameliorative reforms as the progressive income tax and expansion of federal control commissions. And in his 1935 volume of *Liberalism and Social Action,* Dewey gave evidence of the fact that the flirtation with the class analysis of American society was soon to end.

Anyone habituated to the use of the method of science will view with considerable suspicion the erection of human beings into fixed entities called classes, having no overlapping interests and so internally unified and externally separated that they are made the protagonists of history— itself hypothetical.[23]

Even though Dewey himself would occasionally slip into the language of class antagonisms, once the spectra of science was raised against this point of view, the lesson to others became increasingly clear. Indeed it could be no other way for almost all progressives had accepted as a cure to problems brought about by the abuses of big business, the expansion of governmental power. To therefore adopt a point of view that would have looked on government as the essential agent of the wealthy and managerial classes would have been inconsistent to this fundamental commitment. To accent the point, R. Bruce Raup warned in the pages of the *Social Frontier,* that the progressive theorist should take special care to vigorously assert the differences between his own views and those of the Marxist.

Educators like Raup, Rugg, and Kilpatrick who challenged the class analysis, argued that American society presented no clear-cut class divisions, but instead that a variety of memberships existed within the same individual, thus obscuring any sharp line of difference. Emphasizing the common factors shared by different people they argued for a strategy of change that would begin by building a consensus from among people of seemingly different backgrounds and economic conditions. The primary vehicle for building such a consensus would be education. They further argued that once such a consensus was built, it could find expression through normal and already established democratic channels and procedures. Indeed it was felt that both owners and workers could be persuaded to accept some form of "democratic collectivism" but precisely what form either worker or owner might be willing to accept was not yet clearly specified.

In the February issue, Harold Rugg took Raup's advice and set out to define an alternative to Marxism. Observing that American society was not to be understood by concepts drawn from the European experience, Rugg denied the applicability of the class analysis to American

---

[23] John Dewey, *Liberalism and Social Action* (New York: G. P. Putnam's Sons), 1935, p. 80.

life. Americans, he observed, simply do not think of themselves as members of any socioeconomic class. Rather than dividing themselves into rigidly antagonistic groups, Americans view their country as a land of opportunity where a person, regardless of race, creed, or ancestry, can make of himself whatever he wills. They believe that the boundaries between classes are blurred and therefore that they live in a classless society. The American mind is permeated with the psychology of ownership, and even a majority of the working class, Rugg observed, "hold the outlook and loyalties of owners of property."[24] Thus he concluded that the Marxian analysis does not apply to the social or historical conditions of American society.

As an alternative to Marxism, Rugg proposed that American society was best understood as an interplay of different interest groups, each pressuring the government for one cause or another. And the government's response was best viewed as a fluid one, varying with the changing pressure. "Their requests, demands, or pleas are granted, rejected or ignored in proportion to the volume of coercive threat carried by their lobbies. Thus all of these groups are 'in government' although most of them disclaim it."[25]

While Rugg's argument did little to intellectually resolve the issue, it helped to reinforce the interest group theory as an alternative to a class analysis. Rugg's argument failed intellectually because even if one granted that his description of the perceptions of the American people was correct, it did not follow that the failure of Americans to perceive themselves as members of a particular class, or that their identification with the owning class, was based on a careful analysis of their own position and interest. If one believed, on careful examination of evidence, that America was really governed by a ruling class serving primarily its own interest, but also perceived that most Americans viewed their society in other ways, then the most reasonable strategy for social change would be to try to bring about an awareness of the way things really are. One cannot adequately argue against a purported fact by suggesting simply that the majority of people do not believe in it; nor can one argue that America is not amenable to a class analysis simply because the majority of people do not perceive themselves to be

[24] *The Social Frontier,* February, 1936, p. 141.
[25] *The Social Frontier,* February, 1936, p. 139.

members of any particular class. Neither was it sufficient to observe the government's fluid response to varying pressures. For once it is admitted that Americans do not correctly perceive the nature of their society, then all of the pressures are in fact circumscribed by the way they do see it.

Considering that progressives themselves had occasion to cite the enormous discrepancy in the distribution of wealth, power, and influence in American society, it was indeed the case that the class analysis was dismissed too quickly. Nevertheless, after offering his interest group analysis, Rugg proposed that change could come about through the development of a new consensus brought about primarily through the schools.[26] He did not say how the schools, as public institutions, would be able to override the influence of the very pressures upon itself which the new consensus was expected to resolve. It should be noted, however, that even those who were more friendly to the class analysis also saw the school as a primary vehicle for shifting society in the desired direction and this view of course separated them from the orthodox Marxist.

Even though a few progressives continued to push for the appropriateness of the class analysis, only John Childs, among the mainline progressives, challenged the adequacy of Rugg's argument.

The real irony of the debate can only be understood by estimating just how well the pressure group theory may have been working in quieting and limiting the scope of the class analysis. The warning was sounded more than once that lest the progressives be misunderstood, they should be careful to separate themselves from the Marxists. It is not quite clear who might misunderstand them. Certainly not the American Legion, which would have burned Rugg's textbooks whether they thought him to be a Marxist or merely a left-wing collectivist. Yet in spite of hostility from the extreme right, progressive education had come a long way since Rice's first critique of the nation's schools appeared in *The Forum*. It had become an acceptable program of education in the eyes of even many of the wealthy elite. Indeed Rugg sat on the commission of the eight-year study supported ($70,000) by the Carnegie Foundation and ($1,500,000) by the Rockefeller-based

---

[26] The use of the schools is implicit in the article under discussion and more explicit elsewhere.

general education board. Even the *Social Frontier* journal was not immune from such pressure, and in 1937 the editors (Counts, Grossman, and Woelfel) were replaced. After making a succession of appeals to the Progressive Education Association (many of whose members looked with a prejudiced and conservative eye to activities on their left) to take over the journal and after a series of refusals, as Cremin notes, "the PEA accepted, stipulating that the name be changed to *Frontiers of Democracy* and that a new board of editors be constituted to remove the taint of radicalism."[27]

## V. LEGITIMIZING POWER

The limits of the liberal educator's radicalism can be understood by examining the political implications of the pressure group theory. Ever since the first systematic exposition during this century by Arthur Bentley in 1908, the interest group theory has been used to discourage discussion of the principles by which a society might choose to distribute justice and wealth. Instead it has encouraged an examination of the mechanisms by which a government could maintain social stability, and it has tended to equate social stability with justice.

Although liberals argued that their ideas were a reaction to a *laissez-faire* theory on which an oppressive and unjust society had been built, their own social theory was significantly analogous to the one they sought to replace. Because they believed that adherence to the business morality of the time, supported by *laissez-faire* theory, was inconsistent with the goals of national growth and prosperity, they offered the interest group theory of society as an alternative to a *laissez-faire* point of view.[28] While liberals were quick to remove their faith from the dynamics of a free market economy, they were equally quick to place it in the dynamics of government believing that the structure of American public institutions provided ample safeguards against the exercise of tyranny.

The argument that was put forth by Bentley in his 1908 classic *The Process of Government* formed the foundation of the progressives' later critiques of the Marxian analysis of American society. In the

[27] Cremin, *Transformations,* pp. 232-233.
[28] The interest group theory was also offered as an alternative to Marxism.

1950s, the interest group theory was further refined by political scientists such as Robert Dahl, David Truman, and Daniel Bell. The basic point of the argument was that the stability of a society is correlated with the ability of its government to respond to the pressures put forth by different groups, and implicitly that if a government is flexible and able to manipulate and assuage different interests, it is worthy of support. Even though it was admitted that any individual governmental minister may be biased toward a given interest, it was argued that over a reasonable period of time the dynamics of government work in such a way as to neutralize (within broad limits) the advantage that any single group may obtain over another. Proponents of the theory have generally been vague about whether they are proposing an ideal social order or whether they are actually describing an existing government, such as that of the United States. However, when it is proposed that all groups (with a few minor and rectifiable exceptions) generally have adequate access to the government, the implication is that a real state of affairs is being described and further that this real state of affairs approximates the best possible state of affairs.[29]

Except perhaps in its formative stages, the pressure-group theory of government has generally served as a conserving influence in American society discouraging discussions of distributive justice. This is not surprising since the structure of the argument is almost a mirror image of the *laissez-faire* analysis that progressives correctly criticized as serving a similar function. In each case there is a series of countervailing pressures acting upon the other and, in the long run, canceling out the undesirable effects of the other. The difference between the two theories lies only in the particular institutions and roles that are thought to play a significant part in the dynamics of society. In the first instance the key roles are played by independent businessmen, laborers, and consumers whose conflicting self-interests are thought to work themselves out in the marketplace to the ultimate benefit of society as a whole. In the second instance the principal actors are groups that are usually, but not necessarily, motivated by economic considerations. Such groups are represented by business and labor associations, ethnic or sectional groups, and by a variety of others. In the second theory the participation of the individual in a variety of conflicting groups is stressed more than

[29] For an example of this see Robert A. Dahl, *A Preface to Democratic Theory* (Chicago: University of Chicago Press), 1956.

in the first. In each, however, the fact of multimembership is seen as an important element in maintaining political stability and social wealth. Thus if wages are lower than desired the wage earner later reaps the benefits when he buys goods. For the *laissez-faire* theorist, such pressures are played out in the marketplace where goods are bought and sold. The pressure-group theorist believes, on the other hand, that such conflicts are played out in the legislative and executive halls of government where a balance is achieved between them.

When progressive educators like Rugg adopted the pressure group concept, they saw it both as an alternative to Marxism and to *laissez-faire* capitalism. It was advanced as a way to remove power from the business establishment and to place it in the government. What they failed to emphasize was that the theory is an argument for political stability, but not necessarily for political justice. In a world in which all decisions are made by groups pressuring the decision-makers in government, then those who will be favored are those who can muster the most pressure, and these are, of course, the already favored groups.[30] Certainly, for example, progressives were correct in perceiving that there was a possible consensus that could include businessmen. For if, as was the case, business suffered at the ups and downs of an unsupervised market, then clearly an increase in the regulatory power of government was not antagonistic to business interests, and especially to big business. It is doubtful, however, whether a shift in the locus of decision-making would also be accompanied by a corresponding shift in the distribution of social justice and rewards.

The conservative implications of the theory were clearly present in the 1908 statement of it offered by Bentley as he chose to identify the ruling class with the interest of the ruled.

Except in the case of a subjected population immediately under the heel of the conqueror under conditions of most primitive oppression, the ruling class is to a certain extent, the chosen (that is, the accepted) ruler of the ruled class, not merely its master, but also its representative; and the despot at the top of the system is representative both of his own class, and to a smaller but nonetheless real, extent of the ruled class as well.[31]

[30] For an elaboration of this point, see Robert Paul Wolff, "Beyond Tolerance" in R. P. Wolff, B. Moore, Jr., and H. Marcuse, *A Critique of Pure Tolerance* (Boston: Beacon Press), 1969, pp. 3-52.

[31] Arthur Bentley, *The Process of Government* (Cambridge, Mass.: Belknap Press of Harvard University Press), 1967, pp. 314-315.

The theory entails a methodology that allows many significant factors to be overlooked. The important elements of analysis for Bentley are not the real interests of the governing group, nor whether the real interests of the governed are represented by the governing class. It is simply assumed that at least in a limited sense, they are represented. Instead the important elements to be considered and analyzed are the mechanisms by which interests are represented, for it is the variations in mechanisms that distinguish a despotic from a constitutional government.

Thus for the pressure group theorist, the key consideration in evaluating a political regime is not to be found in the kinds of decisions that it makes, nor in an examination of the economic interests of those who are making such decisions, but instead in a study of the legal and institutional mechanisms through which such decisions are made. As long as the desired procedures are available it is assumed that the political regime is just.[32]

Bentley admitted that officials may represent particular interests even in a society in which access is relatively fluid. Nevertheless he persisted in his belief that as long as the lines of access are generally available to differing groups, the particular interests of the governing class will be overridden whenever an opposing interest is felt with sufficient intensity or is held by a group of sufficient size.

It was not until the 1950s, however, that political scientists elaborated the way in which the size of an opposing group or the intensity with which an issue is felt can alter the decision of the ruling class. This aspect of the doctrine was worked out by Robert Dahl and others revealing further the conservative overtones of the doctrine. Dahl's *Preface to Democratic Theory* began with an implicit acceptance of the just character of American society and its institutions, but it proceeded to argue that American democracy had been poorly described by those who accepted the doctrine of minority rights, majority rule as its foundation.

---

[32] There is an important connection here with Beard's writings. While Beard in his early writings focused his attention on the interests and backgrounds of the founding fathers, the assumption that comes across in both his later writings and his textbooks is that the mechanisms of American government were progressing to the point of including an ever-wider and more disparate number of groups into the decision-making process.

Dahl identified the traditional view with Madisonian principles established to prevent the tyranny of one group over another—either a minority over the majority or the majority over a minority. Furthermore, the traditionalists believed that if one group is unrestricted by external threat it would, in fact, tyrannize over the other and thus they argued for an elaborate system of checks and balances whereby no group could exercise tyrannical power with impunity. As a consequence, the traditional view served as a justification for a weak central government.

Dahl then pointed out the problem that the traditional view had in defining democracy in any exact terms. There is no stable criterion, he claimed, for natural rights, just as there is no clear statement as to who decides whether or not such rights have been violated. If it is the majority which defines natural rights, then tyranny becomes possible in the very process of formulating the definition—the tyranny of the majority over the minority. If, on the other hand, it is a minority which defines them, then tyranny may exist in the other direction.

Dahl believed that the problem could be resolved by recognizing that "natural rights" is a fluid concept that changes over a period of time. Natural right must not be looked at as an absolute and pre-existent concept discovered once and for all by John Locke or Thomas Jefferson. It is not so fixed and definite that it can be used to measure the quality of any society at any time. Instead, such "rights" are constantly in the process of being defined and the stability and the equity of a government depends on the quality of the process, not the product. The quality of the process depended upon two factors: on the mechanisms for differing opinions to obtain a hearing in the appropriate place and on the extent to which people identify with more than one political issue. If a person identified with more than one issue then a defeat for him on one front would not mean a defeat on all, and he would be more tolerant of particular setbacks. "The majority" and "the minority" refer to shifting groupings instead of to stable entities that were the initiators or the victims of tyranny. Nevertheless, Dahl recognized that there were times when single issues became of paramount importance to both individuals and groups and in these instances the quality of a society depended upon the extent to which those who feel these issues strongly could obtain a hearing.

In view of these considerations, Dahl claimed that the problem of natural rights is eliminated. The important question was no longer which group decides what constitutes a natural right, but rather the intensity with which an issue is felt, the extent to which people identify with more than one issue, and the avenues open to groups that do feel strongly about a single issue to muster support for their point of view. The mistake of the traditional justification, he argued, has been to assume that natural rights have a status independently of issues and therefore independently of the intensity with which an issue is felt. The problem for political society was not to define natural rights but to find a way in which both numbers and intensity could be expressed.

Dahl granted that conflicts between a fluid majority and an equally fluid minority will persist and that there may even be times when a group so firmly defines itself around a set of interests that it begins to constitute a relatively permanent minority. Nevertheless this likelihood is reduced when the factor of intensity is examined more closely. The intensity with which a minority experiences an issue involves more than simply an internal set of privately held feelings. Intensity, he argued, expresses itself in political behavior and where a minority is reasonably large and the issues intensely felt, it is likely (because of voting behavior and the nature of political bargaining) that the minority will prevail over a somewhat apathetic majority.[33]

However accurate the pressure group theory may be as a description of the governmental process, it is also a remarkable argument for accepting the prevailing political decision because it allows one to assume that a defeated minority simply did not feel the issue with sufficient intensity. It confuses political stability with political justice, often shifting rapidly back and forth between these two ideals. As an account of political stability, it is reasonably accurate. As an account of political justice, it is questionable. The argument rests on a seemingly reasonable, but questionable premise: that an individual group is always best qualified to judge whether or not it is treated justly and that the final proof of its judgment rests on its ability to convince others (either a majority of the people or the key governmental decision makers) of the truth of such a judgment. Both sides of the premise are questionable, but the second is more obviously so than the first. If, for example, the majority

---

[33] There are, of course, other possibilities whereby different alternatives that are felt with equal intensity, rule each other out. These are the issues that cause great instability. Whether they arise frequently or infrequently is believed to depend on more than simply the mechanisms of politics. But in the generally optimistic atmosphere in which this point of view was put forth, this was thought to be a remote possibility for American society.

is deriving some significant material benefit from the oppression of a minority, then it seems more than wishful thinking to believe that the majority would compose an impartial jury in deciding the issue, especially if the minority is convinced that the only appropriate avenue for addressing its grievances is through the established channels.

On the other side, while it may seem reasonable to suppose that a group is generally the best judge of its own oppression, it does not necessarily follow that each member of an oppressed group will always express or even recognize the *fact* of oppression. (This is especially true where attempts to establish criteria for oppression are discouraged as they are in a pressure group theory.) There are many instances whereby a group is willing to stoically accept its condition at one moment while at another it recognizes it as oppressive. This is why often one of the most difficult tasks of the leaders of a political movement is to bring people to a recognition of their condition as oppressive. To support this point, one need only look at the liberal literature on rising expectations to show how people's judgments of their own condition change as new factors are introduced.[34]

In order for a group to recognize itself as oppressed, it must understand more than simply the facts and hardships of its present position. It must, among other things, understand that there are other possibilities, however remote these might seem, and it must understand too that its plight is not necessarily a reflection of the natural order of things. Nature does not tyrannize, only man does that. If people believe that their condition is the result of a God-given destiny or an unchangeable genetic makeup (as the worshippers of IQ scores would like) or some other unalterable cause, they do not protest. If they perceive that their position results from the natural order of things, flowing from the rational processes of the universe, they may stoically articulate their plight, but they will not protest it. Protest and resistance occur when people begin to think that things could be other than they are and when they begin to identify human agents as the cause of their condition. One sign of effective oppression is that the oppressed believe that their condition could not be other than it is.

On one level the pressure group theory did serve as a progressive, if not a radical force in American society. For the theory does direct an

---

[34] The liberal cites such evidence as a note of caution about raising the expectations of poor people too rapidly, rather than to cast doubt on the pressure group theory.

examination of the mechanisms by which existing groups can articulate their interests to the political body at large. Thus when discontent reaches a heightened state where grievances are articulated through other than established channels, as was the case during phases of the labor and the civil rights movements, the theory can (and has) served as a force to broaden the scope of established channels. But this was after the fact, applying generally to articulated and organized grievances and having as its *first* concern the reestablishment of social stability.

For progressives to have accepted the pressure-group theory was to fail to see that the quality of social life is not primarily a function of decisions that eventually become issues for political campaigns or formal legislative debates. Political instinct means more than simply having a knack for getting elected. It also means having a sensitivity for certain kinds of issues and not for others. It is rare, for example, that a politician will question the appointment of a person to a regulatory board who comes from the industry that he is supposed to regulate even though such a person's entire frame of reference has been conditioned by his career.[35] Now and then groups may challenge such appointments and on occasion they may even do so successfully, but appointments continue to follow the same pattern belying the belief that different groups can express their feelings in a reasonable, equitable fashion. An advertisement for a new Buick is, among other things, a political act. Add to it an advertisement for Fords, Chevrolets, and Pontiacs, and you have a powerful message telling the public how to spend its transportation dollar. Advocates of public transportation do not receive equal time and cannot afford to buy it. To hire a man in a defense-related industry is a powerful force in political conversion. To assume that groups passionately opposed to a war have the same kind of weapon is absolute folly.

That America was and still is a class society is difficult to dispute given the presence of the super rich and the wretched poor. The adoption of the pressure group view of American society by progressive educators during the 1930s helped to obscure this fact by magnifying the electoral and legislative processes to the neglect of other significant

---

[35] For an elaboration of this point see C. Wright Mills, *The Power Elite* (London: Oxford University Press), 1956.

factors such as the extent to which wealth can direct social and group interest.[36]

Of course what was really at issue during the 1930s among progressive educators was not only the question of the way America should be defined but also the way she should be changed. The class analysis was challenged not so much because it was obviously wrong but because it was thought to be threatening to established channels for orderly change. In this judgment progressives may well have been correct, given the tone of some of the movements that adhered to the class analysis of American society during the 1930s. But there is no magic involved in the class analysis of American society. It does not lend itself to one method of change to the exclusion of others. During the thirties, however, this point was obscured because both the advocates and the opponents of the class analysis associated it with the belief in the necessity of a violent revolution. However, one need not accept the need for the latter in order to see the validity of the former.

## VI. SERVING POWER

Liberal and progressive educators have been associated with libertarian causes in both classroom reform and policy matters. In the area of academic policy, they have often been found at the forefront of questions concerning academic freedom and the freedom of teachers. Dewey, for example, is known for his work in defense of Scott Nearing, Cattell at Columbia, and the right of Bertrand Russell to teach at the City College of New York. Yet while much attention has been given to the various causes which they took up, very little has been given to the *nature* of their defense of academic freedom. In the long run, however, the latter consideration is at least as important as the former in shedding light upon the overall progressive point of view.

The defense of academic freedom was but one aspect of a larger vision of the role of the intellectual in society. The vision was expressed by Dewey in a report during his visit to the Soviet Union. Dewey noted that one intellectual,

---

[36] One must be careful however not to make the opposite mistake and to assume that these processes have no significance. To remove the strictures against blacks voting, for example, was a step forward.

not a party member, told me that he thought those intellectuals who had refused to cooperate wherever they could with the new government had made a tragic mistake; they had nullified their own power and had deprived Russia of assistance just when it was most needed. As for himself he had found that the present government cleared the way for just the causes he had at heart in the old regime, and whose progress had always been hopelessly comprised by its opposition; and that, although he was not a communist, he found his advice and even his criticism welcomed as soon as the authorities recognized that he was sincerely willing to co-operate. And I may add that, while my experience was limited, I saw liberal intellectuals who had pursued both the policy he deplored and the one he recommended. There is no more unhappy and futile class on earth than the first, and none more fully alive and happy . . . than the second.[37]

This lesson was later elaborated in Dewey's "socialist" manifesto, *Individualism Old and New,* where he lamented the plight of the artist in American life who remained outside of and unincorporated into the mainstream of American society. The problem of the "new individualism" was to find a spiritual expression that would correspond to the corporate integration of America's formal institutions. The descriptions of the disestablished intellectuals of the Soviet Union and of the unincorporated artists in the United States was expressing more than simply compassion for Dewey's intellectual and artistic counterparts. Dewey was suggesting as did Plato before him, that the intellectual's place was within the power structure, guiding the political leadership in the governance of society. Unlike Plato, however, who felt there were certain definable limits under which such a role should be assumed, Dewey expressed no limits, and no alternatives.

The vision of the incorporated intellectual is related to the belief about the central role of technology in American society and to the view that the government serves to balance and stabilize conflicting pressures. The primary social need was to rationalize the relationship between power and intelligence by having the critic service the organizational and political leadership.

The promise of technology could be fully realized only if the organizational and political leadership had at their disposal the most

---

[37] John Dewey, *Character and Events,* Vol. 1, p. 404. I am indebted to Joe Hamilton for bringing Dewey's writings on the Soviet Union to my attention.

adequate and refined information available. Technology required an upward flow of information so that the planners and decision makers could consider all relevant factors in deciding on the best possible course of action. In part the public schools and universities were to provide the talent needed for this function.

However, there was another side to this situation and many liberals, both in America and abroad, expressed serious concern about the influence of technological processes on the intellectual development of the general population. The concept of functional rationality, a term coined by the continental social theorist, Karl Mannheim, was commonly used to explain this relationship. Functional rationality referred to the precision with which both men and machines had to be arranged in order to accomplish a given task such as the assembly line production of an automobile. The total process of production was described as functionally rational when each moment in the production process from the work of the machine to the activities of men who ran the machine was so specified and coordinated as to achieve the maximum efficiency of production. The tendency of the new industrial age, Mannheim asserted, was to achieve an ever greater degree of functional rationality. Such an increase was not only to occur within a simple and limited production process but between processes as well. Thus, for example, as the production of automobiles became more efficient, and as more and more automobiles appeared on highways, there was pressure generated to construct more highways, to predict the number of highways needed in the future, and at the same time to make the construction process more efficient.

The drive toward functional rationality therefore stimulated two conflicting tendencies in modern life. On the one hand was the tendency toward greater predictability, coordination, and control with some individuals having an enormous range of information at their fingertips and empowered to make decisions affecting the lives of millions of people. While on the other hand there was a tendency towards increased mechanical specialization with more and more people performing simplified, fixed movements and therefore in need of less and less information to carry out their work.

Liberals like Dewey and Mannheim were especially concerned about this latter tendency because they believed that the way people produced their goods significantly influenced the way they thought about their world. They believed that when most people were required to perform only a few simple and segregated activities, there was no compelling reason for them to want to know the relationship between these and other activities. Thus they would come to feel impotent and irresponsible and would come to view their own actions as only the effects of the action of others. Thus they were thought to be ready tools for manipulation by some unscrupulous demagogue. The remedies that were suggested to correct this tendency, however, were often rather pedestrian. Sometimes they involved expanding the worker's awareness of how his particular function was linked to the total process of production. At other times suggestions were made concerning the ways in which the pent-up emotions of the working class could be sublimated into harmless channels. Some suggested that the answer to the problems created by functional rationality was to help the worker to feel a part of a small primary group, thus giving him a feeling of belonging.[38] Others suggested enlarging the job that each worker had to perform and thereby decreasing the monotony of the line.[39] And a few braver souls proposed that workers be given more direction and control over the production process.[40] Clearly a number of these proposals were designed with the improved conditions of the worker in mind, but the success or failure of each of them was judged primarily by the influence it had on productivity and cost and the quieting of dissent. The solutions to the problems of functional rationality were not to violate the norms of production.

In the liberal scheme of things the relationship between the intellectual and the manager was paramount. Standing in contrast to the functional rationality of the laboring class was the substantial rationality of the managerial elite whose concern was the production process in its entirety and its relations to other processes. But the quality of management depended upon the intelligence of its decisions, and to liberal thinkers this meant that it depended upon the extent to which the decision maker had access to scientifically collected information together

[38] See, for example, Elton Mayo, *The Human Problem of an Industrial Civilization* (Boston: Division of Research, Harvard Business School), 1946.

[39] See, for example, Charles C. Walker and Robert H. Guest, *The Man on the Assembly Line* (Cambridge: Harvard University Press), 1952.

[40] See, for example, Charles P. McCormick, *Multiple Management* (New York: Harper), 1938 and Joseph N. Scanlon, "Profit Sharing Under Collective Bargaining: Three Case Studies," *Industrial and Labor Relations Review,* Vol. 2, No. 1, Oct., 1948, pp. 58-75.

with the extent of his awareness of various options. It was the specific function of the intellectual to provide such information and to articulate the available options.

Liberals might disagree specifically about whether the intellectual's responsibility could be best met by serving the governing elite or the industrial elite, but the essential role of the intellectual was to provide information and alternatives to the elite, to disseminate the opinions of the expert, and, as Mannheim was to suggest, to sublimate through the arts, the excess energy of the masses.

The role of the intellectual did not mean that he was never critical of industrial or governmental decisions, nor did it mean that when he was critical, he only addressed his grievances privately, rarely bringing them out in the open. What it did mean was that liberals strongly believed that the proper place for the critic was within the established structure. This is not to say that they themselves were always accepted by the political powers or that they were negligent in their criticism of them. It is to say that when they were not in close relation to political power, they felt misplaced or, in Dewey's terms, not yet fully incorporated into society.

## VII. THE CRITIC FROM WITHIN

Industrial development and growth required the intellectual to serve two different and seemingly conflicting roles. One, the intellectual was to inform the political and industrial leadership, providing them with the best possible information in order to help them form intelligent decisions. Two, the intellectual had to be free from undue political pressure so that he might refine his information and form his own judgment about the viability of different alternatives. For only when he was free in this way, it was argued, could there be reasonable assurance that his judgment issued from the canons of science and intelligence rather than from political expediency.

The liberal's critique of the university issued in part from the need to resolve this tension. As the training ground for future intellectuals the liberal believed that the university was too removed and distant from the everyday problems of American society and that it was unable to properly serve as a vehicle for social change. The model of the progressive university was the land grant college that, through its farm extension programs, served the needs of the community. Cremin, for example, cites the University of Wisconsin as the progressive model where, by 1900, professors were already increasingly becoming "advisers to the state administration, in the sciences, engineering, finance, education and agriculture"[41] and where the idea was to effect a "true union of politics and education."[42]

Liberals did not, however, view the intellectual as merely the servant of power. Rather his role was perceived as that of a guide working closely with the political leadership helping to chart the course and advising about alternatives. Thus he had to be an equal partner in this relationship, free to follow his own ideas wherever they might lead and to state his point of view without fear of retaliation.

The idea of academic freedom was designed to maintain both sides of this relationship as it was proclaimed that the intellectual best serves society when he is free to pursue his own inquiry to its most reasonable conclusion. Yet the ideal relationship between intelligence and power established certain limits to academic freedom that are not strictly based on the canons of reason and intelligence. Dewey's position is a case in point.

Dewey's position on academic freedom was expressed in an article he wrote in 1902 for the *Educational Review*. He began the article by observing that issues of academic freedom are usually found in those disciplines that have not yet achieved the full status of a scientific inquiry and where many pronouncements are still open to public debate and consideration. Nevertheless, Dewey reported, it is still possible for a scholar to speak out on the controversial side of an issue if he approaches the problem "in such an objective, historic, and constructive manner as not to excite the prejudice or inflame the passion even of those who *thoroughly* disagree with him."[43] The intent of the statement is puzzling since clearly issues of academic freedom will never arise if prejudice or passion are not inflamed, but its effect is to place the burden of proof on the academic style of the intellectual dissenter even to the point of holding him responsible for the reactions of those "who *thoroughly* disagree with him." Presumably a passionate reaction was

---

[41] Cremin, *The Transformation of the School,* p. 164.
[42] Ibid., p. 168.
[43] John Dewey, "Academic Freedom," *Educational Review,* January, 1902, Vol. XXIII, p. 7.

to be taken as evidence of some kind of deficiency in the presentation. After all, Dewey reminded his readers, the scholar "needs tact as well as scholarship."[44]

In the process of elaborating his ideas on academic freedom, Dewey quoted approvingly a statement by President Harper of the University of Chicago which established the conditions under which the "privilege" of academic freedom may be judged to be violated:

(1) A professor is guilty of an abuse of privilege who promulgates as truth ideas or opinions which have not been tested scientifically by his colleagues in the same department of research or investigation. (2) A professor abuses his privilege who takes advantage of a classroom exercise to propagate the partisan view of one or another of the political parties. (3) A professor abuses his privilege who in any way seeks to influence his pupils or the public by sensational methods. (4) A professor abuses his privilege of expression of opinion when, although a student and perhaps an authority in one department or group of departments, he undertakes to speak authoritatively on subjects which have no relation to the department in which he was appointed to give instruction. (5) A professor abuses his privilege in many cases when, although shut off in a large measure from the world and engaged within a narrow field of investigation, he undertakes to instruct his colleagues or the public concerning matters in the world at large in connection with which he has had little experience.[45]

The major effect of many of the prohibitions is to restrict the promulgation of ideas to the public until they have received general acceptance by the academic community.

Dewey's willingness to downplay the threats to academic freedom that may originate from outside of the scholarly community and the extent to which he placed the burden of proof on the style of those who promulgate new and controversial ideas can only be understood in terms of his vision of the proper relationship between the man of intellect and the man of power. He assured his readers that no threat to academic freedom was to be found in interference by the "moneyed benefactors" and that more often than not, the charges of abuse levied against indi-

[44] Ibid., p. 8.
[45] Ibid., p. 9.

vidual scholars are the result of their own "self-conceit" or "bump-tiousness."[46]

Dewey's article on academic freedom should not be read in isolation from the events that were happening at the University of Chicago at that time. Dewey came to Chicago in 1894 as Chairman of the Department of Philosophy, Psychology, and Pedagogy. In 1895 professor Edward W. Bemis resigned under pressure from President Harper for what many suspected to be his outspoken liberalism.[47] Dewey's comments on academic freedom, coming seven years after the Bemis case, are not necessarily to be interpreted as referring directly to that affair. Nevertheless, by placing the burden of proof on the dissenter, by claiming that benefactors do not interfere with the governance of the university, and by citing Harper's remarks approvingly, the consequences of his article was implicitly to sanction the stance that the institution had taken. While there was no direct evidence to indicate that Rockefeller had in fact interfered in the Bemis case, as Dykhuizen notes, "Rockefeller interests . . . were suspected in many quarters of attempting to influence instruction at the university and of forcing . . . the resignation of Professor Bemis."[48]

Subsequent scholars, more aware than Dewey of the extent of Rockefeller's general influence on Chicago, have treated these remarks of Dewey on academic freedom rather kindly. For example, George Dykhuizen finds Dewey's exhonoration of the financial supporters to be merely a matter of misplaced optimism:

Dewey could scarcely have had so optimistic a view had he been aware of the numerous letters which President Harper received from Frederick Gates, private secretary to Rockefeller. These letters reveal that Gates was very much on the alert for anything said by liberal faculty members which might cast reflection on his employer or which ran counter to conservative social

---

[46] The article that follows Dewey's in the same issue of the *Educational Review* provides an interesting commentary on Dewey's general complacency. It asserts that the benefactors of a university have the right to dictate the content of instruction. See Alton B. Parker, "The Right of Donors," *Educational Review,* January, 1902.

[47] The charge, brought out after the resignation, was incompetence. For a more elaborate treatment of this incident, see Clarence Karier, *Shaping the American Educational State* (New York: Free Press), forthcoming.

[48] George Dykhuizen, "John Dewey in Chicago: Some Biographical Notes," *The Journal of the History of Philosophy,* October, 1965, Vol. III, No. 2, p. 219.

thought. In one letter Gates asked President Harper whether "you can yourself afford to appear in this magazine" now that it has become a "by-word and laughing stock" as a result of its opening its columns to articles attacking the Standard Oil Company.[49]

And it is likely that had Dewey known of Rockefeller interference he would have reacted with indignation. It was more than misplaced optimism, however, that lead Dewey to place the burden of proof on the self-conceit or bumptiousness of dissenting faculty members and to fail to see the possibilities of control by the financial supporters of the university. Dewey's stress on the *style* of the dissenter is simply one aspect of the larger task of the intellectual to attach himself to political and economic forces that could affect change in the social world. The lesson of the Soviet Union was clear. The intellectual who alienated himself from the sources of power was an unhappy and futile man.

The close relationship between the university professor and the outside community was initially developed in the area of agriculture. As the nature of American society changed, connections grew in other areas as well, such as science, industry, foreign relations, and urban affairs. As the context of the relationship altered so too did some people's evaluation of it. Among the activities over which concern was later expressed were those involving the Committee for Cultural Freedom, a liberal organization whose membership included a number of Dewey's followers. The activities of this committee illustrates the fact that it was often difficult to serve "science" and "intelligence" while serving power at the same time.

The American Committee for Cultural Freedom was founded in 1951 by Sidney Hook, Arthur Schlesinger, and others to promote the liberal anti-Communist point of view. In 1952 Sidney Hook was succeeded as chairman by George Counts. The members of the committee had been active on a number of fronts attacking "Communist infiltration" into key areas of American institutional and intellectual life. Led by Sidney Hook, one of the foremost exponents of Dewey's pragmaticism, members of the committee argued that membership alone in the Communist party should be sufficient to disqualify a person from

---

[49] Ibid., p. 220.

teaching.[50] Hook's position was that membership in the party committed one to following a doctrinaire line and therefore violated the teacher's "primary loyalty . . . to the ethics and logic of reasoned inquiry or to those processes which constitute intellectual freedom."[51]

In the years 1966-1967 *The New York Times* and *Ramparts* magazine revealed the length that the Central Intelligence Agency was supporting a number of liberal, anti-Communist organizations, among them the American Committee for Cultural Freedom (supported since 1953). The response from the left was to cite such support as evidence of the essential hypocrisy of liberal intellectuals. Others who had been loosely connected with the exposed organizations felt that they had been duped and expressed anger at the leadership and shame for their own failings and complicity.[52] A few, such as Sidney Hook and Arthur Schlesinger, expressed no regrets whatsoever believing that the expenditures were justified and that the acceptance of them had not involved any compromise of integrity[53] because, as they put it, the CIA had never censored any individual member and each person remained free to express his own point of view. But, as Christopher Lasch points out: "These statements need to be set against . . . the rules that guided the international Organization Division of the CIA: 'Use legitimate, existing organizations; disguise the extent of American interest; protect the integrity of the organization by not requiring it to support every aspect of official American policy.'"[54] Such disclaimers should also be set against the fact that to allow a person's sincerity to count as justification for the committee's activities is to vitiate Hook's argument for denying Communists the right to teach since it is not at all unlikely that someone

[50] For a more complete description of the activities of the committee see Christopher Lasch, "The Cultural Cold War: A Short History of the Congress for Cultural Freedom," in Barton J. Bernstein, *Towards a New Past* (New York: Vintage Books), 1969, pp. 322-359. Much of the discussion here follows Lasch.

[51] Sidney Hook, *Heresy, Yes: Conspiracy, No* (New York: The John Day Co.), 1953, p. 174.

[52] For a variety of liberal responses to this incident see "Liberal Anti-Communism Revisited: A Symposium," *Commentary*, Vol. 44, No. 3, September, 1967, pp. 31-79.

[53] See for example both Sidney Hook's and Arthur Schlesinger's response in *Commentary*, pp. 44-48 and pp. 68-71.

[54] Lasch and Thomas Braden as quoted by Lasch in *Towards a New Past*, p. 354.

teaching the party line also may sincerely believe it is true. And Hook himself cites cases where a teacher quit the party once he ceased believing its doctrines, rather than being committed to teach what he no longer believed. Nevertheless, the relation with the CIA was defended because it provided the means to disseminate liberal, anti-Communist ideas. That it also gave a respectable forum to other ideas that were strictly CIA initiated was not considered to be a matter of importance.

However else this incident may be judged, it is reasonably clear that Hook's argument and the activities of the committee were consistent with much of the liberal tradition. And whether or not "the primary loyalty" of the knowledgeable members of the committee were "to the ethics and logic of reasoned inquiry,"[55] they were indeed committed to the full incorporation of the intellectual into American society.

## VIII. SUMMARY COMMENTS

Perhaps nothing reveals a particular political stance better than the way a person describes a social event. The liberal looks at the critic who had once spoken abrasively from outside the power structure operating now from within and he remarks on the ability of this society to *incorporate* radical thought. The radical looks at the same process, describes it as *co-optation* and speaks against the power of society to control and quiet dissent.

The issues that divide the liberal from the radical are not minor ones. The liberal intellectual is concerned with the feasibility of a solution, and it is because of this, for example, that the question of style is so important. Feasible solutions are not those that alienate the dominant political and economic powers. But feasibility has its own problems. Sometimes a solution is feasible because enough people think it is such, and sometimes unfeasible solutions soon become feasible as people change their minds. The obvious solution to the Vietnam war, for example, should have been to have gotten out before involving a large number of troops. That solution was not feasible in part because politicians did not believe it was acceptable to a large number of Americans.

The critic who speaks from outside established channels of power may have an easier time recognizing solutions that are not yet feasible,

[55] See, for example, *Heresy Yes, Conspiracy, No,* pp. 192-193.

and he may be better able to challenge the conventional consciousness out of which many problems are generated. In this light the question of style is not necessarily an insignificant one for it can reveal major points of differences about power and legitimacy. It is only when the symbols of power are effectively challenged that the general population may come to believe fundamental political change is possible when before they would only begrudgingly and abstractly admit that it was even desirable. The French Revolution was preceded by Rousseau's attacks on the child-rearing practices and the educational system that had become symbols of the ruling class and, to a lesser extent, the dissent in American society has been sometimes coupled with a rejection of the soap bubble,—the symbol of American materialism. The liberal point of view, wedded as it is to existing symbols and institutions, is not able to push matters this far. Moreover, the liberal ideal of equality of educational opportunity attached as it is to the liberal's concept of the university is in fact designed to fulfill Dewey's ideal of the incorporated intellectual by facilitating the movement of intelligence into the political structure.

# CHAPTER SEVEN
# Education in a Just Society:
# The Limits of Liberal Educational Reform

## I. INTRODUCTION

Among revisionists scholars of education, there has been a large-scale disenchantment with public education in the United States and with the liberal scholarship that supports it. The most serious charge is that the schools have been consciously designed as instruments of manipulation and social control and that these have been masked by the rhetoric of equality of opportunity. The preceding chapters in this book have lent support to that charge by showing how much liberal theorists and reformers used the schools as instruments for industrial development and state planning, but they have also pointed out that this is not inconsistent with the idea of equality of opportunity.

This chapter is designed to explore and to evaluate the thrust of the revisionist charge against the liberal reformer. After some preliminary remarks the chapter proceeds to examine the charge of manipulation in detail showing the extent to which the charge is applicable to liberal reformers as well as some of the ways in which they might be defended against it. The conclusion to this section is that the charge is valid, but it can be mitigated by a number of considerations. After some concluding remarks on the problem of manipulation, the chapter examines the revisionist critic from the liberal point of view. The material for this examination is drawn primarily from earlier chapters in this book, and its purpose is to help sharpen the critical focus. The last sections extend this focus by examining the principle of equality of educational opportunity and the limits of educational reform and by suggesting a different principle as the guide to educational development.

## II. THE ISSUE OF MANIPULATION

The revisionist critique of educational reform differs significantly from traditional liberal historical examinations of twentieth-century education because it issues from a different point of judgment. Prior to the middle of the 1960s, for example, many of the most influential examinations of progressive reform were written by educational historians who were sympathetic to the movement and the harshest criticism of progressive reform was developed in polemical works generally written by people to the right of the political spectrum. The traditional interpreter of progressive educational reform accepted the point of view of the progressive reformers while critizing only their political effectiveness. Much of the academic debate centered around the question of whether or not progressive education was alive or dead but whatever side of this issue a historian might take, the assumption was often that whether living or dead, the value of the movement could not be denied.

The traditional liberal interpretation of progressive reform has viewed the movement as an attempt to loosen up the rigid structure of schools and as a way to provide members of the lower class with the tools needed for upward mobility and self-respect in a new and difficult industrial situation. As Lawrence Cremin has described the movement:

Actually, progressive education began as part of a vast humanitarian effort to apply the promise of American life—the idea of government by, of, and for the people—to the puzzling new urban-industrial civilization that came into being during the latter half of the nineteenth century . . . In effect, progressive education began as . . . a many sided effort to use the schools to improve the lives of individuals.

And then quoting Jane Addams as indicative of the movement's intent:

We have learned to say that the good must be extended to all of society before it can be held secure by any one person or any one class; but we have not yet learned to add to that statement, that unless all men and all classes contribute to a good, we cannot even be sure that it is worth having.[1]

Whereas Cremin views the progressive movement as an effort to improve the lives of individuals in the emerging urban-industrial complex, revisionists now view it as an attempt to establish more sophisticated methods of social control. Paul Violas reflects this point of view when he comments,

The new liberals supported policies that moved the nation toward the acceptance of a compulsory corporate state in which the individual would be simply a part of the greater collective unity. The key concern became the development of more effective means of social control in order to eliminate conflict and to establish the harmonious organic community. Classical liberalism . . . gave way to a newer version that emphasized community and positive freedom—freedom that meant psychosociological control of the individual within a controlled community.[2]

Then commenting on Jane Addams, Violas, in contrast to Cremins, highlights a different aspect of her ideas.

The rejection of coercion and forms of physical force as a method of social control formed a significant aspect of the new liberalism Jane Addams espoused. She laid the blame for "Much of the maladministration of our cities" on the fact that American governmental theory "depended upon penalties, coercion, compulsion, remnants of military codes to hold the community together." Such methods were survivals of a more primitive past; for the present, she argued, "There would seem to be but one path open to us in America. That path implies freedom for the young people, made safe only through their own self-control." Thus Miss Addams, like

---

[1] Lawrence Cremin, *The Transformation of the School: Progressivism in American Education, 1876-1957* (New York: Vintage), pp. viii-1x.

[2] Paul Violas, "Jane Addams and the New Liberalism," in Clarence J. Karier, Paul Violas, and Joel Spring, *Roots of Crisis: American Education in the Twentieth Century* (Chicago: Rand McNally & Co.), 1973, p. 68.

many other twentieth century liberals, defined freedom as control. Freedom depended on "self-control." The independent, autonomous, individual self was to be submerged in the collectivity of the group society. Only when he desired what the group desired would the most effective kind of social control, the internalization of group norms, be effected.[3]

Separating the new history from the traditional one are issues that themselves are philosophical as much as they are historical, issues that have to do with the nature of man and his freedom. However perceptive the new criticism may be in exposing the elements of social control and manipulation in progressive reform, the defender of liberal education might claim that the critique rests on an impossible view of human freedom. If human beings lived in total isolation from each other, if the activity of one person did not affect the activity of all, if it were the case that desires never conflicted and did not require adjudication, and if adjudication did not at least presuppose that the parties to a conflict had to accept the same arbitrating body, then perhaps one could speak of freedom without at the same time speaking of control, but then one would not need to speak of human society.

The traditional defender of progressive education does not necessarily have to deny the charge that some of the proposed reforms had a component of manipulation to them in order to maintain his defense of the progressive educator. He might simply point out that there are a number of situations where a worthwhile goal is sought and where some of the people involved in achieving that goal may not know all of its ramifications before the goal is accomplished. For example the education of small children always has a certain end in view that the children themselves are not capable of understanding completely until the process is complete. In this *weak* sense of the term, much of education can be called manipulative although the fact that it is so labeled is not a *sufficient* reason for dismissing its value. If the revisionist objects that youngsters can do better by pursuing their own interests without any adult guidance of supervision,[4] then the traditionalist can reply that the burden of proof falls on the critic to show why this should be called education and to demonstrate that there is a reasonably good chance

---

[3] Ibid., p. 75.

[4] While this may be one possible implication of the revisionist critique, it is not intended here to represent the response of any particular individual.

that a child left to his own devices will develop sufficient insight to protect himself from manipulation later on. If the critic assumes that children have a natural drive to know, that this drive is sufficient to bring them to a deep understanding of themselves and their relation to other human beings, then if he should be proven wrong, the consequences of his error will be suffered by others. Thus it is that his own point of view may conceivably have the actual consequences of restricting the freedom of others.

The revisionist critic is also subject to the charge that in highlighting the manipulative aspect of progressive reform, he has failed to consider sufficiently the social and political pressures that provided the context in which such reforms were proposed. To emphasize his point, the traditional liberal historian might cite certain hypothetical situations in which an act of manipulation seems justifiable and then claim that the progressive response fit such situations. Consider, for example, a rather typical situation among nonindustrial, developing nations as a case in point. Suppose that the leaders of a new nation are confronted with a problem of traditional tribal antagonisms, a situation where individuals place their primary loyalty in a local tribal rather than a national group. Suppose too that the national leaders are aware of the likelihood of a natural disaster that will bring about a severe food shortage for one of the major tribal groups. They decide that unless tribal loyalties can be shifted from the local to the national level, the food shortage will be accompanied by great famine and countless deaths. In order to forestall this possibility, they establish a national system of education, and offer as an inducement promising positions in a national civil service for those who attend public schools. Besides teaching certain skills that are important to national life, the schools also deemphasize tribal traditions and substitute in their place, national ones. Clearly the action of the national leaders could be called manipulative, in the sense that those who choose to send their youngsters to school may not be aware that its primary purpose is to alter their children's frame of reference and as a likely consequence, to alienate them from their family. To put the matter in an even more sinister way, the leaders of the country are manipulating the population so that the young will come to see things from their own point of view. However, even granting the fact of manipulations (and, of course, placing aside the complicated history of colonial conquest and the resulting artificial national boundaries), some might wish to claim that in *this* situation there was no better alternative, and that manipulation was thus justifiable.

## III. MANIPULATION AND ITS EVALUATION

The force of the revisionist critique is sometimes diminished because it fails to take into account some of the distinctions that need to be made before the charge of manipulation can thoroughly be assessed. The ethical problems involved in an act of manipulation are best judged in terms of degrees, for not all manipulation is equally pernicious. The act of manipulation consists of both an action whereby someone does something to another person and a goal that requires a desired response from the other party. The goal is often one which the manipulator has a much larger awareness of than does the person who is being manipulated, and to which the manipulated person has not yet fully assented. Judgments that are made about any specific act of manipulation have to take into account both the extent to which deceit is involved, the nature of the goal, and the alternative avenues and consequences.

In some limited situations it is possible to manipulate someone to accept a goal that is in his own personal interest, but which for one reason or another, he would not undertake by himself. In these cases, if the situation has been assessed correctly, that is, if a person is brought to act in his own self-interest, if no one else is obviously hurt by his actions, if the consequences of his not acting might be severe and if no alternative was available to the manipulator, then the single act of manipulation can be excused and possibly even commended. If, on the other hand, the act of manipulation is performed for the self-interest of the manipulator then, even if the party being manipulated is not seriously injured by the act, there is a good reason to render a negative judgment. Furthermore, acts of manipulation that are performed on those who are *unable* to fully understand the consequences of the action are judged differently than those performed in situations where a person is capable of a complete understanding but simply is deceived (even assuming the manipulation to be in the other person's interest). Indeed there are times when, because of the value that is placed on the goal, we are reluctant to even term a certain act manipulative. For example, in Ivan Illich's recent book on deschooling society he criticizes liberal institutions for their manipulative character in terms of the extent to which they shape attitudes and action. However, when proposing certain substitute institutions that he believes to be nonmanipulative, he recognizes there will be the need *"to cultivate"* certain attitudes consistent with these institutions and to discourage others that are inconsistent with them. The difference between "cultivation" and "manipulation" may be somewhat subtle, hinging on whether or not approval is given to a stipulated goal.

The complexities that are involved in judging even an act that is agreed to be a manipulative one are sufficient to warrant a careful examination of the differences between educational reformers. Many traditional liberal historians instinctively want to make a distinction between some of the educators like Snedden or Bobbitt, who were primarily identified with the efficiency movement, and others such as Addams, and Dewey, who are more closely identified with progressive educational reform. Within limits this distinction is a perfectly reasonable one. There is very little in the writings of Snedden, for example, to indicate that he questioned the justness of existing institutions or that he was willing to provide the critical tools needed to appraise them. This is not the case with other liberal progressives of whom it may be said that they believed they were providing critical tools which could be used to improve existing institutions.

The difficulty with the traditional view, however, is that it focuses so heavily on the clear and obvious distinctions between the two groups of educators that it fails to perceive and address the ethical problems that are involved in progressive education generally. Thus the progressive reformer is pictured as striving for a more humane treatment of children in schools and for the development of a curriculum that will further the growth of critical insight and problem-solving skills. The picture is not wrong; it is taken out of the major works of progressive educators, but it is clearly one-sided. In accepting the progressive's point of reference, the traditional historian has been able to deemphasize many events that could have cast progressive reform in a different light. Robinson's recommendations for a history to comfort the children of the working class as they continued to carry on the menial labors of their fathers, or Dewey's treatment of the Polish community have been available to scholars for many years, but because they have been difficult to reconcile with liberal rhetoric, they have not been emphasized. Nevertheless, they are representative of a clear strain in progressive theory, and it is this strain that brings the issue of manipulation into sharper focus.

Individual acts of manipulation must be judged on the basis of factors that relate to the situation in which the act occurs, and, providing that certain contingencies are present, such acts might be excused and on occasion, even commended. But the important point is that such acts must be judged and that there is a strong burden of proof that rests with the manipulator. The basic problem with progressive theory is that, in its implications, it removed this burden and thus came close to justifying manipulation as a norm rather than an exception.

The reason that acts of manipulation carry with them a burden of proof can be understood from the fact that a more neutral meaning of the term refers to a relationship between men and things. An artist manipulates his material in order to conform it to a certain idea that he has in mind.[5] A mechanic manipulates a piece of machinery so that it will perform a particular task. In this process the thing itself is assumed to possess only the quality of resistance without initiating a direction of its own, and, from its point of view, its present state is morally indifferent with regard to its future states.[6]

The neutral meaning of "manipulation" when applied to things, reveals why the term takes on a morally pernicious meaning when applied to people. People are thought to be free in a way that things are not. When a person resists attempts to shape him in one way or another it is because he has already *chosen* an end that he finds incompatible with these attempts. He may in fact be mistaken either about the compatibility of his ends with those being imposed on him or about the relative merits of the incompatible ends, but the recognition of his freedom requires that his choice be respected. To respect his choice means that in the absence of overwhelming reasons to the contrary, any attempt to move him from one state to another should be above board and should appeal to his own capacity for insight and reason.

---

[5] I am indebted to David Nyberg for suggesting this example.

[6] The phrase "from its point of view" is meant only as a recognition of the fact that from the point of view of human beings the present and future state of the thing may not be morally neutral at all. If, for example, the mechanic is repairing a gun that he intends to use in a criminal way, then the future state of the thing has moral implications for people. When the object of manipulation is not a thing, but another human being, then the moral point of view becomes paramount.

The belief in man's freedom can be defended from a number of different points of view. From a traditionally conservative point of view, it can be defended as the requisite assumption for ascribing responsibility to the acts of individuals and therefore as necessary for any social and juridical system. It may also be defended on a moral basis as the recognition of the essential personhood that each of us would like to see extended to ourselves, and therefore that we should extend to others not only in our personal interaction with them but through the institutions that we establish as well.

Although the particular point of view from which human freedom is defended has a great many ramifications for human and political relations, the particular status that has been accorded this value is more directly related to a critique of liberal educational theory.

## IV. MANIPULATION AND PROGRESSIVE EDUCATION

The pragmatic tone in which liberal, progressive education was cast prohibited thinking of human values, including freedom, in anything but provisional terms, and this way of thinking together with the expanding powers of bureaucracy, reduced the moral constraints on manipulation.[7] For Dewey, values had two significant characteristics. First they arose out of problematic situations as a way to assess the

---

[7] This explains much of Dewey's involvement in the Polish Study as well as his appeal to social engineering as the best way to bring the misguided pacifists into line during World War I. See, for example, Dewey's "Conscription of Thought," in *The New Republic,* September 1, 1917, pp. 128-130. Here he argues against the *efficacy* of force to remove dissent. Also significant is Dewey's "Conscience and Compulsion," *The New Republic,* July 14, 1917, pp. 297-298, where he argues against the pacifists on the grounds of the inefficacy of pure conscience. Note, for example, "If at a critical juncture the moving force of events is always too much for conscience, the remedy is not to deplore the wickedness of those who manipulate events. Such a conscience is largely self-conceit. The remedy is to connect conscience with the *forces that are moving in another direction.* Then will conscience itself have compulsive power instead of being forever the martyred and the coerced" (emphasis mine). It is questionable whether Dewey would have any room for the moral prophet unless he were successful in developing a political movement behind him. Certainly this statement would allow little room for the pacifism of World War I.

various alternative solutions, and hence they were provisional—relating to the specific situation out of which they arose. Second they were subject to assessment by scientific methods and thus they were objective in character. The provisional nature of values lead liberals in general to pay more attention to the methods for resolving conflicts than to an examination of the values that were being expressed through them. However, the stress on objectivity provided a special status to the expert decision maker who was thought better able than most to assess the impact of different social and educational policies.

Whether or not this approach to values is ultimately defensible depends greatly upon the context in which it is being applied. When, for example, one is attempting to assess the impact of certain social policies, and the impact of a given set of attitudes upon a specific goal, then it is reasonable to speak of the values that people express as provisional, and to address the issue of changing peoples' values. For example, the value that people had once attached to savings and to delayed gratification did have its origins in specific social factors—in the need to build up capital and in the conditions of scarcity that were generated by this need. Assuming a later situation where capital has been built up, it is not unreasonable to suppose that the values associated with delayed gratification might become dysfunctional to the goal of continued economic growth, although whether the goal is a reasonable one will depend on other factors. When, however, the context pertains to an examination of the very ideas that have served as the basis of social organization the emphasis on the provisional nature of values and on the appropriate method for resolving value conflicts served as a deterrent to a deep-seated analysis.

The emphasis on a method of conflict resolution must necessarily be initiated in terms of the values that are expressed in the conflict itself. Its goal is not to alter the principles under which institutions are governed but rather to bring certain disorders into functional alignment. Manipulation becomes a philosophical problem only if one does believe that there are higher order values that the emphasis on conflict resolution and the functional integration of institutions is masking. It is, for example, in this sense that the school can be seen as a manipulative institution for progressives whose emphasis on functional disorders led them to believe that the problems were basically rooted in attitudes drawn from another era. The primary mission of the school was to address problems at this level.

The difficulty of the progressive theorist arose from placing what indeed might be considered provisional values on a par with other, more fundamental values. Some things that are valued, such as saving, a college degree, free enterprise, etc., do seem to have reference to rather specific situations, and when those situations change, it seems perfectly intelligent to reassess those accepted values. Other things that are called values such as personal freedom, education and just institutions have reference to certain domains of human activities. They are more abstract in nature in the sense that they are consistent with a number of possible activities and while their actual composition is in part determined by cultural and historical factors, their very nature provides barriers to certain kinds of activities. All societies, for example, recognize human life as a prime value in terms of the strictures that are placed against taking a life. The strictures do not prohibit the taking of a life under every and all circumstances, but they lay down rules that limit the kinds of situations (for example, self-protection) under which another life may be taken with impunity. Implied by the very procedures for judging situations in which a life has been taken is that the burden of proof lies on the shoulders of the person who has taken the life to show that he has done so under one of the acceptable conditions.[8]

Using the above example, we can now get a better hold on the ethical problems involved in the question of manipulation. If it is held that values are both objective in the sense that the relative merits of

[8] This statement should not be taken in any way to contradict the juridical principle of a reasonable shadow of doubt. The point is simply that there are always procedures for judging guilt or innocence in a life-taking situation while in many other areas of conduct the question of guilt or innocence simply does not arise. The juridical principle refers to the way the evidence is to be judged and is culture specific. A similar argument about the nature of certain values has been made by Stuart Hampshire, "Morality and Pessimism," *New York Review of Books,* Vol. XIX, Nos. 11-12, January 25, 1973, pp. 26-33. Hampshire directs most of his argument against the utilitarians, but insofar as utilitarianism is expressed by a belief in the provisional nature of all human values, the argument holds for the pragmatic underpinnings of progressive education as well. The major difference between pragmatic and utilitarian ethics is whether there is one standard (such as pleasure and pain) that is universally applicable for measuring values. The pragmatists deny that this is the case, placing the greater weight on the appropriate method for resolving value conflicts.

differing evaluations *can* be publicly acknowledged, and that values, as they are held by particular people can only be held provisionally, then one has a strong justification towards manipulating people to accept the preferred values. This point can be illustrated by stating the case for the provisional nature of values in one of its strongest forms. Suppose that one believes, as modern behaviorists do, that human values are simply the product of one's upbringing and conditioning, and that a different upbringing could well have generated different values (this point of view is not that far from Dewey's except that he wants to emphasize the plurality of background conditions that contribute to the formation of human attitudes and then again to emphasize the need for an intelligent method to resolve some of the conflicts that arise). Now if one believes that another person's values are simply a matter of circumstances, that under other conditioning agents those values would have been totally different, and if one also believes that the present values are, for certain reasons, dysfunctional, then there is certainly no reason to avoid manipulation. In fact there is no other choice; manipulate in the "right" direction or manipulate in the "wrong," but manipulate one must. Neither pragmatic philosophers nor progressive educators would quite accept this formulation, nor would their thoughts on manipulation be quite this explicit. Dewey would, for example, stress the uniqueness of the conditioned person, and the progressive educator would place his stress on reflective problem-solving methods. While the behaviorist would downplay as illusion the *feeling* that people have of actually choosing one alternative over another, the pragmatist would give it recognition but would want to avoid the question as to whether such feelings have reference to real states of affairs—that is, whether the feeling that we freely choose actually indicates a free choice or simply a delusion. Whether human choice was ultimately determined by prior conditions, or whether it was a truly unconditioned and hence a free act, was less significant than whether the world in which choice might be made was seen as an opened or a closed one.

From one point of view the difference between the strict behaviorist and the pragmatist is a very important one. For the behaviorist, what is important is the performance of certain actions but whether those acts are performed voluntarily or not is an empty question. The problem is to develop a series of conditioning techniques which will increase the probability that the desired actions will be performed with reasonable consistency.[9] The pragmatist's stress on individuality, on the person standing as the product of past conditioning but nevertheless standing here and now, meant that the emphasis had to go beyond the fact of behavior and had to express as well the deeper dimensions of attitudes and dispositions as they are now and again manifested in behavior.

On one level, the emphasis on attitudes and dispositions in both pragmatic philosophy and progressive education reveals a respect for persons and their uniqueness that is absent in behavioristic theories. This respect is present, for example, in the emphasis that progressive educators placed on group discussion and problem solving in the classroom, and on the increased emphasis placed on student participation in decisions about classroom goals. The difference is also present in one aspect of educational policy making that can be loosely traced to elements in the progressive platform, and this is the concern for enlarged community participation in the formation of educational policy.

On another level, however, while the stress on individuality and the increased degree of participation in decision making that sometimes follows from it must be said to have ethical advantages in contrast to the strict behaviorist position, it does not by itself rule out manipulation. Indeed, the acceptance of the provisional status of values together with the belief in the capacity of science to objectively adjudicate value disputes provides a warrant for manipulation in which increased participation may be seen as one possible technique. The term co-optation, for example, when used by community or radical groups, is an expression of just this possibility. Co-optation does not refer merely to taking up another group's cause for the sake of personal gain. It refers also to the process of coming to see the problems through the eyes of another, more influential group, when in fact it is still believed by the person making the charge that the prior point of view is more valid. An invitation in the deliberations of that group may possibly provide the vehicle for co-optation to take place. This was obviously the case when Dewey proposed the establishment of a commission of prominent Poles to

[9] The extent to which this point of view dominates modern education should be obvious from the emphasis on behavioral modification and behavioral objectives. What may be less obvious is the extent to which these practices may very well be contributing to the problems of modern education by taking away from both teachers and students a sense of unique personhood and individual responsibility.

oversee Polish affairs and to report to the government any possible causes of disorder that might arise. It accounts too for the feeling of discomfort that a person might have in watching some progressive classrooms as the teacher moves the students to assent to a project that she has already decided on.

Progressive and liberal reform, both in education and in politics, took root against the background of social Darwinism and while it was intended to counter many of the implications of social Darwinism, it accepted a number of others. It is in the context of its reaction to the conservative aspects of social Darwinism that the manipulative aspects of progressive thought is to be understood. Social Darwinists like Sumner attempted to articulate the laws governing human behavior and evolution, laws that they believed were analogous to those governing animal behavior and evolution. The thrust of their findings supported the established *laissez-faire* institutions and were antagonistic to the reformist impulse and, therefore, to directed social change. Manipulation here was accepted as an inevitable aspect of the relations between people (as was coercion) within a settled social system, but it was not thought realistic to drastically change the social system either through manipulation or any other means. Liberal theorists, however, correctly saw social Darwinism as the last breath of an already dead social system. Technology itself had brought about the very change that the social Darwinist claimed to be impossible, and as technology grew the institutions which attempted to govern it became ineffective. The recognition of this situation was the major insight of progressive theory, and the reinterpretation of social Darwinism was the major conceptual instrument for dealing with it.

Pierce and Dewey persuasively argued that the laws of human evolution did not rigidly govern human behavior by wedding it to existing institutional forms but were guides to be used in changing human beings and their institutions. The problem was only to decide in what direction and within what limits behavior and institutions could be altered, and the answer was that change was to be judged by the functional integration of one part of the social structure with another. Because the dominant and unyielding part of modern society was believed to be the growth of technology, technology was proposed to be the focal point of functional integration. The school had many roles in this process, but its major one was to teach people that the new technology was the reality around which their lives were to

be organized and to teach them too to take up their place in its development. Reformers of all persuasions accepted this as the primary function
of schooling. Some, however, like Snedden and Bobbitt envisaged technology as fixed with the roles already predefined, and therefore focused
their attention on developing the skills and behaviors needed in the new
industrial society. Others, like Dewey, saw technology as open and its
direction as predictable *only* within limits. For them, the role of the
school was to establish the flexibility needed to function in such uncertainty.

Nevertheless, the acceptance by progressives and liberals of technology as the organizing principle of modern society provided a significant place for manipulation. The principle of functional integration
requires only that those elements in the total social system that are
openly at odds with the requirements of technology be treated so as to
reduce existing tensions. It does not require that the principles embodied by the existing institutions be evaluated by any means other than
their integrative qualities. Nor does it establish any principles to guide
the direction toward which tensions should be reduced since it requires
no examination of principles but only the articulation of generalizations
by which to guide the alteration of behavior and institutions.

The dominance of functional integration and technology as the
organizing focus of educational reform accounts for most of the seeming anomalies of the progressive education movement. When, for
example, Dewey endorsed the curriculum of P.S. 26 or Robinson proposed a special history for the children of the working class that would
make them content in their lowly positions, they were advocating proposals that would advance the functional integration of attitudes with
technology. Later, during the depression years when progressives called
for economic and political reforms to counter the effects of a *laissez-faire*
economic policy, they were calling again for the functional integration
of various parts of the social structure. The focal point might shift from
time to time from changing attitudes to reforming institutions, but the
goal was always to bring together units that were growing apart.

With social science as the vehicle and functional integration as the
goal, the moral aspects of manipulation were seen as the remnant of a
distant and inadequate metaphysics. The evolution of institutions and of
human values was to proceed on a functional basis, and changes were
to be initiated by the managers as they were coached by the social
scientist.

## V. THE
## PROGRESSIVE'S POINT OF VIEW

It could be objected by one favorably disposed to progressive education that the foregoing analysis is too harsh, that it fails to take into account the obvious inclination that many progressives had towards bettering the lot of the poor, just as it also fails to evaluate progressive theory and practice in the light of the real practical problems that existed at the time. This objection is worth exploring at some length in order to clarify the criticism that is being made.

Those who wish to defend the progressive ideal in this fashion could begin by observing that any practical act, as well as any theory, must be judged in light of the situation and the possibilities of the time; that even though it might be interesting to point towards certain seeming anomalies in progressive education, and to argue from these for a re-examination and reevaluation of liberal theory, the fact of the matter is that these were neither anomalies nor were they central to progressive thought. Instead they were the compromises that progressives had to make with the dominant forces of the time. Not to have made such compromises would have rendered the basic thrust of educational reform ineffective and the plight of poor people and ethnic and racial minorities even more uncomfortable than it was. Take as examples some of the "anomalies" that have been mentioned. Dewey's evaluation of the program at P.S. 26 is neither malicious nor wrong headed. Too many schools for both immigrants and blacks were nothing more than custodial institutions and many of those that were more rested content with teaching a few basic academic skills, and then turning the youngsters out to take up unskilled, low-paying jobs. Moreover, it is not even clear that these schools must be judged as totally inadequate, given the nature of the problem that they had to deal with. It is reported, for example, that "22% of all immigrants who arrived between 1900-1914 were illiterate in any language."[10] To find a school where black children in the slum were not only learning skilled crafts, but where the curriculum was interesting and the work of the youngsters actually benefited the community is remarkable, and such a school was certainly worthy of Dewey's praise. The same argument holds for some

---

[10] *Statistical Abstract of the United States, 1926,* U.S. Department of Commerce, Washington, D.C., p. 75. I am indebted to Jay Wissot and Susan Fox for bringing these figures to my attention.

of the other seeming anomalies: For example Beard chose to downplay the conflict between the settlers and the American Indians at a time when many other textbooks were glorifying the Indian wars. And when the progressives retreated from a Marxian, class analysis of American society during the 1930s they did so with a fresh appraisal of the Soviet experiment in view. The Moscow trials, the Stalin massacres and the Hitler-Stalin pact, confirmed the validity of their opposition and made it impossible for any fair-minded, rational person to find common ground with the Soviet Union. Certainly given these experiences, there should be little question about their rejection of Marxism.

The defense might continue: certainly there is some point to the observation that technology was a focal point for educational reform theory, just as there is some point to the fact that progressive theory found a central place for the social sciences. What is in question is the evaluation that is made of these points. Educational reformers were not unique in envisaging the blessings that technology could hold for mankind. Political and social reformers of many different persuasions saw the same thing, and indeed if this vision was a central plank of the progressive movement, then it must be granted that it was also a central plank of the Marxists as well. Each saw in technology the possibility of eradicating hunger, curing disease, and making the goods of life sufficiently plentiful as to eventually end war. Both the progressives and the Marxists agreed that if the promise of technology was to be realized, the institutions that governed its use and its distribution had to be changed. Part of the problem with the structure of the existing institutions was that control and distribution of technological advances was determined to a large extent according to birth rather than merit. This not only created certain moral problems for those who believed in the democratic creed of equality of opportunity, but it created problems of efficiency as well. The best people were not necessarily the most influential, and therefore much of the potential of industrial society was threatened and with it the vision of universal material well-being. The focus on the schools was indeed largely an attempt to counter this situation by first assuring that every child of unusual talent was provided the opportunity to develop according to his capacity, and second by assuring as well that other children would not be strangers to the new world of technology that they were to encounter. This aspect of schooling accounts not only for the concerns of people like Dewey, but also for those of educators who developed intelligence examinations and efficiency reforms. Nevertheless there is a difference between the emphasis of Dewey and that of the testers and efficiency reformers. The testers were indeed overzealous in their belief that talent identification and vocational training was sufficient for the education of the new citizen. The work of Dewey and his followers was different because they recognized that technology brought many disruptive elements with it, not the least of which was a potential loss of common values and mutual understanding precipitated by, among other things, the high degree of specialization required in industry and government. It was partly for this reason that the curriculum proposed for the schools emphasized vocational programs. They were not, however, programs designed primarily to develop industrial skills, but rather to teach the interrelationships found among different skills, and thereby hopefully reduce the alienation that industrial technology might produce.

The critic might still respond that this program was concerned with nothing more than socializing youngsters thus enabling them to take up a role in industrial society. However, the defense could reply that to a certain extent the charge must be accepted, but when offered as an indictment of progressive reform it requires closer examination. The defender could note that underlying the criticism is the assumption that there exists a vast distinction between socializing someone and educating him, but the distinction holds only in a qualified way. All education involves some socialization in so far as it involves teaching youngsters those insights that a society has developed over a long period of time and which have proved successful in aiding its interaction with its surroundings. It is, in fact, the system of historical insights and the institutions that grew up to sustain them that people refer to when they speak of a particular culture. Some of the more important insights are often taught to children in a habitual way, as if there really were no other possible alternative. Children learn many of the moral codes of the community in this manner as well as certain patterns of speech and certain key values. It is this habitual learning that is usually referred to when someone speaks of socialization, and the contrast between socialization and education is believed to be the difference between rote, mechanical learning and the developing of free, inquiring intelligence and curiosity. But the distinction is not that strong. Intellectual curiosity is itself a habit, one nurtured in some cultures and not in others. It is typified by an awareness of the way things fit together, by a sensitivity to disorders that arise and by a trained ability to develop alternative connections. Abstract thinking, which is so often identified with intelligence, and placed in opposition to vocational education, is merely an instrument, useful in some cultures and less so in others, for projecting possibilities and orientating activity. For example, primitive peoples may not have developed such abstract concepts as "North," "East," "South," "West," and therefore may have difficulty reading a map, but they may yet be highly proficient in navigating a river because of an acute sensitivity to certain environmental cues. This sensitivity allows them to cope with their particular environment. The intent of progressive education was to bring to bear the reflective habits of intelligence and curiosity that are required to cope with our environment on the more unconscious habits usually associated with socialization.

If the objection is now raised that the intent of this reflection, and indeed one of its consequences was to separate the youngster from his traditional culture and prepare him to take up a place in the industrial nation, it must be asked whether such an objection is directed against progressive educational reform in general, or whether it is to be raised against any social change whatsoever. Surely, progressive reform alone did not cause the alienation between newer and older generations, and certainly we can expect that such alienation will continue whether progressive education is alive or dead. If, however, the objection is meant to suggest more, namely that the real function of educational reform was to separate the immigrant child from his parent's culture in order to complete the development of a single nation, then the objection requires further analysis. Certainly some people associated with progressive reform had an undue fear of immigrant groups, and it is not wrong to question how this fear might have influenced their recommendations about schools. However there is little evidence to suggest that this fear dominated those who were most closely associated with the movement. Dewey's involvement with the Polish community may be taken as a case in point. Certainly his document does not imply that Polish people were inferior intellectually to people in the dominant segments of American society. The document like any other must be seen in the context of the times. One may disagree with his support of World War I, but nevertheless one must still admire the rare willingness of an academic philosopher to use his skills to try and clarify the major questions of his time. Apparently he believed that certain conservative elements in the Polish community were hindering America's war effort and he wanted to correct the situation without imposing upon the Poles a totally external and foreign structure; thus the recommendation of a committee of prominent Poles to oversee Polish-American affairs. He might, of course, have decided to take the cultural group as the ultimate and only arbiter of its own affairs, but such a position is not only unrealistic in a society of many groups, each interacting and affecting the other, but it also overlooks the possible desires and wishes of individuals who would wish to move beyond the boundaries of their cultural groups. Certainly there are examples from contemporary times of governments that have encouraged the development of indigenous cultures in order to stunt the development of those skills that would allow individual members to enter the cultural mainstream and demand a larger share of its rewards (South Africa offers one striking example of this.) Such examples justify a certain amount of scepticism towards movements that support cultural isolation as a supreme value.

Public education was offered as a way to develop more peaceful relationships between peoples of different cultures and to bring them to an awareness of the American way of life. For most progressives, however, the term "the American way of Life" was not a parochial one. They did not believe that its basic structure was finished and needed only to be imposed on the immigrant. To them America was, or at least it ought to become, an open society and the immigrant, once made aware of its possibilities, had as much to give to it as he would take from it. This was, for example, the basic thrust of the Bureau of Intercultural Education, and whatever its problems may have been in Detroit, the vision certainly was neither pernicious nor inappropriate.

Perhaps the critic will respond: yes, but a man ought to be free to be what he is without the state trying to shift his loyalties, or develop his appreciation of its industrial wonders. The answer to this is simply that a man ought to be free, but what he *is* is not always clear. The self is indeed the result of a past history, both personal and social and a man is a reflection of that history. To think that a man is any freer when, without reflection, he drags his total history into the present, is as foolish as to think that he is free when he sheds his past for the newest fad that happens along. If one person has a right to be free then so too does every other person, but unless the freedom of one is controlled by institutions that are recognized by all, that freedom exists as a threat to everyone else. In part the new education took as its task the development of this common recognition, and in that sense it was an education for human freedom.

## VI. BEYOND
## REVISIONIST CRITIQUES

The defense of progressive reform tells us as much about the fears which came to dominate the movement as it does about the vision which guided it. Its inability to distinguish Marxism from the Stalinist horrors perpetrated in its name accounts for one of these fears, but this confusion only highlights the progressive movement's inability to establish an independent direction of its own. Nevertheless, if the recent criticisms of progressive reform have been advanced on the basis of an untenable separation between freedom and control, then its defense must be taken seriously. It is to this issue that we now must turn.

The criticism of twentieth-century educational reform must eventually proceed on grounds other than the simple fact that the schools were used as instruments of social control, for the defender of the progressive movement is quite correct in his belief that this criticism may invoke an unsatisfactory interpretation of freedom to make its case. Within limits social control can be defended without denying either the possibility or the value of freedom.

Freedom does not mean only acting out of present desires. Even in the case of a single individual freedom requires that one's present choice not negate the possibility for future choices, and it is thus a questionable act of freedom when one *chooses* to commit suicide or to take a mind-killing drug. Thus freedom, even in the most individualistic sense of the term, implies some element of control—the control that comes from foresight and out of a view of the good for one's future self.

When the context of freedom becomes not a single person, but the interrelationships among different people in the setting of a society, different yet analogous factors take over. One need not believe that people are innately bad or selfish (this was Hobbes' argument) to understand that they might rationally give some of their power over to a governing body and of course, along with that power, the right to enforce the decisions that are made. Among the advantages of people being together in society is the advantage that can come from being able to do more things, to achieve more goods and security together than they can individually.[11] If a person is actually to achieve such advantages, and if he is also to be willing to contribute his fair share to the ad-

[11] This observation has been made by many social theorists and philosophers from Plato to Rawls.

vantages of others, he must be reasonably sure that others will do their part. In small communities such assurance need not require an elaborate structure for there are more immediate, informal, interpersonal controls that can be exerted. The absence of a formal structure of control should not, however, be mistaken for the absence of control in general. In larger societies where many functional relationships take the place of closer, more informal personal relationships the controls become more structured. This does not necessarily mean that there is more personal freedom in the smaller face to face community than there is in the larger society. And even though alienation tends to be a consequence of size, it is not impossible to imagine a large society where face to face communities are the basic primary group and where alienation would be minimized, yet where the relations between primary groups remain impersonal and functional.

The revisionists' emphasis on social control may partially obscure a more serious problem of twentieth-century educational reform by placing the emphasis elsewhere. The defender of progressive education is, in a limited sense, quite correct in questioning the critics charge that educators used the schools to alienate children from their parents and from their parents' community. Again the problem with this claim is not that it is false, Dewey and Blanshard's recommendations that the Polish parochial schools be discouraged is at least one case that supports the validity of the claim. The problem is simply that as the charge is levied, its tone often suggests that the family was some kind of haven for free expression and enlightenment. That suggestion might possibly hold up, but it is not self-evident and certainly requires a closer examination of family life in general. Even if the claim did generally hold true, it would not reduce the desirability of some community agency having the power to act in situations of obvious child abuse (although it certainly would reduce the claim that public schooling made on children generally).

By emphasizing only the factor of social control, the revisionists have been caught in an unfortunate dilemma of deciding who should have real authority over the child. The schools are criticized for undermining the authority of the parent,[12] but because the very same pressures

---

[12] For one expression of this point of view see Joel Spring, "Education and Social Control," in Karier, Violas, and Spring, *Roots of Crisis*, p. 31. Spring's point of view on this issue is not absolutely clear, but the discussion of the

that are exerted upon schools are also exerted on parents, there is little to indicate that the parent's judgment would be essentially different from that of the schools.

The emphasis on parental authority can sometimes prove to be rather uncomfortable. One educator, who a few years ago could enthusiastically advocate "a movement driven by a desire to bring joy and delight to the life of the individual, to enrich experience solely for the purpose of making life more full and lovely,"[13] is more recently puzzled by the discrepancy between the visions of a humanizing educational system held by radical educators and the demands of poor people whom they hoped to represent.

Educational radicalism has been offered as a cure for the pathology afflicting the education of the urban poor . . . In fact, I suspect that what the poor want for their children is affluence, status, and a house in the suburbs rather than community, a guitar, and soul. They may prefer schools that teach their children to read and write and cipher than to feel and to be.[14]

There are some good reasons for shifting much of the control of schools from the educational professional to the parent and the local community. This shift can be defended for example on many of the same grounds that greater participation of the client group in decision making can be defended, but it should not be presupposed that by merely shifting the focus of authority that the education of the young will automatically improve or that the society will become more humane. In view of the fact that schools are the major instrument for preparing youngsters for the world of work, and that many youngsters are directed toward jobs where creativity and curiosity are perceived as detriments rather than assets, it is unlikely that a shift in the locus of authority alone will improve the quality of education. But it is precisely these facts that need to be brought into question.

school as an instrument of social control takes place in the context of its role as a surrogate parental authority. His comment on E. A. Ross is instructive in this regard. "Reliance on education as a new means of control," Ross argued, "was in fact exactly what was becoming a characteristic of American society. More and more the school was taking the place of the church and the family."

   [13] Michael B. Katz, *The Irony of Early School Reform: Educational Innovation in Mid-Nineteenth Century Massachusetts* (Cambridge: Harvard University Press), 1968, p. 214.

   [14] Michael B. Katz, *Class Bureaucracy and Schools: The Illusion of Educational Change in America* (New York: Praeger), 1971, p. 139.

Social control is an aspect of institutions in general, not just of progressive institutions or of schools. Indeed, part of what it means to be an institution is to have certain mechanisms available for affecting a correspondence between individual behavior and the accepted rules. And part of what it means to be an educational institution is to possess the means to establish a general respect for the rules that are accepted. There is an important sense in which early education is analogous to learning a game. In order to learn to play a game one must learn what is allowed and prohibited by the rules even though it may not be necessary to know how to verbalize or articulate the rules. In part early education is teaching youngsters the rules either of an existing society (when it is conservative) or of a projected society (when it is not). Even the members of Summerhill, recognize certain rules even if the student body has an equal voice with the faculty in determining guilt and punishment (which is itself a kind of rule). In view of this function, what is significant is not *that* rules are learned but that they are fair. In the long run, the function of education should be not only to teach the rules but to teach students ways to evaluate their fairness.

The fact of social control is not significant in itself, but what is significant is the direction of that control and the principle it is intended to support. Any effective critique of liberal educational reform must therefore be an examination of the principle that was accepted as the guide for educational innovation and policy; while manipulation is a problem, exploitation is a more basic one.

The major insight of the progressive reformer was that the changing nature of technology demanded structural changes in major social institutions including education and that whatever promise technology held for improving the lot of mankind was being inhibited by lack of planning and functional integration. Education had a key role to play in this situation by developing the intellectual skills and the social attitudes that industrial society was thought to require.

The major oversight of progressive reform was a failure to fully understand the implications of its recognition that every social structure is an embodiment of a set of values and that the institutions in which these values are expressed have a strong influence on determining the desires and inclinations of the members of a society. Thus instead of a prolonged evaluation of the *principles* of social organization itself, the progressives insisted on evaluating institutions *merely* on the basis of their functional integration. Clearly liberal educators shared this over-sight with some of their Marxian counterparts, each believing that one only needed to project the outlines of the future level of technology and that the appropriate values and institutions would reveal themselves as self-evident. Here was the true meaning of progress, and it was one that Marxists and liberals held in common. In order to elaborate this neglect in terms of liberal educational theory, it is necessary to turn again to the social context in which educational reform was proposed.

The defender of progressive reform recognized that one of its driving forces was the realization that the process of social selection had become inefficient in light of technological demands. The entry of talented people into influential positions in the social structure had been inhibited by the stress on a private, unregulated, market economy, and to a lesser extent by inherited wealth. Dewey made this point in a num-ber of places observing that whatever progress industrial development had made was not to be attributed to the men of capital—they were its major benefactors—but rather to the men of science and engineering. He believed that the full exploitation of science and engineering skills was artificially limited by an institutional structure that mainly benefitted the men of business.

Dewey's objection arose out of the *laissez-faire* justification of the existent institutional structures, and it was this that his challenge was intended to address. The challenge was, nevertheless, a limited one failing to go to the heart of the matter. The *laissez-faire* point of view had been used to justify the position of the business establishment by arguing that as businessmen set out to directly serve their own self-interest, the social interest was indirectly, but quite efficiently, served. Dewey merely denied that the social interest was best served by the business establishment and proposed that institutions be altered so as to free technology from its control. His alternative was to change the position of the science and engineering establishments for that of business establishment assuming perhaps that as the interest of science was served so too would be that of society at large. Yet like the *laissez-faire* theorist, no criteria other than functional ones were established to judge whether or not the social interest was being served.

As the vehicle for social selection, the schools were to serve the same function for the modern liberal as the market had served for the older, *laissez-faire* liberal—that of social selection. The dominant and unchallenged value of both the new and the old liberalism was equality of opportunity, and it was this value that was expressed through the institutions of both *laissez-faire* liberalism and contemporary liberalism. The criticism of *laissez-faire* was simply that equality of opportunity had been negated by the very institution that was supposed to support it. The market favored accumulated and hereditary wealth. The schools, on the other hand, were to provide the intermediate stages of equal educational opportunity leading to equal economic opportunity.[15]

Some revisionist historians have challenged the claim that schools have been a significant vehicle for equality of opportunity. Colin Greer for example has argued that regarding immigrant groups, the schools were successful with those whose values already corresponded with the dominant values of American society and that they were not successful for those with variant values. But these analysts fail to challenge the principle of equality of opportunity, addressing only the question of whether or not the schools have actually met this principle. The rhetoric of the school is equality of opportunity and the failure of public schools supposedly has been to live up to its rhetoric. As Greer puts it:

Schools could be an agent for major change in this society. Basic as they are to the maintenance of both the humane and democratic rhetoric of society, and of widescale socioeconomic inequalities, the public schools could be a vehicle for some of us to push the contradictions inherent in the

---

[15] Dewey did not stress equality of educational opportunity as it leads to equality of economic opportunity and therefore inequality of actual economic rewards, but it is an underlying factor in much of his writings as exemplified by the organization of *Schools of Tomorrow* where he mentions without comment how youngsters in Gary are aware of the effect that their work in school has on their ultimate position in the factory. Because Dewey did not address this subject directly, however, one can only speculate about his actual feelings. It does not seem to be stretching his ideas too far, however, to suggest that his failure to challenge the proposals by the testing and the efficiency people specifically on these grounds indicates that his concern was in other areas. Nevertheless that equality of educational opportunity was important to more than simply testers and administrators has been shown by the examination of Warner, Havinghurst, and Loeb, *Who Shall Be Educated* (New York: Harper Bros.), 1944. (See Chapter Four) One of the central assumptions in the book is the need for economic and social differentiation, and the point is that the schools are one of the most effective means to provide the selection necessary.

severe disjuncture between school rhetoric and the social reality to the point of absurdity. Since the goals in the school rhetoric are anathema to the organization and theory of a puritan capitalist society, would it not be absurd and what might happen if the rhetoric became more than words.[16]

Greer's optimism is misplaced. The rhetoric of equal opportunity is not at all anathema to puritanical capitalism nor to any other kind of capitalism. The initial appeal that sold capitalism to many people was the argument that it allowed talent to rise as far as it could without being encumbered by hereditary privilege. Greer's critique is valuable, however, because it does show that the schools were not as successful in assimilating the immigrant into the American structure of values and rewards as is often thought to be the case. It does not, however, sufficiently demonstrate that the schools were insufficient vehicles for equality of opportunity. The principle of equality of opportunity does not guarantee that every person will succeed or even that each group will have the same range of successes and failures as every other group. It merely claims that each person will have a reasonable chance at success and then given a reasonable chance, if he fails, his failure is to be attributed to personal rather than to social factors.

Greer does succeed in casting doubt on the commitment of American society to the goal of equality of educational opportunity, but a society's commitment to an ideal is not judged simply by whether or not the ideal has yet been achieved. The commitment is also judged by whether there has been clear movement towards the achievement of the ideal, and such movement is determined not only by the the the effectiveness of one institution, such as the public schools, but by a constellation of institutions including business, industry, labor, and others. A full analysis of equality of opportunity in American society would require an examination of a number of institutions in addition to the public schools.

The point of the above remarks is neither to confirm or to refute a revisionist analysis such as the one offered by Greer, but merely to suggest that it presents only an aspect of a larger picture, and to suggest

---

[16] Colin Greer, *The Great School Legend: A Revisionist Interpretation of American Public Education* (New York: Basic Books, Inc.), 1972, p. 154. For elaboration and criticism of Greer's views on schools and Equality of Opportunity see Russ Marks' review of *The Great School Legend, Educational Theory,* forthcoming.

too that the examination of American society and education requires an analysis of the ideal of equality of opportunity itself as it fits into the structure of American institutions.

## VII. AGAINST EQUALITY
## OF EDUCATIONAL OPPORTUNITY

Arguments for equality of opportunity have traditionally been advanced on two different grounds. First, from the individual's point of view it was thought that this ideal required that the structural roadblocks to achievement be removed thereby enabling each individual to rise as far as his talents would allow. If the ideal were achieved, then a person, no matter how humble his origins, could achieve wealth and status equal to that of any other person. By deemphasizing accidental factors such as family backgrounds, social class, race, creed or color, individuals would advance by merit alone. Second, from the social point of view, it was believed that equality of educational opportunity provided a way to relieve social tension and possibly violence, by allowing the more intelligent members of the lower classes to relieve their dissatisfaction by rising out of their oppressive situation. Thus it seemed as if equality of opportunity provided the best of all possible worlds: a way to achieve individual fairness while assuring domestic peace and tranquility at the same time.

The ideal of equality of opportunity was associated with *laissez-faire* capitalism before it became associated with a planned society. Initially the market was to be the arena for social selection, a place where each man was dependent on his skills and the attractiveness of his wares for his success or failure. When it became clear to some that success was becoming more a matter of parentage than of skill, reformers began to think of the school as the new vehicle for social selection. Universal education was justified on many grounds, but one of them was that it helped equalize the difference between rich and poor by freeing the talent that was bottled up by hereditary privilege. But when the poor found themselves to be still poor, even after spending the requisite number of years in school, when the school itself became a constant focus of discontent, some began to argue that universal compulsory education was not enough. Compulsory schooling alone did not necessarily mean equality of opportunity. It was at this point that the idea of equality of educational opportunity became thought of as the prerequisite to equality of opportunity.

Both the ideal of equality of opportunity and equality of educational opportunity reveal a common image of social selection. Both emphasize, for example, that the common attribute of human beings is inequality and that the proper role of economic or educational institutions is to identify such inequality so that it may be effectively utilized for social ends. Moreover, both ideals assume that the selection of talent alone is sufficient to assure the social good while differing only about the best vehicle by which to select that talent.

Implicit in both ideals is a judgment about the just distribution of social and educational goods. The judgment is that a just distribution results when one is allotted that amount of education (or in *laissez-faire,* of economic control) that is consistent with one's capacities, and that given unequal capacities, unequal education follows. Just as *laissez-faire* economic policy once identified the market place as the vehicle to sort out inequalities, so the new liberalism has determined that the school should be the vehicle of social selection. Equality of educational opportunity is therefore simply a loose formula for deciding the eventual allocation of educational resources according to the talents of individuals as selected by ideally fair procedures. One of its most common formulations directs society to equalize educational resources during the early years in order to determine the allotment of unequal resources later on.[17] The most heated debates among contemporary educators are not debates about the ideal itself but about whether a certain instrument such as an IQ test is really effective in sorting out the inequalities.

The debate between the liberal environmentalists and the more conservative genetic school has masked the commitment of both to the same principle for the distribution of educational resources. The argu-

[17] As it turns out in actual practice the total lifetime expenditure on education strongly follows along socioeconomic class lines. As Gintis and Bowles have noted: "An individual in the highest socioeconomic decile has three hundred and ninety-seven times the probability (39.7) of ending up in the highest education decile as does an individual from the lowest socioeconomic decile (0.1%). Herbert Gintis and Samuel Bowles, "The Contradictions of Liberal Educational Reform," in Walter Feinberg and Henry Rosemont, *Work, Technology and Education* (Urbana: The University of Illinois Press), forthcoming.

ment is not *whether* genetic factors influence intelligence, but whether they are the dominant influence. To assert that genetic factors influence intelligence by 40 rather than 80%, for example, is to say that performance on an IQ exam or some other appropriate measure is determined *largely* by environmental factors. The proposals to enrich the environment for certain children are therefore proposals to make this factor more equal. And if indeed there were some way to totally equalize the environment, then whatever variations in intelligence that did occur would be determined solely by genetic factors, which would remain stable. Thus, to "equalize the environment" especially in the early years means nothing more than to provide the conditions whereby performance will reflect the genetic factor alone.

To illustrate the difficulties of equal educational opportunity, a brief analysis would be helpful. The goal of the ideal is, of course, not equality. Inherent in the very concept is that people are unequal in capacity, and it is concluded from this that they ought therefore to occupy unequal positions of education, status, and income. What the goal does express is the belief that the procedures for selecting people for different social and economic ranks ought to be able to discount factors other than talent and to allocate equal resources to equal talent. Once this goal is accepted, then the problem is to identify those conditions that result in inappropriate selections, and usually such conditions are thought to exist in one of two places. Either they are to be located in the amount of resources actually allocated for early formal education such as two schools where the expenditure per pupil is significantly disparate, or else they are to be located in certain factors that affect the extent to which the child is able to profit from formal schooling. Assuming, for example, that there are two children of equal intelligence, one of whom comes from a wealthy family and the other from a poor family, the goal of equality of educational opportunity would be to compensate for whatever factors of home life or formal schooling that might inhibit the poorer child from achieving at a level with the wealthier child. Thus a simple compensatory measure would be the type of grants and scholarships that have traditionally been set aside to aid capable but poor children. A more elaborate compensatory measure would be the various preschool and Head Start programs that have been established recently to help bring children to a point of relative equality before they start school.

The commitment to equality of educational opportunity has been followed by attempts to account for discrepancies in the social structure by pointing to discrepancies in one or the other of these two conditions. Either the problem lies in unequal access to formal educational institutions, or else it lies in conditions of family life and social situation that inhibit an otherwise capable child from benefiting from the formal structures that are available. The problem, however, is that the very goal of equality of educational opportunity is in fact a justification for such discrepancies. As John Schaar has observed "it really only defends the equal right to become unequal by competing against one's fellows."[18] Remaining unchallenged is the classification scheme according to which men are assigned different roles in the social structure. The problem is merely to streamline the access vehicle. The structure of status and rewards obtains a quasi- meta-physical status removed from the process of evaluation, and so too do those capacities and skills that are singled out for special citation and reward.[19]

If the goal of full equality of educational opportunity were actually achieved, if the instruments for identifying talent and the institutions for training it were perfected, then it is likely that the society would be even more unequal than it presently is. Talent would be removed from the lower classes, the instruments for control that exist in large bureaucratic structures would become even more efficient, and if certain scholars like Herrnstein are correct,[20] because of hereditary factors, even the small amount of mobility that now exists between classes would diminish. With talent removed from the lower classes, their ability to articulate real injustices would be destroyed and along with it any incentive for others to address social injustices.[21]

In American society, the appeal to equality of educational opportunity has consistently been used to mask basic inequalities in social, economic and political institutions. The schools have been used to hold out the promise of pie-in-the-sky for everyone while the economics of the situation have denied to some even a loaf of daily bread. The prob-

[18] John H. Schaar, "Equality of Opportunity and Beyond," Nomos, IX, Penneck and Chapman, eds. (New York: Atherton Press), 1967, p. 241. Schaar's remarks are addressed to the concept of Equality of Opportunity, but they hold equally well for the concept of equality of educational opportunity.
[19] Cf., ibid.
[20] See Richard J. Herrnstein, "I.Q.," The Atlantic Monthly, September, 1971, pp. 43-64.
[21] Schaar, p. 232.

lem with schools is not that they have failed to achieve equality of opportunity, nor is it that they have not tried. The massive campaign against dropouts is clearly a way of saying that school is the avenue to a good job and financial security, and this message is not totally false. A high school or a college degree is a way of identifying people as employable at a certain level. The problem is that the schools have advanced the idea of equality of opportunity in the context of an economic system that would bankrupt itself if everyone who was employable and wanted to work were actually given a job.[22] Indeed if everyone were to stay in school up to the same level, and were to come out with very similar competencies, employers would have to find some other trait to distinguish the "employables" from the "unemployables." Equality of educational opportunity has been such an appealing idea because people have not wanted to deal with the problem of equality, perhaps assuming that the obvious sense in which people are unequal renders every sense of equality invalid.

Advocates of equality as a social ideal rarely mean to suggest, however, that there are not some very obvious ways in which individuals are unequal. There is, however, a reluctance to grant that large ethnic or religious groups are unequal, not only because the evidence seems contrived but also because such research has too often been put to malicious use (note, for example, the elaborate explanations that were used to explain the fact that for a number of years Catholics were performing

[22] The reasons for this are complex, but they can be seen in a rather common sense way. President Nixon's former treasury secretary Connally pronounced on at least one official occasion that it is unrealistic to expect a rate of unemployment much below 5% in peacetime (he did not seem to notice that the Vietnam war was going on at the time). This pronouncement came close to one of the President's speeches extolling the dignity of work, and the fact that a person can take pride in a job no matter how menial it is. The implied message here, of course, is that there is something demeaning about a man who does not work. Thus on the one side is the Secretary of the Treasury explaining that not everyone can work, and on the other side is the President saying that everyone ought to want to work and should feel badly about himself if he does not. The apparent contradiction is not that severe, however, once it is understood that as long as unemployed people continue to compete for jobs, they act as a hedge against inflation by keeping wages at a reasonable rate. If suddenly people who were unemployed decided that there was nothing wrong with being out of work and stopped looking for jobs, the economy would be in even more serious difficulty than it is. Thus even though everyone cannot be employed it is very important for everyone to believe that they ought to be working.

lower than Protestants and Jews on IQ exams. One of these explanations was that because the intelligent members of the religion entered the priesthood and committed themselves to celibacy, the genetic quality of the masses deteriorated. Of course when Catholics began to score on a reasonable par with these other groups, such explanations were quickly forgotten. There does seem to be an obvious difference in the range of capacities possessed by different men and also in the skills that they are able to learn. To admit that such differences exist among individuals, however, does not commit one to believe that an analysis of intellectual variation along racial lines is anything other than a reflection of the pervasive influence of racist social institutions. It is no more rational than testing whether blue-eyed or brown-eyed people are more intelligent. The significant question is whether the fact of intellectual differences entails any clear directives regarding the expenditure of educational resources, and the answer to this is no.

It may be granted that certain abilities and skills are more highly valued in some societies than in others, and that it is often the case that special consideration and education is given to those who have the desired ability. This consideration is sometimes used to argue in defense of both equality of educational opportunity and of instruments such as IQ examinations which are designed to identify the existence of such talent. Thus it is argued that the doctrine of equality of educational opportunity merely directs society to identify those individuals possessed of the most desired abilities and to then expend a disproportionate share of the educational resources on their education.

Yet the fact that different societies value different abilities and thereby spend a disproportionate amount of resources in training those with such capacities is not so much an argument for how resources ought to be allocated as it is an observation about general social tendencies. It is reasonable to suppose, for example, that militaristic societies do value militaristic skills, that maritime societies value navigational skills, and so on. From such an observation, however, little follows. The observation does not tell us whether and to what extent such skills ought to be valued, nor does it provide any real principle for assessing the allotment of educational resources. For example, while the skills of the nuclear physicist and the engineer may be among the most highly valued in American society, certainly the ability to analyze the propaganda put out by private groups and governmental agencies might be an even more important skill in terms of the maintenance of human freedom.[23] And if the development of a skill such as resisting propaganda is thought to be valuable, it does not, by itself, tell us how educational resources ought to be spent. Perhaps the inverse of equality of educational opportunity would be the most appropriate formula: spend the greatest amount of resources on those youngsters whose intellectual capacity is such that they are least likely to develop this skill on their own accord.

Liberals offered the doctrine of equality of opportunity and equality of educational opportunity as a substitute for hereditary privilege and wealth. The appeal of these doctrines must therefore be seen in the context out of which they arose. Certainly allowing each person to rise as far as his or her talents would allow seemed an advance over a social system that alloted education according to family background and social status. And even if the ideal has been misused as a justification for the *status quo,* as recent critics have charged, that fact would not deny whatever validity the ideal holds. Thus liberals looked on equality of educational opportunity as an approximation of a just and equitable society. Nevertheless, once the historical context and motivation is removed, the ideal falls short of true justice and equity.

The basic idea of justice to which the advocates of equality of educational opportunity appeal is the notion that contingent factors, such as family background, social class, race, sex, or religion ought not to be a barrier to social advancement.[24] The argument is that justice requires that contingent factors be taken into account in the allocation

---

[23] Noam Chomsky, in *American Power and the New Manderins: Historical and Political Essays* (New York: Vintage Books), 1969, pp. 313-314, sees the development of the skills needed to resist governmental propaganda as one of the legitimate functions of schooling. Critics of public schooling, such as Ivan Illich, might of course respond that this task cannot take place in the schools, given their relationship to existing structures of power. Illich may be correct, but it does seem premature to decide what can and what cannot take place in public schools before some debate about what constitutes education and therefore, what ought to take place. Illich's de-schooling proposal has an important place in debates regarding the allocation of educational resources, but without some guidelines as to what constitutes an educative experience, his proposals guarantee no more freedom, no less manipulation than does the existing structure of public schooling.

[24] For an elaboration of this point and of the criticism that follows see Herbert Spiegelberg, "A Defense of Human Equality," *Philosophical Review,* Vol. 53 (1944), pp. 113-123.

of social rewards, and that wherever possible, such factors should be redressed. It is this notion, for example, that was such a powerful force behind the arguments for compensatory education since the contingency of race had posed an extreme barrier to educational and social achievement.

In assessing this argument it is necessary to give recognition to two considerations. First, in terms of human justice the ideal of equality of educational opportunity is a significant advance over the notion of simple social stability that was often used to justify the allocation of educational privilege on the basis of birth and social class. Second, while it will be argued here that the principle of equality of educational opportunity is somewhat off the mark of a just society, it must not thereby be concluded that all of the programs that were advanced in its name should be dismissed out of hand. If compensatory programs have the effect of reducing the barrier that racial considerations presented for quality education, then to that degree they are valuable programs.

The basic structure of this argument for equality of opportunity—that contingent factors ought to be compensated—can be accepted as a reasonable precept of social justice. The problem arises when we are asked to accept only certain factors as contingent and to ignore others that seem equally accidental. Certainly fairness does seem to dictate that accidental factors such as family background, status, wealth, race, sex, or religion ought not to be a hindrance to the development of a man's talents and that wherever possible, these factors should be compensated. Thus if it is decided that the environment in which a child is growing up is deficient in some important way, such as lack of medical attention, inadequate verbal stimulation, etc., and if it is believed that this factor has operated as a hinderance to educational achievement, then it is reasonable to expect that the factor should be compensated. This aspect of equality of educational opportunity can be accepted without great difficulty for it is consistent with our intuitions of fairness and justice. To accept this, however, is not to accept the whole idea.

The proponents of equality of equal educational opportunity are willing only to accept certain factors as contingent while denying contingency to other factors which seem equally accidental. Wealth, social status, economic class, and religion have been traditionally accepted as contingent factors, and more recently race and sex have been added. Other factors, such as the native intelligence of a person, are treated as if they were not accidental at all but instead, essential attributes of a person.[25] The image that guides the liberal idea of fairness is an image where the essential aspects of personality, such as intelligence, may be imprisoned by accidental factors, such as family background. The schools and other social agencies then serve as a pardoning board, reviewing each case in order to decide who has been unjustly imprisoned and therefore should be released. If, however, intelligence is judged to be commensurate with family background, social class, or other "contingent" factors, if performance is judged to be an indication of real ability, and not the result of an accidental barrier, then the imprisonment is judged to be both fair and inevitable, and the prison gate remains locked.

It is unclear, however, why intellectual capacity should be considered any more accidental than other factors.[26] Certainly a person does not choose his own intellectual capacity any more than he chooses his parents or his race. A person may or may not choose to do something with that capacity, but that is a somewhat different consideration. Some may want to respond that the difference between factors such as social class or family background on the one hand and intellectual capacity on the other is that the former can be changed whereas the latter cannot. The response, however, is not adequate. A person can no more change his family background than he can change his intellectual capacity (assuming some ideal instrument by which such capacity could be measured). And while he may change his social class during the course of a lifetime, he cannot alter the fact that he was born into a particular social class. It is the factor of his situation at birth that is described as a contingency, not the changes that occur later on. Of course factors such as family background or social class are factors for which education can sometimes compensate, but there is no reason to assume that intellectual capacity cannot be compensated for in a similar way.

The belief that intellectual capacities cannot be compensated is perhaps most commonly supported by a certain notion of educational efficiency. After all, the argument goes, the principle of equality of educational opportunity requires only that each person be educated to

[25] This point was originally made by Spiegelberg in "A Defense of Human Equality."

[26] See Spiegelberg for an elaboration of this point. This is not meant to deny or to affirm the belief that intelligence or rationality constitutes the human essence. It refers simply to the element of accident involved in the distribution of intelligence among different indivduals.

his or her fullest capacity. It would be unjust to do less, but it would simply be wasteful to do more. Certainly it would be foolish to allocate resources to a student whose limited intellectual capacity would not allow him to profit from the expenditure just as it would be equally foolish to absolutely insist that a person take just one more bite after being filled to the gills with food.

It is difficult to argue with the observation that youngsters are possessed of finite capacities for accomplishing different tasks, and that given this observation it may at times be wasteful and perhaps even cruel to insist that a youngster learn something that he is intellectually unable to comprehend. Of course it is certainly questionable whether our instruments for identifying talent, or our methods of teaching are so refined that a judgment of this kind could be made with any real certainty except in the more extreme cases. However, for the sake of analyzing the *principle* of equality of educational opportunity itself, these considerations can be put aside. (Indeed, for the sake of this discussion we might even accept the claim of one educational technician that he has invented a machine that, when attached to an electric socket on one end and to a person's head on the other, can measure IQ in a culture-free way.)

The general principle that educational resources should not be expended in those areas where an individual youngster is incapable of learning is a reasonable guide for determining how *not* to allocate such resources. Unfortunately, it tells us very little about how such resources *should* be allocated. Even granting that for some purposes a youngster can be viewed as a kind of vessel with a finite capacity for learning, and granting too that different youngsters are possessed of different capacities, it is difficult to conclude from this anything about the allocation of educational resources. A youngster may indeed be possessed of limited ability to do abstract mathematics or complicated physics and different youngsters probably do differ in terms of their abilities in these and other areas. But youngsters are possessed of other capacities, perhaps no less finite in volume (to maintain the analogy) but certainly more indefinite in scope. They are capable of learning how to play a tune, build a house, design a dress, watch a film and many other things as well. If it is decided to single out a specific skill, such as abstract mathematics, for special consideration, then the allocation of resources beyond a given student's capacities would be wasteful. Recognizing, however, that there are an indefinite number of abilities, the fact of finite capacities alone does not automatically entail a decision as to how educational resources should be allocated.

It might be thought that the recognition that human capacities are indefinite in scope, even though finite in volume, commits one to the further recognition that each capacity is of equal value and that there are no distinctions between different kinds of learnings. The argument against equality of education is not in fact committed to such a position, but is addressed to the question of the allocation of educational resources. It does not rest on the issue of what knowledge is of most worth. Whether liberal educational reformers like Dewey were correct in their belief that the most worthwhile knowledge was an understanding of the methods of science as applied to physical and social problems is an open question, but there is good reason to believe that some kinds of learning are to be preferred to others. One need only cite, for example, recent radical critiques of schooling, much of which maintains an equalitarian tone, to show that even here a distinction is made between the relative value of different kinds of learning. When, for example, schools are criticized for teaching youngsters to be passive, obedient, and uncritical, the assumption is that learning is taking place, but it is worthless learning. One could then reasonably assume that there is another kind of learning which is worthwhile.

The greatest danger in assuming that all learning is of equal worth is the danger that comes from believing that simply because a child is attending school and indeed learning something there that no deeper analysis needs to take place. Much of liberal scholarship fell victim to this belief when it came to the education of black people and other minority groups even when it should have been clear that schooling was preparing them for subordinate social and industrial roles.[27]

Moreover when, as is the case with university training, some occupational groups, such as future chemists or physicians, are granted access to cultural knowledge such as art, philosophy, and literature while other occupational groups, such as mechanics and bricklayers, are essentially denied access to such knowledge, it is easy to see the elitist tendencies of this seemingly equalitarian approach. The failure to see this simple point accounts for the misguided approaches of the career education movement today.

---

[27] I am indebted to James Anderson and Clarence Karier for this insight.

Perhaps in reaction to the view that anything that goes on in schools is valuable, even if forced on a youngster, some educators have recently expressed the view that any knowledge is worthwhile as long as it initiates out of a real desire on the part of the child.[28] This point of view confuses a motivational activity with an epistemological concern, and could very easily turn out to be as equally oppressive as the view it is attempting to replace. It is quite true that that knowledge that allows people to be free in some significant sense is knowledge that is most worthwhile, and it is also true that in the long run such knowledge cannot be forced on a person but must be chosen freely. It is wrong, however, to assume that anything that is chosen freely is to be considered liberating knowledge. A child's desires can be conditioned by factors other than schooling and his so-called free choice may be anything but a freedom-producing choice.

Freedom-producing knowledge certainly involves choice, but it involves much more. Freedom involves being able to have a reasonable say in the control and direction of one's life as such direction is understood in the context of possible alternatives. This knowledge involves being able to see things in both their depth and their relationships, and to establish patterns to the seeming flux of events. It is perhaps the case that allowing a child the widest possible choice consistent with the development of such knowledge is normally the best pedagogical strategy, but that strategy is to be bounded by the other requirements of freedom.

Equally as important as the motivational concerns is the structure of the knowledge that is eventually chosen. While it is unrealistic to believe that freedom-producing knowledge can be encompassed by a single set of courses or by a list of behavioral objectives, it is not unreasonable to sketch some of the considerations that should influence the development of the content and methods of such a structure. One might think of a curriculum as simply a system of knowledge most closely related to different aspects of life. In this ideal sense the sciences are those areas of the curriculum that address the issue of the interrelationship between life and its environment (both physical, social, and psychological) while the humanities address the issue of how

[28] See, for example, John Holt, *How Children Fail* (New York: Delta Books), 1965, p. 180. He advocates that the school "should be a great smorgasbord of intellectual, artistic, creative, and athletic activities, from which each child could take whatever he wanted, and as much as he wanted, or as little."

this interrelationship has influenced the development and articulation of human thought, feeling, and practice.

If some knowledge is more intrinsically valuable than other knowledge, then there is every reason to encourage people to acquire that knowledge in a reasonably efficient and systematic way, and if public education were in fact a vehicle for such knowledge, then that would be a powerful argument in its favor. Whether schools can actually serve this function under the existing system of social, political, and economic inequities is a serious question and deserving of an appropriate analysis. The final judgment, however, will rest on how much real freedom can be a by-product of schooling, and whatever that judgment might be, it is questionable whether schools should be accepted as the only avenue for adequate education.

The point is not however whether some knowledge is of more intrinsic worth than other knowledge, or even whether people's capacities differ in the areas that might be the most likely candidates for such knowledge. The question is whether the different levels of knowledge and the varying capacities are sufficient to justify an unequal allotment of educational resources. To argue that these are a sufficient justification is to assume that nothing is lost when funds are spent on one person of high capacity rather than in some other way. But here again an analogy might help clarify the difference. Simply because someone has the capacity to enjoy caviar does not by itself mean that this capacity should be satisfied if it means that one who is able to enjoy only beefsteak must go hungry. What is being sought is a principle by which to establish the appropriate educational expenditure, and the fact of unequal capacities, or even of different levels of knowledge is not sufficient to justify the inequalities that are implicit in the principle of equality of educational opportunity. If, for example, certain kinds of knowledge, such as mathematics or science, are looked upon as tools by which people are able to amplify their powers, then clearly this knowledge is of greater value to an individual than the kind of knowledge which enables one to perform only a limited and defined set of tasks.[29] Further, the more capable the person of understanding and using such knowledge, the more power it provides him and hence the greater its value.

---

[29] The idea that certain kinds of knowledge amplify an individual's power was recently expressed by Carl Bereiter, "The Future of Individual Differences," *Harvard Educational Review*, Vol. 39, No. 2, Spring, 1969.

Nevertheless, few would argue that an individual, simply because he is capable of exercising power, should be granted it. It is generally, but wrongly, assumed, however, that simply because some individuals are capable of learning something, thereby increasing their power, additional social resources should be expended to teach them it.

A reasonable case can be made that some of the most important kinds of learning are only secondarily related to intellectual capacity. If, for example, it is necessary in terms of individual integrity as well as social justice, for individuals to resist the unjust or irrational demands of superiors, then it is important for youngsters to learn that it is sometimes necessary to refuse to bid for the rewards that people in positions of authority are able to hand out. Of course, as the schools increasingly adopt behavioral techniques predicated on increasing a student's passion for such rewards, this kind of moral lesson becomes more difficult to learn in the formal educational setting.

Because an individual's capacity to attain knowledge and to use it to his own advantage alone cannot be accepted as a valid argument for equality of educational opportunity, the ultimate argument for unequal allocation of educational resources must eventually rest not on the advantage that such an allotment makes for any particular individual who receives it, but rather upon some benefit that is gained by society as an aggregate. Advocates of equality of educational opportunity might then argue that by providing additional allotments to individuals of special talent, the general social well-being is raised. A version of this argument was wryly expressed by Martin Mayer in a recent article on the impact of open enrollment. Mayer observed that the opponents of open enrollment could dismiss its advocates with the curse that:

They should cross the river on a bridge designed by an engineer from an engineering school where students were admitted by lottery; and that their injuries should then be treated by a doctor from a medical school where students were admitted by lottery; and that their heirs' malpractice suit should then be tried by a lawyer from a law school where students were admitted by lottery.[30]

This particular argument for equality of educational opportunity like the others has a certain intuitive appeal. Certainly no one wants his appendix removed by Shakey down the block simply because someone

---

[30] Martin Mayer, "Higher Education for All?," *Commentary*, Vol. 55, No. 2 (February, 1973), p. 47.

has decided that educational resources should be allocated more equally. Yet the argument also requires some analysis before it can be decided whether it provides sufficient support for the principle of equality of educational opportunity. The assumption on which this argument rests is that the social good is the natural result of selecting people of outstanding ability to occupy important positions in the social structure. In part this is an empirical judgment and in part it depends on the meaning that is given to "the widest social good." If "the widest social good" is taken to mean not only the good of the people who have the financial resources to take advantage of the level of skills and social resources available but also those of lesser means then the argument is questionable. Even an extension of Mayer's comment might be sufficient to illustrate this point. Many of our most gifted engineers spend their time designing, super-speed highways, comfortable automobiles, and safe jet airplanes so that middle-class and wealthy people can travel from coast to coast in quiet, safety, and convenience while many poor people consider themselves fortunate if there is a bus available to take them to work. Many of our most competent doctors are engaged in medical practice and research that benefits the rich disproportionately to their numbers, while overseas medical research sponsored by American institutions often spends the greatest amount of resources examining and researching diseases that the few rich can be expected to die from—heart disease, or ulcers—while allocating a much smaller percentage of their resources to the diseases that poor people die from, such as dysentery. The general neglect of sickle cell anemia, a disease of black people, the use of syphilis sufferers black and poor, from Tuskegee, Alabama, as a control group to better understand the degeneration of the disease raise serious doubts about the belief that talent will naturally serve "the widest social good."

The disproportionate allocation of resources to the wealthy is sometimes justified on the basis of the spinoff effect. A cruel but generally accurate paraphrase of this argument is that someday perhaps the poor peasant will reach the point of social advancement where he too is dying of ulcers or heart disease. Or, perhaps as someone seeks a cure for these diseases he will unwittingly come across a cure that will rid the system of the dysentery causing amoeba. Such spinoffs do occur. After all, where would the Teflon pan be without the space race, and all those weed killers without Vietnam. Spinoffs do occur, but they are nothing to bet on if one is a peasant suffering from dysentery or had been a black man with sickle cell anemia before the civil rights movement.

The appeal to the spinoff effect is nothing more than another version of the idea of the invisible hand that was first offered by Adam Smith as the cause of all that is good and just in social affairs. Now, however, instead of the invisible hand working in the economic marketplace of goods and services, it is said to work in the marketplace of talent—the school.

It may be reasonable to place the idea of equality of educational opportunity in historical perspective and to argue very much the same way in which one might argue for the defense of capitalism as a historical phase. With capitalism the argument is often made that industrial potential had reached such a stage at the dawn of the industrial revolution, that the freeing of initiative and the reduction of traditional binds could not help but eventually improve the lot of mankind. Similarly with the expansion of knowledge and technique it might be argued that the freeing of talent from the binds of class and hereditary privilege could not help but have a beneficial effect on the lot of mankind in general. Whether or not this argument is eventually accepted as valid, it can help to place the idea of equality of educational opportunity in some perspective by serving to highlight the fact that it is a subordinate principle that can be replaced when the historical conditions are no longer appropriate—when it becomes a retarding factor in the development of human well-being.

The arguments for equality of educational opportunity as the principle guiding the allotment of educational resources does not hold up under careful examination. The problem is to find a substitute principle that is consistent with our sense of fairness and justice. The persuasive power of the principle of equality of educational opportunity rests on its close, but inadequate approximation to the principle of equality. The problem is to apply the principle of equality to education without ignoring intellectual differences and yet without assuming that such differences alone are sufficient to warrant unequal expenditures of educational resources.

The idea of equality as a *general* principle begins with the notion of respect of persons as members of the human race. The idea of mutual respect is of course a long-standing one expressed in different forms by various religions and philosophical systems. Respect, however, can be a cheap idea, easily granted without loss or sacrifice. We could begin by accepting the claim that people are entitled to equal respect, promise that it will soon be forthcoming and then go about with business as usual—nothing changed, nothing lost nothing gained. This is the easy way out, but it is also sham equality. If a person is entitled to respect as a person, then he is also entitled to those conditions and resources (including educational resources) that makes respect for him, not simply for some abstract personality, a real possibility. Equality begins with the recognition of the importance of respect, but it does not end there.

A person is respected for what he does, and what he does is influenced by the resources that he has at hand. If a person is entitled to equal respect, then *prima facie,* he ought to be entitled to equal resources. This is no less true of educational resources than of any other. And if it is believed that a person cannot sufficiently profit by using those resources in the established schools, then there ought to be alternative routes available for him.

The general principle of equality is not a difficult one to understand, and it can easily accommodate the recognition of differences in both background and talent. It means that no institution, whether it be an economic, a political, or an educational one, is to be either established or maintained to provide special privilege or undue hardship to any person or group. In education this means that variations in family backgrounds, race, social class, religion, sex, or *intelligence* are not sufficient to warrant a claim for additional resources or to deny a claim for the average allocation.

The argument for equality is not to be construed as a denial of the fact that the level of knowledge can influence the level of material life for the better, although it does deny that in any but peculiar historical circumstances is the relationship between the level of knowledge and the level of civilization a necessary one. Nevertheless it is the case that a certain level of knowledge provides certain possibilities for the structure of society that may not be available at a lesser level. Moreover, it is recognized that the level of knowledge and the quality of material life in certain areas are influenced by the ability of those who receive extended training in the area. It denies, however, that this congruence is the sole determining factor, and therefore it also denies that intellectual capacity alone is sufficient to justify a claim for unequal resources.

There is, of course, reason to believe that the level of material life might drop if the total allotment of educational resources were divided equally without discrimination and that this drop would be reflected even in the level of the least advantaged members of the present generation.[31] Therefore a change from the principle of equality of education opportunity to the principle of equality does not require that educational allotments be absolutely equal in every instance but instead that there be a shift in the principle under which unequal allotments are granted.

Two related rules are appropriate guides for the distribution of unequal allotments under the principle of equality. The first states the general conditions under which an unequal allotment may be designated (the general rule) while the second specifies the conditions under which an individual may be said to have a legitimate claim to an unequal share (the specifying rule). The general rule is that a disproportionate share of educational resources is justifiable whenever a socially important skill is needed and when the training required to maintain that skill is in excess of the average expenditure for the population as a whole. The term "skill" should not be read narrowly as involving simply the more vocational arts, but even more important, it includes the critical and aesthetic skills necessary to maintain and establish certain levels of sensibility and consciousness. The general rule differs from the equality of education opportunity only in point of emphasis, for it is to be interpreted as directing educational institutions to base unequal allotments only on the knowledge needed to exercise a stipulated skill and to avoid the elaboration of knowledge as simply a device to arbitrarily screen out candidates from a certain educational program. The advocate of equality of educational opportunity will want to leap from this general rule to a conclusion about who should receive the additional allotment whereas the advocates of equality require the specifying rule. This rule states that a person is entitled to a disproportionate share of the educational expenditure when there is reasonable evidence to indicate that he is able to reach a specifiable (but not elaborated) level of professional competence in a socially important skill, and when he demonstrates that he is willing to apply a disproportionate share of

[31] The phrase "least-advantaged member" is borrowed from John Rawls. Although this part of the essay leans upon Rawl's notion of justice as fairness, it is not clear that Rawls would necessarily accept this formulation for education since he seems to rely somewhat more heavily upon the idea of fair competition with regard to educational institutions and therefore perhaps with regard to the division of educational resources.

his energy towards directly and consciously improving the general well-being and specifically the well-being of the least-advantaged member of the society.

The specifying rule does not require that unequal allotments be distributed according to intellectual capacities alone although the ability to achieve a minimum and realistic level of competence is accepted as a necessary condition for a claim. Moreover, this principle suggests some ways in which the accident of intelligence can be compensated: for example, by the way in which the application of skills is directed.

The impact of the principle of equality is to shift the burden of proof in the determination of educational allotments. Under the principle of equality of educational opportunity the burden of proof rests with those whose intellectual performance is below the norm to show that their performance is only an apparent indication of their intellectual capacity, one relating to factors of race, family background, social class, etc., but not to real intelligence. Under the principle of equality, everyone is entitled to an equal allotment while even the obviously intelligent are required to justify an unequal share.

The principle of equality, like the principle of equality of educational opportunity, is to be thought of as the guiding idea behind the organization of educational institutions, and for this reason the act of justifying an unequal allotment is to be thought of as an institutional, not an individual activity. All institutions place the burden of proof somewhere by the very fact that they incorporate norms that govern an individual's behavior. Alterations of institutions of course do not necessarily entail an alteration of norms, as for example when two institutions are brought into functional relation with each other under the same norm. Nevertheless when a change in the governing principle does occur, it is accompanied by a shift in the burden of proof. When, for example, the strictures governing usury were loosened, thereby shifting from the principle of stability to the principle of growth, the burden of proof was taken off the moneylenders. In contrast, the educational reforms of the last century have not involved a shift in the principle under which education institutions have been organized but have involved the adjustment of schools to other aspects of society, such as technology, under the articulated principle of equality of educational opportunity.

The organizing principle is reflected in the status and emphasis that is given to certain key aspects of an institution. Under equality of educational opportunity a large proportion of educational resources is put into the development and articulation of various means of selection, and of articulating the ranking of individuals to agencies that use the schools as a source of training and recruitment. Among the consequences of this emphasis is the false identification of test scores and grades with educational standards, and the belief that evaluation is to be conducted for the purpose of social selection rather than as a natural and sustained part of the process of education. It is this emphasis which gives so much control to governmental and industrial agencies. Under the principle of equality, it is likely that the shift in emphasis would bring under public scrutiny the levels of skills that are stipulated as a requirement for the practice of an activity that, under the general rule, has been selected for an unequal allotment of educational resources. The goal of such scrutiny would then be to enable the largest possible number of people to be potential candidates for such an allotment, and thereby to assure that accidental factors, such as intelligence, are minimized as the criterion of selection while at the same time maintaining the level of skill required for reasonable competency.

The fact that the principle of equality places the act of justification at the institutional rather than the individual level means that the demonstration of a person's willingness to apply his skills according to the principle is a function of the structure of educational institutions and of the commitment that is made by the fact of applying for an unequal allotment of resources and having it granted. At the very least the burden of proof that is placed on those who receive more than the average allotment means that the skills that are developed are to be thought of as skills that are owned in joint partnership with the public, and that some limitations, as determined by fair procedures, might be placed on the time, place, and circumstances in which an individual chooses to exercise such skills. Whether and where such limitations are to be applied would depend on the type of need required, the effects on the development of certain skills, and the compensatory needs of the less talented members of society as determined by existing social conditions.

It is important not to misconstrue the question of freedom and its limitations for those who are allocated an unequal share of educational resources. Certain freedoms such as free speech, the vote, the right to privacy and to free assembly are rights that have been accepted as belonging equally to each person by virtue of his citizenship alone, and these rights must be maintained.[32] The goal of equality affirms the values of these freedoms by accepting them as basic social values. However, because it does recognize such freedom to be a basic social value, it requires that *prima facie,* it ought to be distributed equally. Nevertheless, the process of education can be influential in extending an individual's freedom by leading him to an awareness of certain otherwise unrecognized alternatives that have a bearing on his individual life style and also by extending to some certain rights that are not extended to all. Among these rights are those that are thought necessary for the carrying out the responsibilities of specific social positions. The right that a minister has to maintain confidence in the midst of public inquiry, or that a newsman ought to have to protect his source, or that a physician has to be judged by his procedures and not his results, are obvious examples, as are the rights necessary to carry out the responsibilities of teaching and learning. The principle of equality does not negate these rights. It only refuses to recognize the accident of intellectual endowment as a sufficient justification for a person using the educational resources of a society to increase his freedom at the possible expense of the freedom and well-being of his fellows.

## ✓ VIII. A CONCLUDING EVALUATION OF TWENTIETH-CENTURY EDUCATIONAL REFORM

In many ways progressive education comprised the most liberal wing of educational reform in the United States during the twentieth century, and as such it perhaps best expresses both the promises and the limits of schooling in American society. It was to the public schools that people looked for the hope of a new tomorrow, and for the development of a new citizen who would break the binds of the past and realize the promise of the future. Progressive educators such as Dewey, Counts, and others had a vision of what might be and they saw the school as the place where that vision could begin to become reality. ✓

When progressive education is abstracted from the larger social

---

[32] It must be recognized, of course, that many of these rights are under severe threat for many people in a society such as our own where the great distortion in wealth renders some much more influence in the political process thereby vitiating the idea of one man—one vote, if that is to be interpreted as each man should have a generally equal influence on the political process.

forces that spirited its development and is looked on in a restricted sense as a series of proposals designed to reform the classroom, it is difficult to deny the validity of some of its insights. For there is considerable evidence now to support the progressive view that education does not have to be a dull mechanical enterprise and that within limits and under proper conditions children do not have to be coerced in order to learn important and difficult subjects. If nothing else, progressive ideas helped motivate a deeper examination of the learning process both in terms of the development of children and the structure of the curriculum as it attempted to shift the burden for educational failure from the child to the process of schooling itself.

A complete evaluation of progressive reform, however, cannot rest content with abstracting the movement from the larger forces that spirited its development. For it is in the context of these larger forces that the progressive ideal took on its individual coloration and became different for children of different classes. Progressive education was one aspect of liberal educational reform generally. It was initiated and designed to use the schools to meet the various needs established by industrial development and to smooth over the dislocations caused by an ever-expanding technology. The idea of liberal educational reform was the ideal of equality of opportunity and as translated into the schools this meant that education was to become the basic instrument for realizing the "American dream." But the ideal itself was limited more by the needs of industrial society than by the requirements of justice itself. And it was for this reason that progressive pedagogy was translated in different ways for different children as the "realities" of other aspects of American life brought home the need for different goals and different expectations.

One does not have to be insensitive to the hopes that people placed in industrial development nor must one view the machine as a monster intent upon consuming people as nourishment for its own growth in order to see the fallacy of the liberal progressive vision. If one is concerned to establish a more humane society, then he ought to work to establish that society in the very places where people live and work. If one is intent on having man's work and his machines serve real human needs, then he ought to see to it that a man's work serves *his* human needs and not assume this to be an inevitable by-product of letting talent rise to the top. And if it is believed that the requirements of technology and the nature of work are destroying the humanizing and educative functions of the family and the community, then one should reexamine the requirements of technology and the nature of work. The school is not a messiah. If the child is ignored or dehumanized at home and on the block, it is unlikely that the school will save him. If parents are treated like slaves at work, it is unlikely that they will demand that the school treat their children as free and intelligent human beings. Schools reflect more than they guide. They are molded around the norms of the communities in which they are found. If the community is racist, then so is the school. If the work of the father or the mother is dull and uninteresting then they likely will become dull and uninteresting people and so will the child. There are no *inevitable* benefits to technology—no matter how diligent the school. If technology is to serve real human needs then it must be governed by just human principles, and when this occurs there will be less need to worry about schools.

# INDEX

Academic freedom, 227–234
Addams, Jane, 237–238, 241
American Committee for Cultural Freedom, 231–233
American Federation of Teachers, 131
American Legion, 214
Anderson, James, 114, 115, 272
Army Alpha and Beta Tests, 59

Bagley, William C., 183, 185
Bancroft, George, 178
Barnes, Albert C., 103, 104
Beard, Charles, 14, 173, 177, 186, 187, 191, 192, 193, 200, 218
  Progressive history, 178–185
Beard, Mary R., 183, 184
Bell, Daniel, 2, 167, 216
Bemis, Edward W., 230
Bentley, Arthur, 215–218
Bereday, George, 209
Bereiter, Carl, 274
Bernstein, Barton J., 232
Bernstein, Richard J., 18
Bestor, Arthur, 145–153, 155
Blanshard, Brand, 104, 107, 108, 256
Bobbitt, Franklin, 63, 241
Bond, Horace Mann, 115, 116
Boring, Edwin G., 58
Bow, Warren, 125, 128
Bowles, Samuel, 23, 263
Bradshaw, Helen, 104, 107
Brameld, Theodore, 131, 211
Bullock, Henry Allen, 114, 198, 199
Bureau of Intercultural Education, 121–133

Callahan, Raymond, 62, 63, 64
Cambell, Jack K., 38
Cardinal Prinicples of Secondary Education, 144
Carnegie Foundation, 143, 214
Carter, James G., 28
Cattell, James McKeen, 58, 182
Central Intelligence Agency, 232–233
Child Centered Education, 25, 26, 29, 136, 137, 143
Childs, John, 210, 211, 214
Chomsky, Noam, 268
Class Analysis of American Society, 210–215

Classical Curriculum, 59–60, 67–69
Coleman, James, 165
Commager, Henry Steele, 195
Commission on the Reorganization of Secondary Education, 144
Committee of Ten, 36–37
Conant, James Bryant, 153–161, 164, 165
Counts, George, 14, 111, 202–208, 210, 211
  on education, industry and equality of opportunity, 100–103
Cremin, Lawrence, 23, 26, 69, 100, 110, 143, 144, 198, 204, 215, 228, 236–237
Cubberly, Ellwood P., 196, 197
Curry, J. L. M., 112, 113, 114, 115
Curti, Merle, 197, 211

Dahl, Robert, 216–220
Darwinian theory, 29, 30, 31
  influence on 20th century educational theory, 41–55
  impact on educational psychology, 57–58
Dewey, John, 2, 3, 5, 6, 14, 18, 19, 57, 147, 167, 170, 171, 201–202, 207, 210, 211, 212, 224, 225, 234, 241, 243, 246, 247, 256; on academic freedom, 227–231; comments on P.S. 26 in Indianapolis, 108–111, 117; criticism of the reflex-arc theory, 65–67; on ethics and evolution, 49–55; Polish study, 103–108, 109; response to the testing and efficiency movements; 75–80; on the role of history, 172–177; views on relation between knowledge and interest, 94–97; on work and education, 80–91
Dewey, Evelyn, 88, 90, 109, 110
Distribution of knowledge, 137–139
Dondineau, Arthur, 125–126, 129
Drost, Walter H., 73
DuBois, Rachael, 121–125
DuBois, W. E. B., 119–120
Duhem, Pierre, 75
Dwight, Timothy, 68
Dykhuizen, George, 230

Educational science, 26–28
  at turn of Century and before, 28–40
  Twentieth Century educational science, 40–47

science and reform, 47–54
Efficiency movement, 62–64
  ideological aspects of efficiency
  movement, 72–75
  liberal reactions to, 75–80
Eliot, Charles W., 37, 116
Ellul, Jacques, 20–21
Equality of (Educational) Opportunity, 21,
  93–94, 100–102, 132–133, 137–139,
  235, 261
  evaluation of, as an ideal, 262–282

Fox, Susan, 250
Freedom, 15–21
  liberal analysis of, 242–243, 255–256

Gardner, John W., 156
Gary, Indiana, Schools, 88–91
General Education Board, 143, 215
Giles, Warren, 126
Gintis, Herbert, 23, 263
Goddard, Henry, 58, 71
Graham, Patricia, 144
Greer, Colin, 23, 260–262
Guest, Robert H., 226
Gutek, Gerald L., 204

Hamilton, Joe, 224
Hampshire, Stuart, 245
Harlow, Ralph V., 194
Harris, William Torrey, 29, 30, 31, 32, 33,
  34, 35, 36, 39, 40, 41, 43, 52, 113, 149
Hartz, Louis, 194
Havinghurst, Robert J., 137–138
Herrnstein, Richard, 265
Hofstadter, Richard, 171
Holt, John, 273
Hook, Sidney, 211, 231–233

Illich, Ivan, 240, 268
Integration, 132
Intellectuals, 223–234
Interest Group Analysis of American
  Society, 210–223
IQ Examinations, 33, 263–264, 267, 271

Jencks, Christopher, 163, 164
Joncich, Geraldine, 59

Kallen, Horace, 121

Karier, Clarence, 70, 72, 196, 230, 272
Katz, Michael, 196, 257
Kilpatrick, William H., 14, 117–121, 211,
  212
Kimball, Solon T., 97
Krug, Edward, 196

Lasch, Christopher, 232
Life Adjustment Movement, 143–153, 155,
  156
Lippmann, Walter, 57
  reaction to testing movement, 76–78
Loeb, Martin B., 137–138

McCormick, Charles P., 226
McClellan, James, 97
MacCracken, H. M., 68
Manipulation, issue of, 236–262
Mannheim, Karl, 5, 8, 20, 225, 227
Marks, Russell, 71
Marx, Karl, and Marxism, 36, 203–207,
  211–215
Mayer, Martin, 275, 276
Mayo, Elton, 226
Mead, George Herbert, 14, 48, 49, 57
Merriam, Charles, 208–209
Mills, C. Wright, 19, 222
Myrdal, Gunnar, 2, 109

National Advisory Committee on Civil
  Disorders, 161
National Association for the Advancement
  of Colored People, 109, 117
National Education Association, 27, 36,
  100, 101, 113
Negro Education, 111–121, 198–199
Nevins, Allan, 195
Neill, A. S. (Summerhill), 9, 258
Nyberg, David, 242

Ogburn, William F., 79, 191

Parker, Alton B., 230
Parker, Francis W., 30, 33, 34, 36, 37, 38,
  39, 40, 113, 116
Payne, Joseph, 68
Peirce, Charles S., 48
Polanyi, Michael, 9
Posser, Charles A., 144
Pragmatic Philosophy, 246–247

Pressure Group Theory, *see* Interest group
  analysis of American Society
Progress, 191–200
Progressive education, 13, 14, 15, 26
  conflict between technological and
    communal values, 97–99
  in context of liberal educational reform,
    135–137
  evaluation of revisionist criticism, 225–
    262
  problem of manipulation, 240–250
  progressive point of view, 250–254
  revisionist and traditional interpretations
    of, 236–238
  social context of progressive reform,
    94–97
Progressive Education Association, 142,
  143

Rankin, Paul, 129
Raup, R. Bruce, 212
Rawls, John, 279
Rice, John M., 26, 27, 28, 29
Robarts, James, 28
Robinson, James Harvey, 173, 177, 178,
  185–190, 191, 192, 193, 194, 199
Romares, John, 58
Rosemont, Henry, 7
Rugg, Harold, 14, 211, 212, 213, 214

Scanlon, Joseph N., 226
Schaar, John, 265
Schlesinger, Arthur, 231–233
School text books, 194–196
Science of education, *see* Educational
  Science
Silberman, Charles, 158–165
Snedden, David, 73–75, 76, 241
*Social Frontier Magazine,* 211–215
Soviet Union, 154, 160, 204–208, 224
Spaulding, Frank, 63
Spencer, Herbert, 48
Spiegelberg, Herbert, 268, 270
Spring, Joel, 70, 256

Subject matter approach, 25, 29, 136–137,
  141–143
Sumner, William Graham, 43–47, 48, 49,
  50, 51
Szoke, Ronald, 68, 181

Taylorism, 62
Terman, Lewis, 58, 76
Testing movement, 58–62, 140–141
  ideological aspects of testing movement,
    67–75
  liberal reactions to, 75–80
Thorndike, Edward L., 14, 141
  ideological concerns, 67–71
  problems with his justification of nature
    of learning and intelligence, 64–66
  views on intelligence, 58–61
Toulmin, Stephen, 174
Transferability of learning, 60–61
Truman, David, 216
Turner, Frederick Jackson, 170–171, 194
Tuskegee Institute, 114, 115

U. S. Office of Education, 144

Violas, Paul, 70, 196, 237–238
Vocational Education, 69

Wales, Fred G., 129
Walker, Charles C., 226
Wallace, Michael, 171
Warner, W. Lloyd, 137–138, 140, 161
Warren, Charles, 112, 113
Washington, Booker T., 114, 115, 116
White, Morton, 172–173, 175
Wirth, Arthur, 98
Wirth, Louis, 8
Wissot, Jay, 250
Wolff, Robert Paul, 217
Woodworth, Robert, 60

Zeran, Franklin, 144